"If you could spend an evening with Phil Downer and his family, play games with his children, dine with them in their home, or sit and talk with them in their rooms as I have, you would not only purchase this book, you'd make it your mission to get it in the hands of every parent you know. I want every family in America—in the *world*—to read *A Father's Reward*. There is a way to turn our nation around, and it begins in the home. Not only will this book give you a vision, it will show you how that vision can become reality."

Kay Arthur
Executive Director, *Precept Ministries*

"Phil Downer is a man who walks his talk. He is a focused father who is as busy as any man I know, but his children are way up on his priority list. In my book, that's a man worth hearing."

Steve Farrar
Men's Leadership Ministries

"Phil Downer writes what he lives, and he lives an uncompromising righteous life. Every father should read this book and learn from Phil's example as he follows Christ. It's a winner!"

Neil T. Anderson
Freedom in Christ Ministries

"If you're looking for a wonderful handbook on how to be a godly father, this is it. Phil Downer, with his customary honesty and practicality, has given a gift to fathers who struggle with what it means to be a father (or know someone wh glad you did."

Steve Brown
KeyLife Network

"Phil Downer is a great parent and a wonderful writer. His new book is 'must' reading for dads, whether their kids are doing great, just okay, or deep in crisis. I wish every parent in America would read *A Father's Reward*."

Bill Armstrong
Former Senator from Colorado

"The greatest reward in a man's life is for his children to grow up and continue walking faithfully with Christ. That's not easy without a guide to help navigate the minefields of current culture. Phil Downer's latest book, *A Father's Reward*, is not just important, it is *essential* for any father who cares about the spiritual welfare of his children."

Larry Krider
President, The Gathering

"The first line caught my attention: *Ozzie and Harriet are dead*. Phil Downer goes on to blow the image of the 'perfect' family and explain the real meaning and reward of fatherhood. Fathering, he candidly points out, is filled with joy and frustration, but the molding of a great father must take place in the furnace of daily life. His warm, purposeful, and honest approach to the topic will encourage and challenge you as the father and gatekeeper of your home. You'll find his bold statements concerning discipline and trust to be refreshing and practical. I highly recommend this book to every father, parent, and newlywed."

Gary Carlson
Publisher, *The Christian Businessman*

"Phil Downer's book is a call to arms for fathers to embrace their God-appointed responsibility as the spiritual leader, nurturer, and protector of their families. In the raging cultural war, he sounds the alarm loud and clear that the major battlefield is in our homes, fought over the minds and lives of our children. As the father of four and grandfather of eight, I found this book enlightening, encouraging, and convicting."

Clayton Brown
Investment Banker

A FATHER'S REWARD

PHIL DOWNER
with Chip MacGregor

HARVEST HOUSE PUBLISHERS
Eugene, Oregon 97402

A FATHER'S REWARD
Copyright © 1998 by Phil Downer
Published by Harvest House Publishers
Eugene, Oregon 97402

Library of Congress Cataloging-in-Publication Data
     Downer, Phil, 1947-
     A father's reward / Phil Downer.
     p. cm.
     ISBN 1-56507-773-3 (Softcover)
     ISBN 1-7369-0021-7 (Hardcover)
     1. Fathers—Religious life. 2. Fatherhood—Religious aspects—Christianity. 3. Child rearing—Religious aspects—Christianity.
     I. Title.
     BV4529.d69   1998
     248.8' 421—dc21   98-5764
                                       CIP

Printed in the United States of America.

98 99 00 01 02 / DH / 10 9 8 7 6 5 4 3 2 1

I would like to dedicate this book to God's most incredible gift to me after the Lord Jesus: my devoted and faithful wife, Susy, who made a decision to trust God and rebuild our love, and who is now my loving wife, co-laboring parent, and fellow soldier in the battle to win and disciple people around the world. She is my partner, lover, and favorite companion.

Most importantly, Susy's commitment of most every waking hour to our children has been the underpinning of our family. I will be forever thankful for her sacrifice, forgiveness, eternal perspective, and plain old hard work which keeps me and our family on track for Christ.

While this book is focused on the father's role, little of its content could have been accomplished without a partnership with Susy. Not only have we been co-laborers in the discipling of our children, but also in the recording of our journey through the pages of this book.

I love you, Susy.

—Phil Downer

For Bob Bever, a great father and a great friend.

—JCM

Acknowledgments

I especially want to acknowledge two couples who have provided stalwart encouragement for Susy and me to do this book: Scott and Karen Melby and Richard and Christy Bacon.

I would also like to thank the many people who have built into our lives, especially those who discipled and mentored us in the early years, including Liane Day, Jim and Mary Gail Lyon, Paul Johnson, Dave and Judy Hill, Joe and Gladys Coggeshall, Ted and Edith DeMoss, Bruce Wilkinson, Charles Stanley, Bill Gothard, Joe Stowell, Howard Hendricks, and Kay Arthur.

Acknowledgment is due to those special individuals who have incredibly supported Susy and me with great encouragement throughout the years in a variety of ways: Paul and Rena Olschner, Jackson and June Wingfield, Richard and Christy Bacon, Bill and Judy Hardin, Mike and Beth Felix, Daryl and Cathy Heald, Scott and Karen Melby, Bill and Elizabeth Mitchell, Wil and Kristi Armstrong, Senator Bill and Ellen Armstrong, Jack and Phyllis Cauwels, Hugh and Nancy Maclellan, Ron Blue, Pat MacMillan, Clayton and Charlotte Brown, Winston and Judy Parker, Jim and Bev Henry, Jon and Charlotte Faulkner, Pete and Peggy LaRochelle, Tom and Del Francescon, Robert and Celeste White, Kevin and Gail Ring, Brad and Lynn Smith, Fred Zillich, Andy Read, Bob Tamasy, Dave Stoddard, Charlie Williams, Craig Kiggens, Rick Bealer, Bruce Witt, Yvonne Eubanks, Jackie Troxel, Anne Miller, and Derrick Merck.

Finally, I would like to acknowledge the incredible help and vision of the entire Harvest House team in the production of this book. Thanks to Bob Hawkins, Jr., Bill Jensen, Carolyn McCready, Julie Castle, and Teresa Evenson for their expertise. A special thanks to my editor, dear friend and fellow soldier, Chip MacGregor, whose creativity, input and ability to boil down the words of a verbose lawyer, I so greatly appreciate.

All proceeds from this sale of this book go to CBMC, whose ministry stretches throughout the world.

—Phil Downer

Contents

Contents

Part One:

Ozzie and Harriet Are Dead

Stepping off the plane in Denver, I was welcomed by my brother-in-law, two business colleagues, and my 14-year-old son. While I shook hands with my friends, it was clear my son had something important to tell me. He was literally jumping up and down with excitement.

"Dad!" he cried. "I can't wait to tell you what I did last night!"

"Okay, Paul," I replied, winking at the other men in the group, "what is it?"

"I did my first joint!"

Suddenly conversations ceased.

With acute embarrassment I glanced at my friends, who were suddenly all looking at their shoes, grimacing. I opened my mouth, and no words came out. With a mighty effort, I got hold of my emotions. Turning to face my son head-on, I angrily muttered, "Paul . . . you'd better tell me what you're talking about."

My son, still smiling innocently, looked at me as though he was pleased as punch. "Well, Dad, you know how I've wanted to build a bookcase for the new room? Last night I learned how to do a hand-mitered joint!"

"Oh," was all I could reply, until I noticed the snorting sound coming from my brother-in-law, who sounded like he was having an attack of some kind. His whole body was shaking, and he was trying so hard to keep from laughing out loud that he was having trouble standing up. "Well,

Paul, that's great!" I finally managed, noticing the relieved smiles on my friends' faces. My son still didn't know what everybody thought was so funny, so he just started telling the story of learning to use a miter box and backsaw. By the time he was finished, we had all looked at each other and shared a sigh of relief.

"It's refreshing," one of my friends told me later, "that your boy could get so euphoric over learning to use a simple tool . . . and amazing that he would bother telling you about it."

"It's not so amazing," I assured him. "We talk a lot. Paul had learned something new, and wanted to share his discovery with me. Doesn't your son do that?"

My friend, who is a godly man and a leader in his church, looked at me with a pained expression in his eyes and said, "Phil, my son never talks to me anymore. And if he told me he'd tried a joint, I would know it wasn't the kind made of wood." After a pause, he added, "I wish I could have that kind of relationship with my kid . . . but I guess I never really felt very close to my own father."

"Hey," I told him, "welcome to the club."

I'm no perfect father. You don't have to take my word for it—ask my kids, they'll tell you. My dad never had time for me, so I didn't really have a model to follow other than watching "Ozzie and Harriet" on TV. When I first became a dad, I had no idea what to do. I was afraid of babies and disgusted with diapers. Somehow I figured if I worked hard and wore a tie regularly, everything would work out—after all, it always did for Ozzie and Harriet.

I soon realized that Ozzie and Harriet are dead. Boys don't come home from school and stand around the kitchen drinking milk and talking with their moms anymore. There are a million other diversions that are far more interesting. Girls don't leap into Daddy's arms to say good night—it would appear too unsophisticated. In an activity-filled, pleasure-seeking world, I've got a lot of competition for my kids' attention. So if I wanted to keep a close relationship with my kids, I realized I was going to have to do something different. And if I want them to grow up to be Christians, I'm going to have to disciple them. I decided years ago I had better learn a few facts about fathering if I were to have any chance of succeeding.

I

Slip-Sliding Away

And the people served the LORD all the days of Joshua, and all the days of the elders who survived Joshua, who had seen all the great work of the LORD which He had done for Israel. Then Joshua the son of Nun, the servant of the Lord, died . . . and all that generation also were gathered to their fathers; and there arose another generation after them who did not know the LORD, nor yet the work which He had done for Israel. Then the sons of Israel did evil in the sight of the LORD (Judges 2:7,10).

I was sitting there in my favorite chair, quietly enjoying a cup of hot coffee. Soft music was playing in the background, and a roaring fire lit up the room. Susy was seated across from me, having just made my favorite dinner. My six children, who had immediately leaped from the table to do the dishes, were now sitting quietly all around me—one straightening my pillow, another refilling my cup, each of them like quiet angels waiting patiently to serve the master.

And then I woke up.

My life isn't really like that, though I think I saw that life one time on an old Bing Crosby Christmas special. The trouble is that most of us have this image of what makes the perfect family, and we desire to be perfect parents, but then

13

our kids show up and ruin the whole picture. Don't get me wrong, I've got great kids. But they aren't quiet angels, and I'm certainly not an archangel. Some days I wonder when I'll ever get a handle on this fathering business. But I've had the wonderful opportunity to be in many Christian homes around the country, and I've had the opportunity to observe a great number of families. I travel about one hundred nights a year for speaking and ministry engagements, I'm involved with a lot of Christian men, and when I travel I often ask to stay in their homes. Things always look great for the first five minutes. Everybody is there, the home is beautiful, the Bible is on the table, the guy is involved in ministry, and everything looks swell. Unfortunately, if I stay longer than one day, I often find that the home is little more than a food-and-laundry depot.

What many families really have is a bunch of individuals who have agreed to share a few things like washing machines and telephones. Eventually, Johnny and Jill can't get along with only one phone, so they get a second line. Then they add a business line, buy portable phones, and stick in a stereo, a computer, a satellite dish, and Super Nintendo, so that nobody really has to connect with anyone else in the family for longer than the time it takes to check each other's phone number. Johnny and Jill got along fine the first day with the computer, but then they started fighting over it, so they each got their own computer, and eventually Dad got his own, too.

Each teenager has his or her own bedroom and bathroom, there are televisions in three different rooms of the house, and through the Internet each person can connect with people all over the world. But nobody seems to be connecting with anyone *inside* the house. And Dad is killing himself to support the whole operation. There is a pool in the backyard, church activities on weekends, and school or sports meetings nearly every night. Everybody in the family goes to church, but at different times and with different people, so that no one is ever sure who went where and with whom.

Dad's Brave New World

They don't even realize it, but their family is being torn apart. Even with all the church activities, the family is coming apart at the seams. They are not learning how to live together as a family. The kids are growing up with so much protection from personal relationships that no one really knows what is going on inside their heads. Instead of being eager to maintain unity, the children never learn to be unselfish. Rather than working out their differences and conflicts with their siblings, they simply pack stuff between each other, so they do not have to deal with one another. We are delivering into the Christian community people who are inept at dealing with relationships, incompetent at resolving conflicts, and unable to reach other people with God's love. They are consumers, nothing more.

Actually, we have become a country of consumers. Manufacturing is down; consumerism is up. Our acquisitional propensity has altered everything about our lifestyles, including our perspective on the family. In 1900, this country was 85 percent agrarian-based. Children were admired, desired, productive, and considered assets. Today we are service-based. Children are often not admired or desired, but endured. They are not considered an asset, but a tremendous cost. They are not a benefit, but a great liability. Too many aren't wanted.

What happened? In the agrarian society, children worked with Dad and Mom. When Dad went to work in the fields, the boys went with him. They learned the principles of sowing and reaping. They learned the principles of delayed gratification. They would plant this season and reap next season. They learned that if you did not spray for insects, you lost your crop. They discovered that if you did not protect your crops in cold weather, you could lose everything. The kids learned how to work and produce, so they were productive.

Now kids just learn how to consume. Many kids have the consuming skills of an adult, but they do not understand the concept of producing. They've been raised with a "give-me" mentality. Our country is at risk because we are raising kids who spend more than they earn. They think that by purchasing something below retail they have "saved" money . . . and they learned that idea from their parents.

Our culture also has witnessed a progression of Dad away from the home. At the turn of the century, the father spent time in the home. His children learned from him, regardless of personality type. In many homes his words, stories, and songs were the basic source of entertainment. By the 1950s, the father was still in the home, but he gave entertainment over to Walt Disney. Dad was consumed with his work. While he may have been in the house, he was there working on his priorities. Mom was home, but Dad was working. He was not interacting with his children, becoming primarily an authority figure instead. While that tended to lend stability to the family, it also made the father fairly remote. During the 1960s, Dad left the home during the week in order to get ahead in society. He began traveling and getting involved with all kinds of things that kept him away from his family. There were more meetings, more demands, and less time for developing a relationship with his kids. The father stopped being the one who drew the family together and became strictly the provider who took care of the consumers.

The father used to be the individual who was most responsible for shaping and developing character in the children. While Mom was the nurturer and care-giver, Dad was the strength and model in the family. But all that changed when men began devoting themselves to their careers over their kids. Instead of Dad coming home and filling the children in on his life, Dad stayed at the office late, thinking that "providing" had superseded "developing." The family became segmented. Mom and Dad no longer met at the door with a kiss, kids crowding around asking, "What happened today?" because Dad was not home in the evening. The dinner hour was not a gathering of the family because Dad had a business meeting and the family was scattered. CBS took over the news just as Disney took over the entertainment, so we all sat in front of the television in the sixties and let Walter Cronkite become our source for information, not Dad. Dad had entered a brave new world, in which he wasn't needed as a dad so much as a supplier of toys.

In the 1970s, Dad left home for profit, and Mom started to go to work. We found that we could find a lot of comfort in things, so possessions became important. Dad was no longer in the home, and Mom was lonely, so Mom left the home, too. The advent of television and the rise of consumerism forced the father to begin focusing on acquisitions over relationships. Rather than providing for his family, he began providing *things* for his family. Dad substituted *things* for himself, and that caused further division in the home. By the 1980s, the family had started to break up. Dad wasn't living with Mom, and the care-givers of the kids were baby-sitters and strangers other than Mom and Dad. Sports figures and rock stars became the admired icons of a generation, so that it was considered quaint to honor one's father. Twenty-two-year-olds began making 100 million dollars for playing basketball, and it became pretty hard for Dad to compete with a media star who plays ball or makes music videos for a living.

In the 1990s we have entertainment with Disney, news with CBS, celebrities as heroes, and the computer as a second parent. Television became the primary parent in the 1980s, but in the 1990s the Internet has supplanted TV as second parent. Dad is not a significant figure. Not only is he not around, kids often don't even know who he is. Some dads are in different states. Many have completely abandoned the home. Now the kids have new dads—some have two or three dads. The generation that is being raised will have more spouses than they do children.

A Biblical Alternative
Some people think it's crazy and old-fashioned, but a family doesn't have to be a collection of individuals. If the

father will step up and begin fulfilling the role God has for him, he will find that he can still be the strength of the family. He can still be the shaper of his children's lives. When you have a family that works as a biblical unit, with Mom and Dad in their biblical roles, discipling their kids, the children develop a God-consciousness, and the family develops a biblical worldview. That sort of biblical alternative isn't the product of a wild imagination either, for I've seen it at work. When God becomes a normal part of your family, everything changes. You'll find yourself actually wresting control away from the culture, and you'll see the lives of your children change forever.

It's amazing how many people God brings to your doorstep when you follow the biblical alternative. They want to know why you are different, and how you got that way. We have sat at baseball games and heard people say, "Your family supports one another. You are excited for one another. Your kids are excited when their brother or sister gets a hit. *Your son even cheered for your daughter to win.* How did you get that?"

It used to be that running a Christian business was the way to effectively reach people. I think that is still true, but I really believe that the Christian family will be the primary apologetic unit for the next ten years, witnessing Christ to the world. If you have a Christian family that is operating with love and devotion as a discipleship ministry team, you've got the most effective outreach resource around. The future is not going to be the church reaching the lost as much as Christian families reaching their communities. People are still impressed when they see a loving Mom and Dad and kids. It's different, but appealing, and it attracts them to Christ.

Influences from the East
Bill was an alcoholic who destroyed his marriage. He started a 12-step program and got "dry," then came to Christ about two years later. Today he is a godly man, involved in ministry all over town. He and his wife are

involved in outreach, and Bill is very involved in community sports with his kids. An elder of his church and
involved in men's ministry, he is just a phenomenal, active
guy. But when you get with Bill and his kids, you realize the
family is not as strong as it appears. When Bill's kids are
with him, they are very sweet and polite. But when Bill's
kids are away from their dad, they are just like all the other
kids. They cuss like their peers. His son is involved in discussions about pornography. His daughter is sexually
active with her boyfriend. And the younger boys spend
their time playing with some of the most evil-looking toys
I've ever seen. Bill's life is best described by the words of
Isaiah 2:6: "For Thou hast abandoned Thy people, the
house of Jacob, because they are filled with influences from
the east."

That is what is happening with America on the brink of
the twenty-first century. We are *filled* with influences from
the East—everything from consciousness-raising and mysticism to yoga and nature worship. When we allow those
influences to shape our kids, it moves them away from
God. What Bill has done is let the culture tear his kids'
hearts away from God. They sit in front of the television
and watch shows that deal with mysticism and sensuality.
They hear phone numbers you can call to speak with psy-
chics. They go to movies that are absolutely satanic, with
reincarnated monsters and all kinds of devil worship. They
say the movie "was great except for those two scenes."
That's like saying the food was good except for those two
cockroaches! They play video games in which they pretend
to be evil characters, destroying one another in a struggle
for power. And they have been plunked in front of the television *while Bill is involved in his godly activities*. His home
looks wonderful, but he has allowed it to be corrupted by
the culture.

American society used to be guided by Christian principles, but now we can talk about everything in our classrooms except Jesus Christ. Our colleges can offer classes on
yoga and transcendental meditation, but cannot post the

Ten Commandments on the wall. Friends with the Gideons have told me they can hand out Bibles in state classrooms across Russia, but are banned from many campuses in the United States. Our culture has worked to get God out of our lives, and the mistake Bill made was that he allowed the culture to dominate the lives of his children. He permitted television, teachers, and the mainstream media to "disciple" his children, and in the process poison their minds.

Whatever Happened to Discipline?

My friend Curt is a godly man. He is not the "drive-through-the-next-challenge" kind of guy, but a thoughtful, pensive sort, on the computer early in the morning doing exegesis of Scripture and involved in teaching men how to study their Bibles. He is a very reflective, meticulous man, and he teaches others in great depth. Curt's problem, however, is that he has failed to discipline his kids. His spiritual life is in good shape, but the lives of his children are in chaos. Hebrews chapter 12 says that a father has to discipline his son. A culture without discipline will soon fall apart.

I was not disciplined in my life. My mother spent time in an insane asylum (that's what they called it in the fifties) after a second suicide attempt. I found her one day on the floor, lying in a pool of blood. My father was involved with another woman, to whom he introduced me in the driveway as my "new mom." I didn't think there was anything wrong with my old mom, and I was really crushed by the experience. Rather than offering me discipline, my father let me do as I pleased. One of the worst things that happened to me was that I was allowed to roam the neighborhood totally undisciplined.

In the fifties and early sixties, roaming the neighborhood was deemed "safe," and I did not have any supervision. I went wherever I wanted, my parents fighting till all hours of the night, and I would go to bed with a real sense of fear as I heard them screaming at one another. I would wake up and throw back my covers, and they would sometimes still be screaming. I was ostracized and made fun of by neighbors. I didn't feel I belonged anywhere. That experience created deep insecurities and fears in my life, *and that exact thing is happening all over the nation in other families*. My dad felt too guilty to reprove me, and he did not want to have an adult in the house who could see what he was doing, so I grew up totally without discipline or input from him. On top of that, my sweet mother had read Dr. Spock, who had convinced her that she needed to let me express my frustration, so I built a pattern of using anger as an expression for embarrassment, insecurity, and anything else I didn't like.

My friend Curt has let his kids take the leadership of his home. He is afraid to disagree with them, and afraid to disappoint them. So while he, a spiritual giant, has been discipling men and studying the Scriptures, he has allowed his own kids to rule over him. That is exactly what was prophesied in Isaiah 3:5, where it says, "The people will be oppressed, each one by another, and each one by his neighbor; *the youth will storm against the elder,* and the inferior against the honorable." We have entire communities where people live in total fear—not of gangs, or the Mafia, or of hardened criminals. They live in fear of the 12-and 13-year-old neighborhood kids who roam the area, growing up without discipline.

I want to write this book to Curt and others like him, because I have found that growing up without discipline was a great curse. I had to learn discipline the hard way: by flunking out of college, joining the Marines, going off to war, and having a drill instructor pound it into my head. I saw men who were undisciplined die in Vietnam, and I don't want my kids to end up that way. I want to teach our children discipline, for when you discipline a child properly, it turns his heart toward you and ultimately toward God.

Back-Row Brats

Have you ever gone to church and looked at the back row of the balcony? Sometimes going into churches as a guest speaker, I have noticed the godly parents sitting in the front with their leather Bibles all underlined, nodding with approval at the sermon. Meanwhile, their kids are sitting in the back row with looks of rebellion on their faces reflected in the way they dress, giving no attention to anything going on in the service. They are only there under duress. After church the parents nervously come up to me and say, "Oh, I want you to meet Gordon and Gail." Then they immediately begin making excuses for their kids. "We send them to the finest Christian schools, but they are just going through a phase. We're not sure why, but we are just trying to keep them in church. It seems the church doesn't appeal to them any longer." They've got a couple back row brats, and they don't know what to do about it. That's the way it was with us and our first child, Abigail, until friends gave us Dr. James Dobson's *Dare to Discipline* when she was about two. That book really turned us around.

Too many men have left the raising of their families to their wives, abdicating the responsibility to get involved by disciplining the kids. When they come home after long hours at work, they feel guilty having ignored everyone, so they try and buy the kids off by taking everyone to a movie. Often Mom is left trying to run the family—until she decides she's had enough and leaves to find a job where she can feel that what she does is valued.

Isaiah 3:12 warns, "O My people! Their oppressors are children." Imagine that the oppressors of a land are its children. So often in troubled families, those that are oppressing, that are guiding the family away from the Lord, are the children. In the next line of Scripture it adds, "and women rule over them." In other words, men allowed the kids to cause problems and oppress the family, then stood by while the women decided to take charge and rule the homes. One family we know is in tremendous crisis. The parents and younger kids are now forced to visit two of the older children—one is in jail, the other is in a juvenile home because he was "unable to cope with living in a family." As I see that family, I realize that could just as easily have been Susy and me. As I talk to the parents about how they got into that position it becomes very clear: the father was building a business, working 12 to 16 hours a day, and the Mom was left home with a big family. Though they had Christian parents, the kids turned into back row brats. The Mom was just not able to do all that was expected of her, and the family fell apart. It all could have been avoided if Dad had done his job.

What Do You Worship?

Isaiah 2:8 points out the problem with American businessmen: They worship what they do with their hands. The verse states, "Their land has also been filled with idols." Of course, we do not bow down to wooden objects anymore, but the next line notes, "They worship the work of their hands, that which their fingers have made." When we devote all of our time and attention to our jobs, we are worshiping the work of our hands. Men are doing that around the country, abdicating the responsibilities they have to disciple their children and follow God's pattern for their lives. They are leaving that for their wives to do, and it isn't getting done. That's not the wives' fault—they were never called to be both mother and father.

I was one of those self-centered businessmen who worshiped my work. Through my ambition and anger, I nearly destroyed my marriage. The truth is, I loved Susy, but I wasn't very nice to her. We had gotten married while undergrads at Southern Methodist University, attended Emory Law School together, and got great jobs after graduation. I became an elder in my church and a successful lawyer with a growing firm, but inside I was filled with bitterness and emptiness. Then one day a man invited me to a Christian Business Men's Committee (CBMC) luncheon to listen to Paul Johnson talk about his life. Paul was a contractor, and I was suing a contractor at the time, so I thought I would listen to what he had to say.

Although Paul talked about issues in his business, he primarily focused on the meaning of his life and the struggles he faced. I listened carefully, for I knew I was facing the same struggles. Then he offered an answer—a way to have peace with God right away. That's exactly what I wanted. Though I had a nice house, a great income, and an important job, my life was in constant turmoil. My deep insecurities were keeping me from experiencing a rich, full life. The fact is, I had myself on the throne of my life. And while I tried changing by reading self-improvement books and trying transcendental meditation, those efforts never achieved the goal of offering me peace, joy, and forgiveness.

When I met Jesus Christ, everything changed. I realized I had put myself in control of my own life, and the results had been disastrous. The only solution was to surrender control to God—something I struggled with, since I like being in control. The business world had taught me that the more control I had and the more power I wielded, the happier I would be. It was a lie. I was worshiping myself, and I was miserable. When I decided to turn control over to the Lord, things started to change. I recognized God came to earth in the person of His son Jesus Christ, dying on the cross, paying the penalty for my sins. He was buried and on the third day rose again according to the scripture and lives today. I confessed my sin and told God I wanted to change. I received Him by faith as my Lord and Savior and he forgave my sins, healed my marriage, and gave me a whole new perspective on work. In our country today, men are walking away from their responsibility as fathers to pursue success at business, and the results are obvious in the lives of their kids: selfishness, rebellion, anger, violence, and loneliness. Throughout history, when men have neglected their families, society has fallen apart.

You don't have to look very far to find biblical examples of this. Consider the nation of Israel: Upon seizing the Promised Land, everybody must have been excited, having seen the Lord give their nation great victories and provide them with adequate leadership and guidance through the years. Joshua's generation loved God and had seen Him work in their midst. But Judges 2:10 says that they failed to pass along to their children the stories of the faith, so that they grew up knowing nothing of the Lord. When Joshua and all the people of his generation died, the next generation did not know God. Immediately some problems set in. Judges 18 reveals how the people of the tribe of Dan failed to settle their own lands, so they went out and stole someone else's. Along the way, they stole the Levite's priest, and the golden and graven images, and pretty soon Moses' grandson was setting up statues for idol worship. A generation that had worshiped God gave way to a generation that rejected God.

It is a scary reality that people who neglect God wind up in trouble. A culture that fails to inculcate its values into its children will see a generation of godless, aimless people arise and destroy their land. The implications of that are frightening as we look at our own culture, for I believe we are failing to pass the truth on to the next generation. Many Christian men are under a burden of guilt because their kids do not know Christ, though we really can't be guilty because only God saves people. I am not responsible for the salvation of my kids, for I can't save my kids. But I *can* make the effort to see that they know about the Lord and that they see God at work in my life.

The Book of Judges tells us the next generation "did not know the Lord." That's the Lord's business. The parents can't be blamed for the choices of their children. But the next line reads, "Nor yet the work which He had done for Israel." Now that's an entirely different problem. The parents *can* be held responsible for not telling, sharing, and modeling the truth of the Lord. We as fathers are required to teach our kids the truth. The generation after Joshua didn't know God nor the work of God because the fathers failed them, and for that those parents will face consequences.

Getting in Touch with Your Kids
I have a friend Geoff, who is involved in CBMC with me. He's a godly man and a good example, but he admitted to

me once, "Phil, I don't know what to do with my kids on the weekend."

"Well," I asked him, "What do you do with your kids on the weekend now?"

"They just kind of hang around as I do my activities," he told me.

"What do you do?"

"Well, I do projects."

"What do they entail?"

"Handyman projects," he said. "You know, going to the hardware store, working in my shop. How can I involve a four-year-old kid in that?"

"Geoff," I said, "take him with you."

"But . . . he's only four."

"Find him something to do."

Geoff thought for a minute, then asked, "Well, what *could* he do?"

"Hand him the list. Have him hold the pencil. Let him check things off the list."

"What good would that do?" Geoff asked.

"First, it will get you doing *something* together. Second, it will make him feel a part of your life. Third, it will reveal to him your faith. The way you treat others, the way you spend your money, the way you plan things and accomplish them—they all reveal your faith to your son."

That thought was a revelation to Geoff. He came back to me the next week and said it worked out great. He continued to give his son responsibilities. He let him carry the bag home and unpack the tools. Eventually he taught his son how to swing a hammer. That led to other things. His boy learned how to craft furniture in the home. More importantly, he learned his father's values.

Men often don't know how to get into the arena of relating with their kids, since their own fathers never took the time to talk with them. But every father is called to get involved with his kids, even if he doesn't have a natural aptitude for it. For example, a couple of years ago I rebuilt the porch with my kids. Josh and Anna were 9; Matt, 11;

Paul, 13; and Abigail, 15. Susanna, at 3, was our runner. We worked in the garage together running the lathe, making spindles from raw wood, and making brackets with scroll saws and band saws. Then we assembled these brackets, banisters, balusters, and railings. I used to do everything myself. Now we're painting, sealing, and rebuilding the entire porch as a family team. That is the level of involvement my children have in home projects since I've committed myself to being a dad.

I didn't start out with this much involvement. I had to take a deliberate approach to fathering. After all, I didn't exactly have any role models to follow, so I just started opening up my life as best I could. I got into my porch idea by making a deliberate attempt to go to the next level with my kids. We started out with roly-poly games on the carpet, then moved to camping, which I have hated to do since the Marine Corps gave me all those free camping trips in Vietnam. I'm not too fond of power tools either, since I have little aptitude with my hands. And the last thing I want to do is deal with instruction books, blades that break, paint that has to be cleaned up, and a handful of kids who track the paint all over the house. That is just not my temperament. To come home from a very demanding, challenging, and sometimes frustrating workweek at the law office, and now ministry, to spend time on handyman projects is about as much fun as coming home and being forced to retake the bar exam! It's just not what I naturally want to do on my weekends.

But I became concerned about the development of our kids spiritually, and I realized that they need me to disciple them. I can't just sit there and bark orders to them and expect them to buy into my "Christian virtues." I need to get involved in their lives. If I want to be with them, I need to offer some attraction for them to be with me. I need something that pulls them out of their peer group and makes them want to be with me instead. That is where most men are struggling right now. They come home tired, and the only time they spend with their kids tends to be barking orders and instructions at them over meals before they go out with their friends, or when they're trying to get their kids up in the morning. That is not modeling your faith to your children, and discipline without a strong personal relationship breeds rebellion.

By nature I would rather watch eight hours of sports on the weekend. I would like to come home after work, watch the news, and let my wife wait on me. But God has called me to something greater than that. What I want to do, as one of God's children, is reach the world for Jesus Christ. That is my passion in the Spirit. So as I overcome my flesh and get involved in what God wants me to do, I want to do it with my kids.

The Family As a Team
We are building a team in my home to do exactly that. We are all involved in evangelism and discipleship with our peer groups. The kids and Susy and I are involved with families. It has taken us a long time to get there, and now I would like to give other fathers a blueprint to follow. I want to help parents develop a plan so that all the team members work together as a family. Too many Christians expect to raise their kids in the church and send them to Wheaton College or Biola, thinking that all of a sudden at 25 years old they'll wake up as evangelists and disciple-makers. But that is not happening because we have not been modeling discipleship in our homes, and we have not been walking with them and discipling them in the faith as we go.

I see men and women devoting themselves to empty endeavors. The things we are going to take with us from this earth to heaven are the souls of people and the Scriptures. Nothing else will last. Too often we are abdicating our responsibilities by involving our kids in activities that do not last. The richest and most satisfying experiences I've had include discipling men, discipling couples with Susy, and discipling my own children. It is an exciting opportunity, and I want that opportunity for everybody. If we're going to face the challenge of a culture in chaos, the first thing we are going to have to do is commit ourselves to eternal things and make sure we know how to disciple.*

Second, we have to recognize that our culture is corrupt. Kids are going down the tubes. Instead of impacting society, our children are falling into the trap of the culture. The only way to avoid losing our kids to the culture is to create a godly culture for our children to live in. I'm not talking separation from the world, but integration of godly conviction in a godless culture.

Third, we are losing the next generation, and it's time the church stood up and decided to figure out an effective means for passing on the truth. We're seeing Joshua's generation all over again, leaving behind people who do not know God or the things of God. If we want our nation to last, or a legacy of world-changing faith to last, we are going to have to commit ourselves to building spiritual strength into the next generation.

Fourth, we are losing the Christian mandate of going and making disciples. The Bible offers a battle plan for raising a generation of disciple-makers. I want to help mothers and fathers see the benefits of being focused on a plan that will not only enrich their lives, build a strong family, and build a battle unit for Jesus Christ, but also be a vehicle by which the whole family can reach the next generation and fulfill the "Great Commission." You can start with little babies and end up with an assault team for Jesus Christ.

Here is my dilemma: Susy and I are two average people who have had extraordinary teaching, mentoring, and discipling, and are involved in an effective ministry. We can take no credit for it. We just said yes to some great opportunities. We chose not to have children when we were younger, but when we did, Susy became "super-mom." She

---

* For more information on discipling, I encourage you to pick up a copy of *Eternal Impact,* a book I did with Chip MacGregor for Harvest House Publishers. A visionary and practical book on how to invest in the lives of people, it will give you some great insights into the process of discipling your children.

would get up at five o'clock in the morning and read books,
to the kids, go to work, come home at lunch and read more
books, then rush back to work. I had very little involvement

Building Lines of Communication in Your Home

Communication involves a lot more than words. It is
best founded on trust, transparency, and truth. So when
communicating with your kids . . .

+ Be at the right place at the right time—just as though
  they were important clients.
+ Ask them about their day and be willing listen to
  what they have to say.
+ Begin with a period of encouragement and affirmation.
+ Be willing to share with them the struggles of your
  day without dumping on them unprocessed problems.
+ Ask feeling questions, such as, "How are you feeling
  after the loss of the game?"
+ Discuss positive attributes of your friends.
+ Ask open-ended relational questions such as, "Who
  do you spend the most time with?" "Who do you feel
  listens the best to you?" or "Have I done anything
  that has hurt your feelings lately?"
+ Confess any known interruption of fellowship which
  you've caused.
+ Remember that a gentle hug goes a long way.
+ Sometimes, let silence reign. Your being silent will
  encourage your children to fill the air with feeling
  words and factual statements.
+ Ask them for feedback, advice, or input.
+ If there has been a recent difficulty in the family, continue to ask follow-up questions several days or
  weeks later.

in the whole process. We were on the road to raising children with one foot in the world and one foot in the church, which would have ended in disaster. So when Abigail was four, Paul was two, and Matt a newborn, we sat down and made some key decisions (including Susy quitting her job) that changed our parenting plan—not because we were smart, but because someone discipled us and mentored us, and we just got ahold of some concepts that we found worked.

So now our 17-year-old daughter sits at ball games and talks to women 30 years older than herself about their problems with their teenagers. She is actually mentoring and sharing Christ with older people, and seeing them come to the recognition that they need Jesus Christ. She is talking to Christian moms and dads about how to communicate with their kids. They come to us, point at Abigail, and ask, "Okay, how did you do it? We want that for our family."

When Paul was 13, he loved to play baseball. In between games one night, I noticed he was walking around behind the concession stands with a girl and boy I didn't know. When I was that age, my dad would have had reason to suspect I was smoking cigarettes, drinking beer, or looking at bad pictures. But Paul came back to me all excited about how he had spent his time sharing Christ with some new acquaintances.

Matt, who is thirteen now, is taking his second friend through a *First Steps* Bible study—an investigative study for nonbelievers or new Christians. My children are just the greatest joy of my life, and are living out the principles that men and women built into us over the last 20 years. John, the beloved apostle, said "I have no greater joy than to hear that my children are walking in the truth" (3 John 4 NIV). That is a father's reward, and that is exactly what I am seeing. I don't take any credit for it. Susy and I had been married for five years before I came to Christ and in that time I destroyed our marriage. We both were reached for Christ through CBMC, then God put our marriage back together again and gave us five more years to grow before our first child came along. We prayed for our kids long before they came, and we had great teaching, so we are just on the other side of the power curve.

Spoons and Attitudes

Parents, it *is* possible to have healthy involvement with kids today. I see many men making lousy decisions, thinking they are discipling their children by showing up at their baseball games. It is time we all grow up and decide we are going to start doing things God's way. If He has blessed you with children, He has also blessed you with the responsibility to raise them. That will mean investing in a healthy relationship.

A friend of mine in another city, a Yale graduate, is one of the smartest engineers I know. His eight-year-old son wanted to learn how to throw a baseball. Instead of picking up a glove and going into the backyard, Jason hired a personal coach to show his kid how to toss a baseball. That's a consumer's answer to a kid's need: Hire a consultant. We are living in a world where we just do not understand how to get along with our kids.

I remember when I was trying to figure out how to build a relationship with my children. Growing up, Susy's family had often vacationed at her Uncle Jimmy's farm. They had 1400 acres near Tulsa, Oklahoma. I had heard about all the neat activities they did on that acreage, so I began thinking, "That is what I need. I need 1400 acres to take care of my kids!" Interestingly, though, when I talked to Susy about the farm and asked her, "What did you like most?" her answer surprised me: Uncle Jimmy would get the jeep, a gallon of ice cream, and drive around the field with one spoon, allowing everyone to eat ice cream in the pasture.

That's it. No big adventure, just kids and a gallon of ice cream and a loving uncle. I realized I didn't need 1400 acres, I just needed a spoon and a good attitude. That's when I started to understand the concept that I can do things with kids that don't require a lot of money or cartoon characters. I found a place we called "Stream Park" in downtown Atlanta, five minutes from our house, where we could go and do fun activities. I learned tremendous principles on how not to spend money, and how to do ordinary things with my kids, building relationships with them. I am continuing to do that, and I want to communicate to dads who have no idea what to do that *it is possible*. Any knucklehead can eat ice cream with a spoon while sitting on the grass. If I can do it, so can you. I am not relational, I don't like babies, and I don't have the temperament to hang out with teenagers. I don't have any natural ability for being a dad, but God is accomplishing something in my life. In shaping my kids, the Lord has shaped me. This book was written as an attempt to share my struggles, to state the vision for why to train kids, to share some practical ideas of how to do it, and to offer the results of what happens when you are faithful.

One Year's Difference

I received a letter from a friend who told all about his son: "Steve is reaching out to his friends and impacting them for Jesus Christ. He is discipling people, sharing his faith—we're really proud. We are seeing tremendous growth in his life." I received another letter from a guy telling me about his house being stormed by eight policemen, and having his son thrown on the carpet of his living room, frisked, handcuffed, and dragged out the door at about 2:00 A.M., charged with murder. The son later admitted to the murder and is now in prison. I asked my kids in our family devotion time, "What is the difference between these two letters?" They said, "Well, obviously one of them is a godly kid and one of them is not." Then someone else suggested, "Maybe one of them has a godly mom and dad and one doesn't. Maybe one has a mom and dad and one doesn't, or maybe one is from a poor and disadvantaged family. Maybe another one goes to a good church."

So I told them the truth: "The only difference between the two boys is 12 months." It's the same kid. His father, writing about reaching peer groups, is talking about the prisoners that his son is now reaching for Christ. The young man is in prison for the rest of his life, but he has come back to Christ. The only difference is 12 months. About a year before it all happened, my wife talked to his wife and asked how things were going.

"You know," that lady replied, "Rob is so involved in work and ministry and all that he is doing, that I'm afraid sometimes he is neglecting our son. I wish he would take time to disciple Steve." Rob never did. Now the son is getting discipling from the prison chaplain and his dad as he visits on weekends. Now Steve is memorizing verses and getting involved in people's lives, but he has done it after taking another man's life. Had Rob discipled his son in the early years, things might have been different.

There is a principle that I have come to understand in my life: *I am responsible for discipling my kids*—not the Sunday school, not the youth pastor, and not the Christian teacher. Me. I am not saying that I am better than anyone else, only that it's my job as the dad. I've seen godly people have very rebellious kids, and I want to implement some practical principles that will change the lives of my kids so that I never have to make excuses for them. I don't want my family to succumb to the culture. That's the challenge we Christians in America are facing, and it's time we developed a plan for meeting that challenge.

Each year we keep track of memorable notes, quotes, quips, and stories and include them in our Christmas card. Just so you can get a feel for the Downer family, we'll offer in each chapter some . . .

Quotable Quotes

✦ *Speaking the Truth in Love:* Matthew, on the return trip from a rodeo, said, "Dad, you're the greatest dad in the world. . . . You're not the most *patient* dad, but you're the greatest dad!"

✦ *The Great Trial Lawyer Case:* Upon being informed by Susy, "This test says I'm pregnant," Dad snatches the box to the do-it-yourself pregnancy test, with a view toward finding the loophole. Printed on the back of the box are these words: "This test has proven to be 100% effective in laboratory tests."

✦ *A Treasure Rediscovered:* Our son Paul happened to walk by as Susy, while cleaning the guest room, picked up a rolled-up sheet of paper and put it on the bed. "Mom, you saved my life! You can't imagine how important that is! That's the map for all 22 forts in the backyard!"

✦ *A Bright Future:* In response to Susy's comment on Paul's birthday that ten was such a great age to be, Paul exclaimed, "I agree. Ten! The dawn of life!"

✦ *Annual Award for Cowardice:* After finding his sleeping bag already occupied by one boy during a backyard camp out, Dad was "forced" to retreat to the house and share the heated waterbed with Susy!

Study Questions

1. What comes to mind when you think of the "ideal family"?

2. Over the past 20 years, how has our notion of a "family" changed?

3. How were you shaped by your father?

4. On a scale of 1 to 10, how involved are you with the spiritual development of your children?

5. If someone were to examine your life, what would they say you worshiped?

2

Where Have All
the Fathers Gone?

*T*hus says the LORD, "Preserve justice, and do righteousness, for My salvation is about to come and
My righteousness to be revealed. How blessed is
the man who does this, and the son of man who takes hold
of it; who keeps from profaning the sabbath, and keeps his
hand from doing any evil"(Isaiah 56:1,2).

I am a direct descendant of one of the church's greatest
preachers. I'm the eighth generation from Jonathan
Edwards, the early American preacher who brought revival
to a sin-soaked land by warning sinners that they were "in
the hands of an angry God." Here was a man who took a
strong stand for Jesus Christ, helping to shape a generation
through his faith. Yet by the time I was born, there was no
evidence of any godly individuals in my immediate family
line. Someone, somewhere, dropped the ball after Jonathan
Edwards. What could have been a godly legacy turned into
a spiritually bankrupt generation. In looking into the family, I realized that the fathers had failed to pass on the faith.
When Dad doesn't do his job, the spiritual life of the family
dies.

When God first set up His plan for the family, He left
the leadership of the home and the teaching of spiritual

truth to the fathers. The Lord explicitly instructed the dads to model and talk about spiritual things with their kids. That command, God's central plan for developing spiritual families, is not happening in most Christian homes. Our neglect of it is scary, because we are at risk of losing the next generation. People who know the truth and turn from it always end up in trouble.

Take, for example, Gideon, a champion of the faith. He was God's chosen leader, who believed in the power of the Lord and defeated a mighty enemy with a ragtag army. Gideon is one of the heroes in the Old Testament, but what happened with his son, Abimelech, is one of the most frightening events in Scripture. Abimelech murdered the 70 sons of Gideon, spare one. The godly man's son became a criminal. What a condemnation for one of the greatest leaders the world has ever seen!

Have you ever noticed how few dads seem to have a great relationship with their sons anymore? Have you heard the nightly news report on the millions of single-parent homes in this country, or wondered why there are so many inner-city children with no father in their lives? Have you ever stopped to ask yourself, "Where have all the fathers gone?" At a time when a dad is so desperately needed, why has he disappeared?

The Father As Watchman
A 1996 *USA Today* poll found that only 37 percent of those polled believe our country will be in good hands when the next generation grows up. I find that a real tragedy, for I don't believe this attitude has ever been prevalent in our society before. I don't know of a time in our country's history when such a poll would have shown these results. And it's really not a condemnation of our young people, or our government, or our institutions. It's a condemnation of parents who have failed to do their job. It's a denunciation of fathers who have abdicated their God-given responsibility in the family.

Fathers used to serve as watchmen for the family, protecting their children from evil influences and setting an example of integrity. But the watchmen have fallen asleep, allowing all sorts of destruction to come upon the family. The dads have become weak, acting powerless in the face of Satan's attack. Jeremiah 47:3 gives a vivid picture of this: "Because of the noise of the galloping hoofs of his stallions, the tumult of his chariots, and the rumbling of his wheels, the fathers have not turned back for their children, because of the limpness of their hands." Our culture has seen fathers abandoning their responsibilities as shepherds, leaving their children to face the tumult of the world on their own.

Perhaps with all the downsizing that has taken place in recent years, many Christian men have reason to feel insecure. They live in fear of losing their jobs. They continually hear stories about couples who are divorcing. They are never sure what standard they are supposed to live up to. The problem is that instead of placing their trust in God, too many fathers are placing their trust in man. They are trying to provide for their families through their jobs, instead of trusting God to honor His promise and provide all of their needs. The result is that fathers are leaving their children behind.

A watchman cares for those under his charge. In Jeremiah 3:15, the Lord promises to give knowledge and understanding to "shepherds after My own heart." That is, He can offer us the help and resources we need to protect our loved ones in a violent, evil world. A few verses later, the Lord states, "Stand by the ways and see and ask for the ancient paths, where the good way is, and walk in it; and you shall find rest for your souls" (Jeremiah 6:16). Unfortunately, the people of that day are quoted as replying, "We will not walk in it." God is looking for men who will follow Him, and who will serve as watchmen for their families.

Discipling Your Children

Remember, a dad is a discipler of his children. It used to be that we could trust our Sunday schools to teach our children the stories of Scripture and the application to their lives. Maybe there was a time we could trust our schools to teach our children character. However, if we're relying on our schools and churches to disciple our kids today, we are not doing our jobs. We are watchmen asleep. Our goal as fathers ought to be to help our children see Jesus Christ in us, and then to grow our kids into disciple-makers. But when the watchmen are asleep, the enemy begins making progress.

I am shocked to see some of the things going on in Christian families. I was on a business trip not long ago, and on the airplane was a high-school group heading for a mission trip. I ended up sitting next to a bright, well-mannered young woman. The young people were passing around a book of some kind, reading passages from it and laughing and pointing as it made its way from seat to seat. It finally got to our row, and the young lady beside me took the book and started reading the pages. At first I didn't pay any attention, but eventually my curiosity got the best of me and I looked over her shoulder.

I couldn't believe what I saw. The book was Dennis Rodman's autobiography, and I had never seen such a vile piece of trash in my life. Honestly, I couldn't bring myself to look at the pictures. I've made the commitment of Job 31:1 not to let my eyes fall upon a woman who would cause me to lust, and promised Susy I would not put anything before me that would divert my attention from her. I just don't need that sort of filth in my mind, so I chose not to look at the book.

Then the thought struck me: Why in the world would these young people, who were going across the ocean to minister in the name of Jesus Christ, want to fill their minds with this sort of filth? Later I noticed that some of the kids were wearing Dennis Rodman T-shirts. When I asked a couple of them about it, they didn't seem to think it was a big deal. I was just an old-fashioned church guy, somehow not in touch with their culture. But who needs that sort of "culture"? From what I saw, it did not appear the Lord

Jesus Christ was the predominant occupation in the minds of those young people. They didn't want to fill their minds with Scripture or with the thoughts of God, but with the rantings of a tattooed basketball player with an overdeveloped ego. The guy appears to be everything a father would not want his children to be, *but the fathers and leaders on the trip didn't seem to notice.* It seemed to be no big deal to them if the kids on the mission trip were filling their minds with tripe. Where were the watchmen? Asleep at the gates.

When I was going to Vietnam, I never worried about getting killed. Everybody in wartime thinks they're invincible. Everyone thinks it will happen to somebody else. And that is exactly the attitude many parents seem to have in raising their kids. They think moral catastrophe could never happen to their family. The fathers don't see what they are building into their young kids' lives. Rather than being watchmen, they become businessmen, leaving the kids to watch out for themselves.

One of the principles that I have lived by is to show our children the true results of sin. I want them to learn about sin from *me*, rather than from billboards and televisions. About ten years ago, I took my kids to the Fulton County courthouse and introduced them to a judge. They sat through an arraignment and watched men and women come through in handcuffs, leg irons, and jail coveralls. The people were charged with everything from robbery to assault to prostitution (which I explained was taking off your clothes for money). Then we talked with the judge. He took my kids into the jail and had them smell inside the lockup, lie on the stone bench, and experience the fright that comes when the door bangs shut. A few years later I took them to visit the drunk tank, and they observed people lying in their own vomit—something never portrayed on the Budweiser commercials. Another time I took them to a junkyard and showed them where fast cars end up when people drink. There were beer cans on the floors of these vehicles, and blood on the windshields. We saw what a sports car looks like after hitting a tree. If you really want to teach your kids the truth, *let them see the consequences of sin.* My kids saw exactly what happens to people who get involved in the sin of drug addiction and violence, which helped them understand the consequences of sin. I want to be the first one to introduce my children to the results of sin, so they aren't confused and start to think that sin is fun.

Too many fathers don't know what they are building into their kids. We send our children off to the best Christian schools, clothe them in the latest fashions, and take them to Bible-preaching churches, then turn around and allow them to revel in idolatry and hedonism through the TV. It's like going out and hiring prostitutes, robbers, and drug addicts to come and perform in our living rooms for three or four hours each night. One of the reasons it is happening is because Dad isn't making the effort to be a watchman.

Many years ago Susy and I sat down and watched "M*A*S*H." That program was, and continues to be, one of the mainstays of TV watchers in America, so I wanted to keep track of the messages it was sharing with the viewers across the country. The various types of sin extolled on that show were astounding. Everything dealing with religion was mocked. Father Mulcahey was a buffoon with little genuine faith. Frank, who carried a Bible, was portrayed as a Bible-thumping, fornicating, hypocritical malingerer. Patriotism was bad, excessive drinking was good, and America was to blame for all the deaths in the Korean War. That message is beamed out to millions of homes through reruns every night. As a watchman, I decided we didn't need that sort of destructive message in our family.

Blind Watchmen
The Lord once criticized the lazy fathers of Israel in this way:

> His watchmen are blind, all of them know nothing. All of them are dumb dogs unable to bark, dreamers lying down, who love to slumber; and the dogs are greedy,

they are not satisfied. And they are shepherds who have no understanding; they have all turned to their own way, each one to his unjust gain, to the last one. "Come," they say, "let us get wine, and let us drink heavily of strong drink; and tomorrow will be like today, only more so" (Isaiah 56:10-12).

At the time of the prophet Isaiah, the nation of Israel was in great turmoil. The people needed protection, but those put in charge—the watchmen—were blind and dumb. Can you imagine a watchdog unable to bark? Instead of doing their job, the watchmen of Israel became more interested in partying and selfish pleasure than in protecting the country. As a result, the nation fell apart. The generation of leaders drifted away from wisdom and godliness.

I see a lot of generational drift in our own nation, particularly in the increasing acceptance of sensuality in our lives. I see more and more Christian men giving in to sexual temptation. They are involved in church, but when their business takes them on the road, these men sit in front of the television and fill their hearts and minds with lust and sin. They are living dishonest lives with their wives and children, unwilling to confess their great need for visual protection from sexual temptations.

From the time my kids were old enough to pray, they would remember me as I traveled. They would pray (and still do) that I would not go out with anybody except Mom, that I would not look at women who had no clothes on, and that I would not take my clothes off with women. Even before they knew about sex, they prayed very clearly for their father. You don't have to be 16 to know that you are not supposed to take off your clothes with someone other than your husband or your wife. Those prayers have always been a protection for me. I have often said to my family, "When I am out there, you pray for me, that I'll find protection. Now when *you* go out, who will be praying for you?" Their reply? *"You will, Dad!"* My attempts at protection have helped us build a relationship.

The problem of sensual temptation was evident in Isaiah's day. Isaiah 3:16 says, "Because the daughters of Zion are proud, and walk with heads held high, and seductive eyes . . ." In other words, girls who dressed and acted seductively were held partly responsible for the downfall of the nation. Unfortunately, that is exactly the sort of young women our culture seems to be developing. In America, too many believers are raising daughters who are used to wearing two square feet of material over their private parts, and these girls don't understand what they are doing to men. They don't understand that they are attracting people by their physical appearance, rather than by their godly hearts. They are getting themselves in trouble and leading themselves and boys astray.

I went to speak to a big church singles' group not long ago. The crowd ranged from about 22 to 26 years of age, none of them married, and I was really incensed when one pretty young woman walked in wearing a leather skirt that looked like a tea towel. It barely covered her, and she sat right in the front row. I tried to avert my eyes, but it's difficult never to look at an attractive woman sitting half-uncovered in the front row. My shock increased when I discovered that this was the wife of the man who had invited me to speak at the church! He was a CBMC guy, who really loved the Lord, but his wife was running around looking like a prostitute, and he didn't seem to even notice or care.

As I was getting ready to speak, I silently prayed, "Lord, give me the wisdom to know how to address this." Then the Lord began to fill my mind. I started with some Scripture, then began to talk about the responsibility men and women have to each other to not cause one another to stumble. We are explicitly warned to be careful and not tempt one another.

The more I talked, the more this woman in the front row became uncomfortable. She began to tug on her tea towel, to try and get it halfway over her thighs. But that was mechanically impossible, since the material was not long enough, so she finally leaned over and asked her husband if she could borrow his blue blazer, which she used to cover her legs. Afterward she had some strong words for me, but she admitted that she had not thought through the influence her clothes could have on other people.

I have gone into homes where I have been concerned about the daughters because they appeared so lusty. They walk, in the words of Isaiah, with "seductive eyes," and I wonder why their parents allow it. The problem is that we men are not communicating honestly with our wives and daughters about the way that we are made. For example, when I was in Maui with Susy, and we were admiring a great seascape, there were two people under an umbrella involved in overt sexual activity. It was unbelievable how they were wrapped around each other in plain sight. My eyes went right to them, and I had to force myself to turn away. But Susy didn't even notice them. She was saying things like, "Isn't the beach beautiful!" My wife never saw them—but I never saw anything else! Men are visually stimulated, and the sensuality so prevalent in our culture these days plays to our weaknesses. Dads, if we are to set an example in our homes, we've got to talk with our wives about the way we survive in our culture.

I didn't communicate this well to my wife and daughter, and it caused some problems. They wanted to watch some figure skating on television one night, and I was struggling with the whole thing. I think a lot of women enjoy ice skating because it is beautiful and romantic, while a lot of men enjoy it because women wearing short skirts parade around with their legs over their heads. Anyway, at our family Bible study that next morning, I asked my boys what they spent their time watching when figure skating was on television. "Well, Dad," one of them replied hesitantly, "I really struggle with it, because I end up looking at parts of the girls I should not be looking at."

My wife could hardly believe it.

"I have that trouble, too," I admitted, but by that time Susy was suggesting we "move on to the next topic." But then my two other sons admitted the same thing, and that got her thinking. We spent our morning talking about maintaining a godly thought-life. As men we need to be transparent with our children, teaching them the risks that are evident in our culture. We can't be blind watchmen, standing around while the enemy takes more and more territory. We've got to be willing to stand up for purity and morality, even when it goes against the prevailing culture.

Falling by the Sword

Isaiah goes on to say that the end result of all the watchmen falling asleep is "your men will fall by the sword" (Isaiah 3:25). That is what's happening in America today. Our young men are falling by the sword, as violence overtakes them. A host of destructive behaviors attached to sexual sin is causing death and disease at an age at which young peo-

---

Getting Your Kids to Talk

Most of us fail in the arena of creating a secure relationship and environment which is conversation-inducing from a young person's point of view. Here are some tips:

+ Be fun.
+ Stay relaxed.
+ Rather than rules, give encouragement.
+ Let them pick the restaurant, the meal, and the timing of the event.
+ Start your conversation with a funny, self-effacing story.
+ Be walking in God's spirit and not in preoccupation with business pressures.
+ Tell a compelling account of someone else's life.
+ Pray for God to use your time together to strengthen your relationship.

ple should still be enjoying the pleasure of youth. It's time we faced the danger and talked about it as families. Unless the fathers step forward as leaders, the young men will continue to fall.

Mary, a good friend of ours with three sons, called me in a panic not long ago. She often calls for advice, because she wants to know what to do with her boys. She raised them with little input from her husband, who has been immersed in scholarly research from the time they were babies. They all got good grades, were involved in Bible school and Sunday school, said they loved the Lord, and had made professions of faith. Now she feels she is losing them. "They don't listen to me anymore," she told me. Her youngest is now a senior in high school, and Mary just found out he was out all evening at the senior prom, then spent the night in a hotel room with his girlfriend. "Why?" she asked me. "After all my words and discussions, why would he do something so stupid?"

As I talked to her, it was clear she did not feel equipped to deal with these issues. "My husband is so involved with his work, and he's right in the middle of his Ph.D. dissertation. I can't really expect him to take time from what he is doing to deal with this problem. Emotionally he is so strung out from his work pressures and the demands on his time that he is not going to cope well with this." Over the years, her husband had pretty well separated himself from his sons, giving instruction without a relationship with his boys. But I have found whenever you try to discipline someone without a relationship, you do not get righteousness but rebellion. Her husband was drowning himself in his work, not spending time with the family, and expecting his wife to hold everything together. There is nothing that causes a mom to be quite so hysterical as a father not involving himself with his kids when the kids go into a ditch.

So I called him on the phone. "Mitch," I told him, "your boys are headed for destruction. You may be a success at your work, but do you think that will comfort you when you find out you've been a failure as a father?" Like many guys, he was forsaking gold for rubbish. He was willing to dump his family in order to make a name for himself, thinking he could always check back into the family when-ever there was an emergency. But families don't work like that. Relationships can't be turned on and off. They have to be nurtured.

My generation grew up with the attitude that we would achieve and possess. Men have given their lives to working and gaining a resumé and a reputation among their peers, but in doing so they have left behind the next generation. There is nothing more joyful than having children walking with God in a fruitful and productive way, and nothing more painful than watching your children's lives destroyed by the evil influences of society.

I was in the home three nights ago of a godly couple in their mid-thirties. They make about $200,000 a year, live in a beautiful house with a huge pool, have everything they could ever want, but have never allowed money to get in the way of ministry. He is an engineer, with a real vision for winning and discipling other men. She is a lawyer, with a heart for women who are hurting. Not long ago they had their neighbors over for dinner, saw that the couple was experiencing marital difficulties, and led both the husband and wife to a saving knowledge of Jesus Christ. This couple has a dynamite ministry, and are being used by God to touch the lives of many people. Unfortunately, they don't seem to be touching their own children. When you come into their house as a visitor, the kids do not get up from their chairs. They hardly recognize your presence. They are demanding with the mom. They can usually be found watching a six-foot-wide TV screen that's often playing an afternoon soap opera.

The last time I was in their home, the children were watching a movie in which a nearly naked man was talking about having an affair with his secretary, who at that point was lying provocatively on the bed with a towel wrapped around her. Mom and Dad apparently did not see any problem with it. They didn't even make excuses to turn it off when I was there. Danger signs are everywhere in their home, and they can't see them. They're like blind watchmen, allowing the destruction of their children.

Spirituality and Sour Grapes

What every parent should want is for their child to walk with God and be controlled by Him—not regulated by a bunch of rules from Mom and Dad, but open to God's voice through prayer and Bible study. We want each child to be seeking a godly spouse, for if they marry godly people, they'll have a shot at a great marriage. We would all like our kids to be good fathers and mothers, diligent in their work, and good stewards of all that God has provided for them. We would like them to have a Christ-centered worldview, understanding that this world is comprised of people who have been captivated and incarcerated by the world's system, and have a heart for freeing those people from their bondage through eternal life in Jesus Christ. Every parent wants their children to be disciples of the Lord, so that they

---

Ten Things Your Kids Will Love to Hear

+ "God has a wonderful plan for your life."
+ "I can't wait to see what God is going to do with your many gifts."
+ "You are *so* pretty!"
+ "You are *so* strong!"
+ "Isn't it exciting the great number of opportunities God has given you?"
+ "It is a privilege to be your father."
+ "I'm so proud of the choices that you've made."
+ "I enjoy being with you. You're really a lot of fun."
+ "Thanks for listening."
+ "Great job!"

can in turn be spiritual reproducers and pass on their faith to the next generation.

But with all the cultural problems we face, some Christians tend to sit around and share their sour grapes. They complain about the evil influences, but do nothing to protect their kids from them. They whine about the wickedness on television, but sit in front of the tube night after night. It's time for the fathers to stand up as watchmen. We can no longer complain about what other people have done to us, or what sort of legacy we have been left. There comes a time to take responsibility for our own problems, and as we do that, we can change the course of our family history by cutting off the line of guilt and sin, and starting a line of godliness. It is time for the fathers of America to stand up and take responsibility for their problems. In Jeremiah 31:29,30, the Lord says, "In those days they will not say again, 'The fathers have eaten sour grapes, and the children's teeth are set on edge.' But everyone will die for his own iniquity; each man who eats the sour grapes, his teeth will be set on edge." We need to ditch the sour grapes and start focusing on spirituality.

That's what the apostle Paul did. One of the great father/son relationships in the Bible is that of Paul and Timothy. While Paul wasn't a *physical* father to Timothy, he was certainly a *spiritual* father, treating Timothy as his own son, training him, instructing him, and teaching him spiritual truth. Paul even said that he had sent Timothy out into the world "after the interest of the Lord." Whenever the New Testament talks about discipling, it always uses the metaphor of parenting, because no one can draw closer to us and know us better than our parents. If it is possible to have a close father/son relationship with someone *outside* your home, how much greater it must be to have that sort of close discipling relationship with someone *inside* your own home. Dad, you can be president of this and leader of that, but if your children are walking with God and grow up reproducing your spiritual life in their children and grandchildren, you literally are impacting generations of people.

Missed Opportunities

The Andersons sat in their home, excited about the new ministry with which they were involved. They told me about the people who were coming to know the Lord, and all the excitement of discipling new converts into maturity. Suddenly, in walked their 16-year-old daughter with the news that she was pregnant. With that announcement, everything changed. The Andersons' lives went into a tail-spin. Neither felt equipped to continue in ministry. Both suffered from feelings of failure. They had to admit that there had been some warning signs and guideposts they had missed with their daughter. Now it was too late. The full ramifications really broke their hearts. The father took it the hardest, because he readily admits he failed as a watchman. He allowed peers to overcome parents, and the culture to overcome Christ in his home.

Many of the current generation of young people in church have drifted from their walk with Christ because their parents never showed them how to stay close. We have substituted success for significance, style for sub-stance, and ministry to others for ministry to our families. Too many Christians have a shallow faith, and that shal-lowness rubs off on the lives of their children.

Think about your day: The school bus comes in the morning, taking your kids off to school. You are out the door before the sun comes up. You come home, sometimes after the sun goes down. The children have three or four hours of homework. How do you maintain influence in your children's lives? Most parents in our country have del-egated the responsibility of raising their children to differ-ent institutions, including some very well-meaning people. They've delegated child-rearing to youth groups, youth pastors, and teachers. Then they've gone to work. But they are giving away the very responsibilities they can't delegate to anybody else. The father is the watchman—he can't give that role to anyone else.

Quotable Quotes

✦ *Forgetting the Mission*: While walking past the family room and hearing the grunts and groans of two little boys taking part in ground-level fisticuffs, Susy heard Matthew say in a moment of intermission, "Hey, Josh, I forget, are we fighting or are we wrestling?"

✦ *Extra Skin Discovered*: During a wrestling match on the carpet while implementing a double-twisted choke hold on Dad's waist, Paul exclaimed, "Hey, Dad, where did you get all this extra skin?"

✦ *The Positive Outlook of a Child*: Facing the required removal of four baby teeth in the middle of the All Star tournament, Matthew responded, "Dad, I can't wait to get 'em yanked because all I'll be able to eat is ice cream!"

✦ *Typo of the Year*: In a handwritten note to a valued and beloved co-laborer, Phil mistakenly wrote the letter *b* in place of the letter *y* in this note: "Oh, what a jo*b* it has been to co-labor with you this year."

✦ *Truth over Discretion*: Joshua, age six, to Matthew's all-star baseball coach: "Whoa! Where did they ever find an all-star jersey big enough to fit you?" The coach responded, "Whoever's little brother this is, you're benched for the game!"

Study Questions

1. What would you say are the greatest dangers attacking our children?

2. In what ways is a father called to be a "watchman" for his family?

3. What are the results of having a blind watchman?

4. How can a Christian father realistically protect his children from the evil influences of our world?

5. What practical steps are you taking to leave behind a godly legacy?

3

Raising Godly Kids

*A*nd you shall love the LORD your God with all your
heart and with all your soul and with all your
might. And these words, which I am commanding
you today, shall be on your heart; and you shall teach them
diligently to your sons and shall talk of them when you sit
in your house and when you walk by the way and when you
lie down and when you rise up. And you shall bind them as
a sign on your hand and they shall be as frontals on your
forehead. And you shall write them on the doorposts of your
house and on your gates (Deuteronomy 6:5-9).

The University of Michigan did a study about how many
minutes people spend with their kids. They found that the
average American father spends about 8 minutes a day
with his children, and on weekends 14 minutes a day.
Moms did a little bit better. The average mother spent 11
minutes per day with each child, and 30 minutes a day on
the weekends. Those are what I call "fishbowl parents."
That is, they think about raising children as though they
were raising fish: You put some water into a great big
aquarium, fill it up, dump in the fish, put fish food on top,
and watch them eat. Most fish owners sort of sit back and
watch them go. And that's the way most folks raise kids.

Unfortunately, that's not the system God had in mind
when He designed the family. As a matter of fact, "fishbowl

parents" are going to find a lot of heartache when they discover their method of child-rearing doesn't work. As with
anything important, you get out of it what you put into it.
If you want to be a great pianist, you've got to spend an
enormous amount of time practicing. Without investing the
time, you'll always be a run-of-the-mill piano player. If you
want to be a great lawyer, or artist, or golfer, you've got to
spend a lot of time learning the basics, improving, practicing, and eventually becoming proficient at it. Proficiency
takes time. The same is true of parenting.

Raising good children is a difficult process. As parents,
we begin not knowing much about what to do, and we
learn by our mistakes. But nothing can take the place of
simply spending time with our kids, so that they see how
we live and pattern themselves after us. A short while ago I
asked one of the most godly women I know—a woman
who has raised sons and daughters who love and serve the
Lord—to name the one most important aspect of parenting.
Without hesitating for a moment, she said, "Spend plenty
of time with your children. By doing so you'll create a bond
that can never be broken."

Susy and I have had a tremendous advantage as parents, as many people have poured their lives into ours and
given us much insight and wisdom on raising children. We
were Christians, walking with the Lord, five years before
Abigail was born. We prayed for our children before we
were even sure we wanted to have any children. We prayed
for months before our first was born that God would not
give us children who would not love the Lord. We felt there
were enough people on earth who didn't know Him, and
maybe our time should be devoted to those people, so we
put a lot of prayer into our children before they ever arrived.
You may already be in a position where your children have
seen you not walking with God, but I've learned that it's
never too late to set an example. We do not determine where
our kids end up; the Lord does. We need to be available to
be used by Him, no matter what He calls us to do. When we
make mistakes, we've got to learn to confess them and move

forward. We all live with the consequences of past actions, but God is calling us to begin living holy lives in front of our children, no matter what the past has brought. I've made some terrible errors in my life. Rather than letting them continue causing trouble in my family, I've confessed them and put them behind me. Now my job is to spend time with my kids and reveal God to them as best I can.

So ask yourself: What occupies my time? The places you invest in reveal the things that are most important to you. If you spend it all at work, your career is what you value most. If you invest all your time into sports, that's the thing that occupies your heart. I talk with a lot of fathers who spend the bulk of their time lying in front of the TV, hoping something worthwhile will come on, but it seldom does! In reality, if we ask our kids how they know we love them, we'll find that they evaluate our love by the amount of time we spend with them. If we make time with them a priority, they understand their importance to us.

As a dad, I need to be available, open, and ready to hear what God has for me with my children. My own dad was no fun in my early years. He never taught me, or talked with me, or wanted to spend time together. But the Lord says we are to teach our children to love God by talking about Him and showing our devotion to our kids. I can't just say to my youngest, "Susanna, love God!" She'll look at me and ask, "Who's God?" To help my kids understand God, I've got to know Him, manifest Him in my life, and spend time with my children so they can see and then model the manifestation of God reflected in me. Perhaps there is no better way to help our kids love God than by exploring His character.

He Is Sovereign

There are many characteristics of God, but I want to explore nine and discuss how they relate to fathering. The first is that He is sovereign. He is supreme over all things. Deuteronomy 4:39 puts it this way: *"Know therefore today. . . the Lord, He is God in heaven above and on the earth below; there is no other."* He is in charge of all things. As we look at our role in the home, God has given us authority. We have no authority as parents that God didn't give us. Our goal is that our children would follow God. But if we are not under God's authority, and our children are not submitting to our authority, how are they going to learn to submit to God? What we need to do as fathers is to submit to the Lord, encourage our children to submit to our authority, and trust that as our kids grow and are nurtured, they will learn the blessing of submission to God.

When I try to be sovereign in my home, I am going against God's plan for my family. We need to be willing to submit to the will of God, and show our children through our actions that we submit to the Lord. One goal that Susy and I have had is that we would have an upfront, personal, growing, one-on-one relationship with each of our children. We fail sometimes—a healthy relationship takes constant evaluation. But that's our goal: to build a relationship with each of our children.

My brother-in-law Tom always thought I sheltered my kids too much, loading them down with rules and restrictions. But after I sent my 14-year-old son to Africa, he said to me, "I'll never accuse you of sheltering your kids anymore, Phil." I told him that by being protective, I was trying to build character and competency. So when Susy and I had the opportunity to send Paul to four countries in East Africa with Tim Philpot, the newly elected president of CBMC International, we did so knowing we had tried to prepare him for the battles of life. He was going to have to live out the instruction he had received from his parents.

Shortly into the trip, Paul was struggling with trying not to look at the lewd pictures in a magazine of the man sitting next to him on the airplane. Paul told me later he would struggle, fail, confess, and then struggle again—all the time observing our friend Tim Philpot, who was seemingly unaware of the nudity as he pored through his Bible and prayed about the trip. Paul called home that night and told me he had failed some, but through that failure had recognized the need for guarding one's eyes, "Just like you told me, Dad." He also learned from watching the persevering Tim, who would not give in to the temptations that were close to him. The experience helped Paul withstand other temptations during the trip. If we want our children to grow up and not get burned by sin, we must begin by keeping their hands off the hot stove, and persevere by giving them an opportunity to work close to the stove when they are ready for it. In that way, we are taking *recruits* and training *soldiers* for Christ in the family.

He Is Holy
The second aspect of God's character is that He is holy. 1 Samuel 2:2 tells us, *"There is none holy as the Lord."* As the holy Father, God is entirely righteous. But those of us who are earthly fathers are still struggling with sin. Unfortunately, some of us try to project an image of a "favored class." That is, we have our own standards. We ask our kids to live by rules that we are not willing to live by.

Not long ago, I was in a home where a father insisted his kids turn off the television. "You've been watching too much," he told them. "Besides, most of the stuff on TV is junk." But I noticed, as we moved toward his study, he had his own television on! The message his children received was that it was bad for kids to watch the tube, but ok for adults. That's the sort of message that drives kids away. We need to live by the same rules we ask our children to live by. Paul warned in Colossians 3:21 NKJV, "Do not provoke your children, lest they become discouraged." I think one of the ways dads provoke their children is by having two standards. We expect them to be good and follow God, but we claim the privilege of doing anything we want to do.

We need to learn the Lord's view on righteousness. The world says the way to teach kids about sin is to go out and experience it, but the unexpected result is that when you find out all about sin, it traps you. My friend Carey had an interest in traveling across Russia, so he did an Internet search using the words *free* and *Russia*. It took him to a

screen that read "Beautiful and Free: Sexy Russian Girls."
His curiosity got the better of him, and soon he was brows-
ing through the lewd trash on the Net. His experimentation
became pleasure, and before long he had developed a daily
habit of looking at pornography during the quiet moments
away from his family, even while his wife and children were
readying themselves for church. Carey was filling his heart
and mind with garbage, and separating himself from his
Savior, his wife, and his family. Then one morning his wife
caught him red-handed when Carey was unable to blink off
the smut before she could see what he was doing. That day
was filled with confession, tears, and repentance, in addi-
tion to a recognition that he needed to follow Joseph's example of fleeing from sin in order to escape its grasp.

God is holy and uncompromising with His children.
I've had to admit to my own children examples of when I,
years ago, walked the streets in a bad part of town. Curiosity and a desire to share a few exciting moments left me in
great danger and sin. The truth is, we are never old enough,
mature enough, or strong enough to withstand the grasp of
sin. But I'm glad I told my children the honest truth of that
story, because a year ago, while Susy and I were in Asia on
a ministry trip with 12-year-old Matthew and 16-year-old
Abigail, I passed by a door filled with women who said,
"Come in for a free drink. Just come in for one minute and
take a look." I turned to my kids and asked, "What do you
think? Do you think we should do that? Do you think your
father, president of CBMC, a man who is supposed to be a
godly Christian leader, could survive?"

They both looked at me and said, "No, Dad, you could-
n't survive." And they were right—I needed to run away
from that door. I must admit that the next time I was on that
street, I wanted to go by the same door again and see if I
could catch a glimpse of what was going on inside, but I
forced myself to walk on the other side of the street. Having shared my weakness with my kids, they watched me
closely as I turned my head and crossed the street. (Frankly,
if I had not crossed the street and had instead started

toward that building, I think both my teenagers would have confronted their father with going too close to a known trap of Satan!) The Scriptures tell us to "flee from sin," and I think it's time fathers began taking that literally, and demonstrating the mechanics of fleeing to their families.

Bankers have a lot of problems with counterfeit money, but they don't train tellers by asking them to handle counterfeits. Instead, bankers ask tellers to handle the real McCoy, becoming so familiar with genuine U.S. dollars they can immediately recognize a phony bill. In the same way, we can make sure our children spend so much time with the authentic source of joy and righteousness, the Lord Jesus Christ, that they recognize when somebody offers them a false source. We ought to flood our children's thinking with our own life examples, training them with the authentic holiness of God so they learn not to compare themselves with peers or parents, but with the life of the Lord Jesus. As a bank teller becomes intimately familiar with the authentic monetary scrip of America, our children must become intimately acquainted with the authentic scriptural principles of the Lord.

After giving an instruction such as, "Don't put down the Skil saw on the floor until the blade stops" or, "Don't walk aimlessly through the magazine racks at the airport," I usually follow up with one of my favorite questions: "Do you know how I know not to do that?" My kids have gotten used to saying, "We know, Dad—because you tried it and you got stuck with something you didn't want to have in your mind." I often reply, "That's right. All I'm trying to do is give you the benefit of the lessons learned from my own failure." My lectures are not for the sake of creating perfect children, but rather godly children who are growing in the holiness of the Lord.

We need to teach our kids how to deal with temptation. I started sharing my temptations with my kids early in their lives, not in explicit terms, but in ways they could understand and pray for me. For example, I often stay in hotels that offer pornographic movies in the rooms. I don't watch

How to Build Inward Conviction, Not Just Outward Conformity

✦ Be transparent about your struggles.

✦ Share your failures.

✦ Tell your kids the consequences of your bad decisions.

✦ Talk about times when practices failed and only principles survived.

✦ Pray out loud together.

✦ Offer more questions than instructions.

them, but I will confess I have read the titles. These sound like hard-core, raw pornography, and I asked my sons and daughters when they were just old enough to pray, to pray for me that I would be strong and God would be with me in that room. I ask God that I would live in that room the same way I would live if my kids were all there. I know that back home, the Downer boys and girls are praying that "Daddy will be good." I want to teach my sons and daughters how to deal with temptation, because this world is going to be much worse in the future. God is righteous, and if I'm going to help my family grasp that truth, I've got to live out His righteousness.

Susy often reminds the kids that bad choices bring bad results. We need to be going not in our own way but in God's way. When we go the wrong way, God disciplines us. As a father, I have to be honest enough to admit my own failings to my family. There have been plenty of times I've lined them up on the couch and said, "Well, Daddy has blown it, and I'm sorry. Would you please forgive me for my bad attitude? I've been impatient. I was wrong."

We want our kids to have fun, and to do that they have to learn that sin is not fun. Oh, it's a thrill for a short moment. But unholiness always leads to unhappiness. We need to teach our children that they can have fun without sin. We want to be the first people to teach our kids about the world. I want to be the first one to teach my children about speeding cars. I want to be the first person to teach my children about alcohol, drugs, and sexual temptation.

When one of our teenage friends got arrested at school, we spent a lot of time talking about the fun and acceptance he thought he would have by going along with his friends. As a result of his actions, he reaped pain and brokenness. We talked extensively about Donny's expulsion from school. My son Paul went to see him, took him a gift, shared his commitment as a friend to him, and prayed with him. Paul wasn't condoning his wrong, but affirming their friendship. Through that experience, my kids were able to see firsthand the pain of giving in to peers and getting away from God.

He Is Just

Second Chronicles 19:7 tells us that God's judgments are perfect. I continually remind our children that *God's* judgments are perfect, but *mine* aren't. I sometimes make mistakes. They have learned that, too. We have talked to our kids about discipline, that God has given them to us and asked us to be in charge of them until they are old enough to take charge of their own lives. That's our God-ordained role, and the Lord has said in Proverbs 13:24 that he who spares the rod hates his son. So my kids understand that I need to discipline them when they get out of line.

I've become convinced that the "rod" should be used to separate us from the discipline. We should spank small children when they need it, but using a rod so that they don't see us merely as spankers. The rod separates me from the punishment. I was skeptical about corporal punishment at first, but when a good friend observed our first child's bratty behavior when she was 2½, she loved us enough to say, "If you love Abigail, you will start disciplining her immediately. The younger you start, the easier it will be." That person was right. I took the message to heart and got myself a rod.

You see, I learned the basic principle of discipline in the Marines: *Discipline exists to save your life.* If you blow it in wartime, you can be sorry, but you can't change the fact that a lot of guys got killed. Being sorry doesn't change the results of sin. Discipline teaches us that if we make bad choices, we'll experience bad results. If a father is consistent in discipline, loving his kids and disciplining not in anger but for correction, he'll find the family understands the justice of God. If a dad can forgive and reveal his forgiveness, his kids will grasp the forgiveness of the heavenly Father.

I don't mean that a child should be punished when he makes a mistake. Kids need to experience the natural consequences that come with mistakes. But I have tried to teach our kids there are some things I don't have to explain to them. For example, I don't have to tell them not to blindly throw rocks. When somebody does something that's clearly dangerous, he or she gets punished.

Most parents don't want to be bothered trying to keep their kids in line. But kids are lost, selfish people in need of a Savior. Left to themselves, they'll become little terrors—and eventually big terrors. The only way to prevent that is to demonstrate justice. [Being just takes a lot of strength.] It's very similar to being a soldier—you have to have strength, valor, dependability, and commitment. We are in a battle for our families in America. Many children are unrestrained, and now we have some groups warning us never to spank children. They pretend that spanking is a form of child abuse, instead of a form of correction. But without it, we have uncorrected people terrorizing the land. With a little love and tenderness, discipline becomes corrective, not just a means of hitting back at someone who's hurt us.

We need to listen to our kids, care about them, build self-esteem, and show real openness to their ideas and what they are doing. All that takes time. I remember my dad always had a list of things he wanted to accomplish. If he got the list done he was happy, and if he didn't get it done he wasn't happy. And no matter what happened, he had his list. Unfortunately, I was seldom on it. I remember one time saying to him, "Dad, I've got something really important to tell you." But his answer was always, "Just a minute, Son, I'm doing something." About 20 minutes later I tried again: "Dad, I've got something really important I want to tell you." But he didn't answer. He was working on his list. Eventually, about an hour and a half after I had first tried talking with him, he finally came and said, "Oh, what was it you wanted to say, Son?" I remember looking at my father and saying, "I just wanted to tell you that Susy and I are getting married. 'Bye." Then I left. My father didn't have time, but he had his list.

Dad, your children need to be on your list. If you are going to punish them, you've also got to praise them. If you want to show you're just, you've also got to show that you're interested. Discipline without a relationship develops rebellion. I have a rule at my house: If I can't do it with my kids, it doesn't get done. There are some things around the house that don't get done or I have to do them late at night or early in the morning. If I can't do it with my kids, working beside them, I try not to do it. As they have grown, we have been able to do more complicated projects together like building the porch on our house. But I want to do things with the kids around the house so that they might learn from me.

I also try to have outings with the kids. My wife has really helped me in this area, and if a father will simply ask his bride, "Honey, what should I do with the kids this weekend?" he'll find a plethora of great ideas. My only rule for our outings is that I try not to spend any money. Our society teaches that it takes money to have fun, and children grow up thinking they have to go and *buy* fun. Birthday parties are now elaborate events at which people spend all kinds of money. You go to malls and you have to spend money and buy things to feel good. So when the children were little, I tried not to spend any money at all. As they have moved into the teen years, I have limited my spending to inexpensive meals where we can sit and talk with each other.

When we lived in downtown Atlanta, we often went to a place we called Stream Park. It was about a mile from our house, with a nice stream flowing through it. Over the years we built a fort, laid out stones, and made a rope swing from one tree to another, so that we could swing across the stream and have a good time. We played catch, threw rocks, picked up glass, and learned lots of neat things. We caught some fish and brought them home to our aquarium. We even went out one time, dug a big hole, and buried some treasure. Then we made a very complex treasure map (*"Start at the oak tree with the hole in the trunk. Walk 15 paces to the rock wall. Turn right and walk 4 paces to the sundial. Turn left . . . ."*) One year later, when the cousins came, we let them see if they could find our treasure following the map. Stream Park was a place where we never spent any money. We would just go together and have a lot of fun. We didn't have a lot of rules either. Our goal was to have a good time.

On our outings, I'm often asking questions. One thing I learned in law school is that one of the best teaching methods is asking questions. It teaches people to think, and our children need to learn how to think God's way. When Abigail, Paul and Matthew were probably 6, 4, and 2, while we were visiting Stream Park one Saturday, our son Matthew somehow went under water. It wasn't very deep, so I reached down and pulled him out, coughing and choking. Then I turned to the other children. "Okay, what happened?"

"Matthew went in the water!" they both shouted.

"Okay, but he didn't go in by himself," I noted, trying to be just. "Abigail, did you do anything wrong?"

"Yes," she admitted. "I let go of his hand."

"I was the one who said to run across the stream."

"Right. Where the big ones go, the little ones follow. So . . .what lesson do we learn?"

"Don't set a bad example," Paul said.

"And do your job," Abigail added.

"Oh, and one other thing," I mentioned. "What did *I* do wrong?"

Everyone just stood and stared for a moment. Why, Daddy hadn't done anything wrong, had he? Then my oldest boy said, "Well, you weren't doing a very good job of watching, Daddy."

"That's right," I told him. "So I've learned a lesson, too. Now let's all play *together*, and I'll start doing my job." My kids saw justice in me, and I hope they follow my example.

Just months before publishing this book, I took my three sons on a father/son retreat with some other boys and their dads. While on that outing, I learned some big lessons. After two days of skiing, devotions, and sharing with the other men, we took an interlude to ski with one of my mentors, Davis, a man in his sixties. I wanted so much to have my sons impress Davis that I took my focus off the Lord, putting up impossible standards of performance for my three boys. They had skied and conversed on an adult level with one of the most successful, godly men in America, and I began to pick them apart on some insignificant judgment calls regarding their manners. Instead of praising them, I found myself saying, "Well, that was great, guys, but I really wish you had . . ."

After a few minutes, Paul, my oldest son, began to get red in the face. "Dad," he blurted out, "why do you try to control us?"

"What do you mean by controlling you?" I replied. My question led to Paul's slow but deliberate recounting of how he and Joshua felt I had tried to control their behavior by giving or withholding my approval of them. As a skilled trial lawyer, I quickly developed my case in my mind, thinking up at least ten examples of how I had absolutely not done what he was accusing me of doing, and I began defending myself with words like, "Son, I don't mind you confronting me, but let's get the facts straight."

The more I went on, the more wrong I was. I could sense God's voice speaking to my heart and saying, "Shut your mouth, Phil. You are about to destroy a very important aspect of fathering. Your sons need to feel secure in offering criticism of you even when you don't believe it is fair or accurate." That's when I recognized if I blew it with the boys now, they would distrust their ability to confront me the proper way. I was about to lose ground that I had been working to create. Suddenly, I remembered that God never criticizes me for how I come to Him. He always listens, and He is slow to anger even when I come upset or angry. So I figured if God is willing to listen to me, I ought to be willing to listen to my sons. With that, I shut up and listened. Later I admitted to Paul and Josh that I have always struggled with the sin of overcontrolling people and events. I gave them examples of how I had made mistakes like that in the past, and told them their mother and I had discussed that our biggest challenge was to allow our children increasing decision-making authority.

To be completely honest, while my words were gentle and biblically accurate, my emotions were running wild. All the time I was thinking, "It's not fair! Look what I've done for them. Can't they see how much I've changed?" I asked the boys to give me a time-out for a while, and I had a chance to pray and reflect, asking God to line up my emotions with what I knew to be true from the Scriptures. The apostle Paul says I need to do all things without grumbling (Philippians 2:14), ought not look out for my own personal interests but for the interests of others (Philippians 2:4), and that I should reveal a heart of compassion, humility, gentleness, and patience (Colossians 3:12).

The best way we can show our kids the miracles of God is to show them the miracle of a changed father. I wanted to move from arrogance to gentleness, from control to compassion, from turmoil to trust, and from loneliness to leadership. When I reflect the love and forgiveness of Christ, it rubs off on my sons and daughters and permeates our relationship, giving them a model that will last long after I've gone home to be with the Lord. After two hours, the boys came to me with gentleness and forgiveness that radiated from the warmth of their smiles. I was about to make a comment of reconciliation, when Paul said, "Dad, I could have handled that better. Please forgive me for exaggerating the situation." I quickly told him of my great love and respect for all three of them, and how their confrontation had honored me. Then I assured them my goal was to set them free in Christ so that they could have honest accountability with me whenever it was needed—not just when it felt good.

My sons and I had gone off on a father/son weekend to grow closer to one another, and though the skiing was wonderful, the Bible study insightful, and the prayer time inspirational, it was the confrontation in the ski lodge that best helped me pass on the work of the Lord to the next generation. We left with a closer friendship, a greater trust in one another, and a more mature relationship with one another. My boys and I are fellow soldiers in a battle for righteousness. By beginning with ourselves and our own relationships, we can export what we are building in our lives to a crooked and perverse generation that does not know Christ.

He Is Love

A fourth aspect of God's character is love. We are told in 1 John 4:8 that he "who does not love does not know God, for God is love." To love is simply His very nature. God is characterized by enduring, unconditional, eternal love. Our children are going to learn a lot about love from us.

The world today says, "Love your kids" to a bunch of people who don't know what love is. Love needs to be a reality in our lives if we're going to share it with our sons and daughters. I try to spend time in the morning reminding myself how God loves and forgives me unconditionally, so that I might be a father who can teach his kids to love. My relationship with them is built on unconditional love.

Children learn a lot about unconditional love from watching our love relationships with our wives. They watch very closely to see if there is any problem between Susy and me. We aren't going to teach unconditional love if Dad is always angry. We can't have love in our home if there is a cold war going on. We need to be a *team*, with love among the members, for our kids to comprehend the true value of love.

To make sure our love stays strong, I take my wife on a date once a week. As believers, that means we sometimes miss a good Bible study, or a good service, or even a good fellowship time. But Susy and I have found we need that time together if we're going to do what we need to do. So we go on dates together and talk about the policies and vision for our family. We try not to talk about the checkbook or the calendar. If we need a business meeting, I usually call and say, "Let's go to lunch Friday and talk about our schedule." We go on a date to remain close, to keep communication going, and to discuss the vision of our family: Where are we and where are we going? What is our ministry? How are we going to deal with the job and get all our work done?

Our date is also the time when I court my wife. I really enjoy that. I get to tell her why I appreciate her. I always have a plan and make preparations. It's a fun time—a date, just like we used to do. Once a week it is a joy for us to be together. We don't go to movies or to places with a lot of people. We usually simply sit across from each other in a restaurant and talk. This is the time when I find out how I am doing. "How am I doing with the kids? Do I need to spend more time with Joshua? What's going on with the girls?" My wife can offer tremendous insight.

Similar things happen when I take my kids on dates. They ask questions, get to hear about my life, and learn from me. They rediscover the fact that they're loved because they see God's love through me.

Loving God takes guts. Sometimes I'm just too tired or too worried about the events of the day. Other times I'm just too selfish. I've got impossible things to get done and don't know how I'm going to complete them all. When I was practicing law, I remember coming home in a knot and sitting in a chair exhausted. My kids looked at me. I was too tired to do anything. I wasn't any fun, just sitting like a lump in my chair. "Poor Dad," they all thought, "he's just too tired to spend time with us." Then all of a sudden the phone would ring, and it would be an important client. I would jump out of the chair in an amazing burst of energy. I would pick up the phone and cheerfully say, "Hello! Sure, no problem. I can do that. That's great!" I would be transformed instantaneously into Superman. That only had to happen once or twice and my kids got a message: "Dad does what Dad wants to do." I had to go and ask their forgiveness, for I was modeling selfishness to them and sending them the message that I didn't love them as much as I loved my career.

For that reason, I've found that the first half hour after entering my home is the most important. That's the time I need to be a servant. Often I have stopped a block away from the house and prayed, "God, I want to be a servant. I don't want to go in as an executive, barking orders. I want to go in as a servant to that family." They in turn start serving me, and all of a sudden I'm ministered to, and I find we have great joy in being together. The war of the family is lost, I think, in the first 30 minutes that Dad is home. Go to the TV, go to the book, to the bed, to the chair, or to the garage, and the kids' hopes of being with Dad are dashed for another night. But go right to the family and their needs, and the love overflows. In 30 or 40 minutes I'm renewed and rejuvenated. I have a new enthusiasm and more energy than I ever knew I had. Soon we are rolling around the floor playing roly-poly or some really dumb game. Our kids need to see us sacrifice for them, not just sacrifice for the guy on the phone, if they are going to learn what it takes to be a soldier of the Lord. Love demands sacrifice.

In Vietnam we lost a lot of men. One time, after much of my squad had been wiped out, I remember going to collect a whole new group of Marines. They were right out of boot camp, had become used to being treated like dogs, and suddenly in the jungle they've got a machine gunner saying, "Wow, I'm glad to see you guys." They didn't know how to take me.

But I assured those young men we needed each other if we were going to stay alive. That very afternoon we had to clear an area. Instead of barking orders, telling these inexperienced guys where to go, I went down to clear out their position. I got down on my hands and knees looking for booby traps, knowing where my head was going to go if I hit one. Those guys sat and looked on in amazement. I came back and told them, "It's clear. You can go now." I taught them how to do it, and showed the sacrifice I was willing to make for them. That built an unbelievable team that stood together in war.

God is love, and we need to give that sort of sacrificial, forgiving love to our kids if we expect them to embrace Him. As a father, I am continually looking for new ways I can do that.

He Is Eternal

The fifth quality of God is that He is eternal. In Exodus 3:14, God tells Moses, "I Am who I Am." Most children today have no eternal perspective and no eternal purpose. That's why teen suicide is at an all-time high. It's why young people are willing to throw away their lives for a cheap thrill, and why the approval of peers has usurped the approval of parents. We teach evolution as fact in school, turning life into a haphazard joke without a purpose. The notion that we didn't come from anywhere and really aren't going anywhere discourages kids from debating the value of giving everything up for a moment of excitement.

To battle that attitude, we Christian parents need to build purpose in our children by helping them see the eternal purpose of God. Our kids need to hear that "God has a wonderful plan for your life." The fact is, God can change the world with a single life. He has something great and wonderful to do in each of our lives. It may not seem wonderful in man's terms, and it may not involve big people, big auditoriums, or big money, but if God calls you to do something, you can rest assured it's important. We need to build vision in our children by talking to them about what God wants to do.

That's why Susy and I have placed such an emphasis on involving the children in home ministry. It grows vision, builds eternal purpose, and helps create an eternal perspec-

Transparency or Rebellion

+ Be willing to say you are sorry.
+ Tell your kids about your childhood (without complaining or talking too much about the good old days).
+ Your past sins of fornication, rebellion, or slothfulness make for fruitful ground to discuss current temptations.
+ These times can be very instructive for them as they see the results of some of the temptations they are now feeling.

tive in our home. We want our children to be more influenced by God than by us or their peers, so that tomorrow they will be an influence to their peers for the Lord.

We found that home ministry is the most rewarding thing our kids have ever done. In Atlanta we led a Bible study for young singles in our home, and I think a lot of them came just so they could see a family that works. They came to our house to be around people who loved each other and understood God's purpose for living. They sat and enjoyed the fellowship, and along the way heard God's Word. That Bible study was an incredible time for our family. These young people helped disciple our kids, and our children began to see God's purpose at work in somebody other than Mom and Dad. After the Bible study we would break up into small groups. Abigail always joined one of the groups of women who were praying together. She had her notebook and list, and became more spiritually mature just by hanging out with mature women. We never asked her to do that; she just asked if she could be a part. We are now doing the same thing in Chattanooga, but with couples. The older children, ages 11 to 17, now have their own discussion and prayer time after I teach.

One afternoon per week, Susy had some women over who fellowshipped together and also discussed some aspects of the Bible. This helped the children understand the importance of being with other believers. We want our kids to see that God's Word is the most important book, and His eternal purpose influences all areas of our lives. Home ministry builds vision and demonstrates what we are giving our lives to. It also creates accountability, because our children watch the way we walk in front of them. One night, after a terribly hard day, I was sitting at the table with a frown on my face when my son asked, "What's the study on tonight?" I looked at him with a sour expression before answering, "Joy." Then I realized the mixed message and said to him, "I guess it's a good thing we're going to study it."

There is a spiritual battle going on, and our kids need to experience at least a taste of that battle if they are going to develop spiritually. We need to teach our children to have that sort of eternal perspective. There's a bumper sticker I see around that complains, "Stuff happens" (more or less). I pulled up behind that recently and said to my daughter, Anna, "Do you think that's true?"

"Nope," she said. "God allows things in our lives, and even when we do things wrong, He is still in control." You see, if you teach children God's principles, they learn the truths they need for life.

He Is Omniscient

God is all-knowing. There has never been a time that God did not know everything. The psalmist declares, "O LORD, Thou hast searched me and known me. Thou dost know when I sit down and when I rise up. Thou dost understand my thought from afar" (Psalm 139:1,2). God knows everything—an important characteristic of God we need to be teaching our children. Our period of influence as fathers is short. In a few years our children will be out of the house. We are going to lose our children, so during the time they are in our homes we want to impart faith to them, and let them see in a real way that God knows everything.

He knows our lives, our motives, and our intentions. When I practiced law in Atlanta, I saw men all the time going down the escalator in Peachtree Center to a news shop that specialized in sexy magazines. They thought nobody saw them. Not long ago I was staying in a hotel that was hosting a convention, and I watched a crowd of men cheering and hollering over some pornographic movie they had been watching. I know they wouldn't do that at home or in front of their friends and families, but they were away from home, so they thought nobody could see them. They're thinking to themselves, "Nobody will ever know!" But God knows. We're not keeping any secrets from Him. We need to live in light of the fact that God sees and knows everything, and teach that to our children.

For example, we teach our children to pray *believing* in God. If a father can teach his kids to pray in faith, his job is half done. He can do that by demonstrating prayer. When I have needs, I want my kids to see me on my face before the Lord. I spoke at a conference last week, and before I left we all got on our knees and I admitted to them, "I need to pray, kids. I'm not ready for this. I've been out of town all week, and I'm just not sure how things are going to come out. Would you pray for me? And tomorrow morning, when I'm speaking, would you pray for me? I really need God's help on this." Over the years the children have learned that they have a role in my ministry. They know that I need their fervent prayer.

I taught my children that I prayed over the judge, jury, lawyers, and courtroom before every trial. We continue to pray through both big decisions and little decisions, because we want our kids to understand the importance of knowing and obeying God's will. For that reason, any time one of the children faces a big decision, everybody goes to prayer.

When my son Paul was five years old, he was asked to recite the Christmas story in a big service at church. There would be a dress rehearsal, and then four consecutive nights the whole gymnasium would be filled up with hundreds of people waiting to see the Christmas pageant. Paul would have to memorize 14 verses. He was afraid, but we encouraged him to do it as a growth experience. "Let's pray about it," I urged him. So we did.

We prayed about it for days. When the day came that we needed to make a decision, I was in Washington with a very important client and three other lawyers, working on a very important case. We were right in the middle of a major issue, when suddenly I realized we had to let the church know our decision. So I told the men, "Excuse me for a minute. I've got an emergency." Then I went to a phone, called home, and got Paul on the phone. "We need to make a decision and not put this off. Paul, have you prayed about this?"

"Yes," he told me. "I've prayed about it."

"Do you want to do it?"

"No, Daddy, I don't want to do it."

"Well," I hesitated, not wanting to put too much pressure on the boy, "what do you think God wants you to do?"

"Oh, I think God wants me to do it."

"But you don't want to?"

"No, I don't want to do it."

"Okay, then what are you going to do?"

"I'm going to do it."

I knew he was afraid of being embarrassed, so I promised him we would work on it every night. Susy and I worked with him for several weeks. On the evening of the dress rehearsal, I talked to my son. "Before Daddy goes to court, what does he do?"

"You pray through the room," Paul answered.

"That's right. And you know when we go to a city to speak, and Mom and Dad share our testimonies, what do we always do?"

"You always pray through the room."

"Tell you what. Tonight let's go pray through the room where you'll be speaking."

My son leaped up, shouting, "Oh, that's a great idea!" So we went over to the church. It was dark, but we walked hand in hand around the whole room and prayed for the people, for the place, and for Paul. We stood where he would stand, and we got up onstage and saw how it would look. He was really excited. That was the last time I was with him until his final performance. My schedule took me out of town, but I got back in time to see the closing night. Paul stood up, walked across the huge stage, and recited the Christmas story letter perfect. Later, he asked me, "Daddy, could I do that next year?" I told him, "I don't know about next year. I'm not sure what God is going to ask you to do. But how can you know what God wants you to do?"

"I'll ask Him!" came the response. "I want to do what God wants me to do," my son told me, "because it's exciting." He felt the Lord with him all the time he was onstage. He felt our prayer support for him. My son learned that God knows him and is always willing to guide him.

He Is Omnipresent

God is everywhere. Jeremiah 23:24 NKJV asks, "'Can anyone hide himself in secret places, so I shall not see him?' says the LORD. 'Do I not fill heaven and earth?'" God is everywhere, not limited by time or space. Our children need to understand that the Lord is with them at all times, in all circumstances, even when they are afraid.

It's a funny thing, but one of the ways we have helped our children understand the omnipresent character of God is by playing "monster in the house." In our Atlanta home, everything in the house on the main floor was open. We designated one room as the prison where the kids must stay if the monster catches them. Someone else can tag them and get them out of prison. It's just a silly, fun little game. We've had whole families over to play monster with us. I will never forget one time when I was sneaking around looking for someone and a closet opened—a whole family came pouring out! In the midst of the game, I might say, "I don't know where Paul is, but who does know where Paul is?" Everybody will shout the response: "God knows!"

"That's right! Who knows what Paul's doing?"

"God knows. He's everywhere!"

"Is there anyplace you can go and not be with God?"

"No, no place at all!"

It might be a silly game, but it is a continual reminder to the kids that the Lord is with us at all times. We used to live on a busy street in a downtown neighborhood, so we never let the children go outside unless accompanied by an adult. But one time when we were playing ball, the ball sailed across the street. I said to my eight-year-old, "Would you go get the ball?" She looked both ways, got across the street, picked up the ball, and then couldn't get back. The cars were whizzing by. Every time she would step out, another car would race by, forcing her to step back. Of course, what I wanted to do was run over there, stop the cars, and get my little girl. Instead, I prayed.

She waited very patiently, and finally a space came. All the kids were watching her as she came back across the street. "Were you scared?" they asked. My daughter replied, "Yes I was, but then I prayed and God helped me."

I looked at her and asked, "Were you scared then?"

"No," she told me, "because I knew what to do. You taught me what to do. I just prayed and knew God was with me." Never think the lessons of silly games are lost on your children.

Another benefit of drilling into the lives of our children the fact that God is always with them is the improved job our kids have done with chores. One of my boys said to me recently, "I worked hard at cleaning my room so that you would notice. But you didn't come into my room, so you never saw it . . . but that's okay, because *God saw it*. He knows I did a good job."

It's true: Teach your children the truth about God, and the lessons will change their lives.

He Is Omnipotent

The eighth characteristic of God is that He has all power. As it says in Psalm 147:5 NIV, "Great is our Lord and mighty in power." Our little kids are small, and to them we appear awfully big. Sometimes we need to get down on their level and let them see us not just as powerful, but as caring. I once heard Howard Hendricks proclaim that any father who wrestles with his children twice a week should win an award as "father of the year." He's right! Every kid loves to wrestle, because it forces the father to get down on their level. When we roll around on the floor, and let them mess up our hair, it shows that we're surrendering some of our strength in order to be with them.

When the Father sent His Son to be born as a man, Jesus surrendered some of His power in order to identify with us. Christmas reveals not only God's incredible plan for mankind, but also His love and concern for us. The Almighty Creator was willing to give up power in order to be with us. Sometimes when we are wrestling on the floor, I talk with my children about that. I'm always looking for a way to share spiritual truth with them by cutting it into bite-sized chunks they can swallow.

For example, in Atlanta we would go to the Chatta-hoochee Nature Center. It was a fun time as we hiked along the swamp trail and talked about creation. There were some people there who were clearly worshiping the earth, and that got us talking about the difference between worshiping the Creator or His creation. These people noticed us when my children started talking out loud about God's imagina-tion in making all this stuff. When one of our kids men-tioned to this group of people that we had a pet turtle, it was clear they were upset. "You can't keep a pet turtle," one lady said, "it's just not right."

"Well," I told her, "we use it to teach the kids responsi-bility."

"But the turtle is an animal companion," she told us. "What do you feed him?"

"Lettuce, carrots, and tomatoes," I replied.

"Where do you keep him?"

"In the basement."

"The basement!" she shrieked. "You can't keep a turtle

in the basement! You're going to hurt its shell, it'll turn a different color, and it won't be as healthy or happy!"

I felt like saying, "We'll get it a therapist." Instead, we smiled and walked away, then used the conversation to talk with our children about God's power. He is big, yet He has come to earth to be with us. He walked with us, wept with us, never sinned, and loves every little thing about us. Our kids need to understand that God—the all-powerful God— has surrendered His power in order to touch us, and will approach each individual on his or her level.

Susy created a game to help the children understand power under control. We call it "the ear game." One of the kids would get on my shoulders and grab hold of my ears, turning them this way and that in order to steer me. Whatever they would do with my ears, I would do—move forward, backward, up, or down. They would get on my shoulders and "drive" me around the house. They thought this was the greatest thing in the world, since their big, strong dad was under their direction. They learned that they have volition and that even a powerful Father who loves them will meet them where they are.

Of course, since I am a task-oriented type of person, I often want to stick with a schedule. Occasionally I have put a bad ending on a family outing by sounding impatient and saying, "We've got to go home. It's over, finished. Get in the car." But Susy encouraged me to listen to the children better. So when we were at the park loading up, some of the kids said, "We haven't played ball yet!" Normally I would have said no, but actually the children had made a reasonable argument, so we played ball. Later my son told me that decision had made his day. He saw that I was willing to listen to him, and that allowed the day to end on a wonderful note. When a father allows his kids to observe his power submitting to them in love, they better understand the power and love of God.

After leaving the law practice to take my new position with CBMC, our financial picture changed dramatically. Our inability to sell our large downtown Atlanta home meant the family remained there while I lived in Chattanooga. Coupled with the change in economics from law practice to ministry, it created some trying circumstances. One time we thought we had found the "perfect" house to purchase in Chattanooga, but when we were unable to sell our home, it became clear the Lord was not going to allow us to buy the home we all wanted. The children were upset that we would lose that wonderful house and not be together, and they said to me, "But, Dad, we simply *must* buy that house so we can be together!"

My reply to them included some of the hardest words I've ever had to say in my life. I had to admit to my children that their father was broke. I simply could not buy the house in Chattanooga they wanted so much. Then I told them they would have to ask their heavenly Father to supply their needs, since their earthly father was unable to help them. Painful words, but that act of humility and submission is something none of us has ever forgotten. A few weeks later one of our friends, having just received one of the largest verdicts of his legal career, offered to give us most of the entire down payment for the purchase of the house in Chattanooga. Our children saw firsthand that their heavenly Father would answer their prayers and help the family. The Lord provided for a need in a way their earthly father was unable to provide.

Fathers, we need to get over the pride of trying to project omnipotence to our children. Instead, we need to demonstrate our heavenly Father's omnipotence in all things by surrendering our needs to Him in front of our kids. By humbling ourselves, we bring our families into the process of trusting God. Our uncertainty, instability, and lack of success can be entrusted to the Lord.

He Is Truth

Finally, we need to help our children understand that God is truth. They've got to be exposed to the truth if they are to grow spiritually. Ask yourself: Do most kids know more about Walt Disney or D. L. Moody? Do they know more about the apostle Paul or Michael Jordan? Are they more familiar with the Bible or the latest TV schedule? We need to protect our children in all ways. Many dads want to live in the best part of town, attend the best churches, and send their kids to the best schools, then invite a gang of thieves and thugs to perform in their home on a nightly basis through the television set.

I'm not a television watcher, but last January I turned on the Super Bowl to see how my friend Chip MacGregor's team, the Green Bay Packers (which he keeps telling me is the greatest team in the history of the NFL), was doing. Since I had not seen TV for a long time, I was shocked at the commercials. A soft-drink commercial was a sensual experience. The truck commercial was nothing but sex and violence. The perfume commercial was beyond description. I remember looking at my oldest son and noticing his eyes were the size of silver dollars as he watched the images and listened to the music. We immediately reinstituted our old practice of clicking off with the remote any commercial (or cheerleader routines) that evidenced "the lust of the flesh," "the lust of the eyes," or the "pride of life" (1 John 2:16). The boys were able to respond very quickly with the clicker, and we were all able to enjoy the game without the distraction of the world. Our desire for our children is the same desire we have for ourselves: to be holy. To do that they can't be filling their minds with evil. Instead, they need to be filling their minds with truth.

We need to teach our children the principles of sowing and reaping. If we sow sex and violence in the minds of our kids, we are going to reap tremendous devastation.

As a father, I've decided the best thing I can do is fill my children with truth. They'll hear plenty of falsehoods from newspapers, television, and friends. Part of my job is to counter those falsehoods with truth. Every chance I get, I speak truth to them. We read the Bible together, we talk about spiritual things, and we make sure they understand the facts about God. By doing so, I hope to help them know Him better. I'm planting the seeds of truth. Then I'll trust God to bring a harvest of righteousness.

Sometimes, when it starts to get late but we're not too tired, Susy and I pile everyone in the car and go out for ice cream. As we drive, we pray for families we are seeking to love and get to know better. We include the kids in our prayers, for we want them to see themselves as part of our

Quotable Quotes

+ *A Borrower Gets Her Just Desserts*: A very wiggly, squiggly, stand-up, sit-down Abigail on a long flight to Seattle said, "Dad! I think I got Mom's control top stockings!"

+ *Favorite Quote From A Friend's Family*: Sam, six years old, stood at attention as he received a stern lecture from his father. At the end of the long harangue, the dad asked his son if he understood. The boy, still looking up at his father, simply said, "Dad, did you know you have hairs in your nose?"

+ *Favorite Quote From Our Own Family*: Matthew, then five, caused quite a bit of laughter among a table full of men in the middle of Dad's speech at a men's conference. When asked what caused all the commotion, one of the men responded, "About ten minutes into your remarks, your son elbowed me and said, 'Hey, mister, do you know when this guy will be finished?' "

+ *In Defense Of His Twin Sister:* To Dad, who had just impatiently asked Anna to speak more loudly so he could hear her, Joshua instructs, "Dad, yesterday you asked Anna not to speak so loud, and now you ask her not to speak so softly. Just tell her what you want her to do and she'll do it!"

ministry. It's become sort of a tradition for us to play music while we drive, and one of my favorite Steve Green songs sums up what I want to do with my sons and daughters:

We're pilgrims on the journey of the narrow road,
And those who've gone before us line the way
Cheering on the faithful, encouraging the weary,
Their lives a stirring testament to God's sustaining grace.
Surrounded by so great a cloud of witnesses,
Let us run the race not only for the prize;
But as those who've gone before us,
Let us leave to those behind us,
The heritage of faithfulness passed on through godly lives.

After all our hopes and dreams have come and gone,
And our children sift through all we've left behind,
May the clues that they discover
And the memories they uncover
Become the light that leads them to the road we each must find.
Oh may all who come behind us find us faithful,
May the fire of our devotion light their way,
May the footprints that we leave
Lead them to believe,
And the life we live inspire them to obey.
Oh, may all who come behind us find us faithful.

Study Questions

1. How much time do you spend with your kids? How much would you *like* to spend?

2. What are the biggest struggles you face as a father?

3. What lessons do we glean from studying the attributes of God?

4. Why is it important for a father to also be a servant?

5. If a friend said to you, "It's too late to change—my family is too messed up," how would you respond?

Part Two:

Dad's Home!

My daughter Anna and I have a great relationship, but sometimes I don't take time to listen to her. It's easy for me to get into a "nod-the-head-but-don't-listen" mode. We had planned a night out together to study our Bible, and I told my wife I didn't want to come back until I had really connected with Anna and talked. As we talked at a local Subway, I asked her every question I could think of: How are you doing? What are you up to? How is homeschooling going? What great things have happened lately?

All I got from Anna was "fine," "okay," and "nothing much." Obviously, I hadn't hit an interest of hers. Remembering that she reads all the time, I asked her a few things about books. She still answered the questions with one or two words.

"What is your book about?"

"A family."

"What about the family?"

"They're struggling."

"What are they struggling with?"

"The farm."

I probably asked her ten questions about the family before she finally realized I was not going to stop until she told me about her book. She could see her dad was really interested in hearing about the story, so she started to open up. We had already been there about an hour and a half, and typically at this point I would have packed everything up and gone home, but I was not going to leave until we had an in-depth conversation. When it finally occurred to Anna that I really cared about her book, she almost exploded with words. She told me all the anecdotes, stories, characters, and details of the story. She completely forgot about dinner. She went on about her book for an hour. Since that day, our relationship has been much closer. Instead of feeling like a father who never takes the time to communicate, now I know my daughter sees that I care about what's going on in her life.

4

Building Relationships

So then you are no longer strangers and aliens, but you are fellow citizens with the saints, and are of God's household, having been built upon the foundation of the apostles and prophets, Christ Jesus Himself being the cornerstone, in whom the whole building, being fitted together is growing into a holy temple in the Lord; in whom you also are being built together into a dwelling of God in the Spirit (Ephesians 2:19-22).

Growing up in an era when big boys didn't cry, with a father who was working around the clock to provide for his family, I learned early that if you gave away your feelings you got hurt. My goal was to not give away my feelings. When I was 12, I decided I would never hug my father or cry again. I made good on that commitment, even through Vietnam.

I didn't cry when my men got killed. Even when I had the blood of my best friend on my uniform, I didn't show that it bothered me. I never cried or showed I cared. I did everything I could to keep everyone from getting close to my emotions.

As a young man, I remember sitting in movie theaters during a particularly sensitive moment in a drama and making jokes in order to distance myself from any emotion that would cause me to feel what was going on. As I went into marriage, I carried this baggage around with me. Susy couldn't get close to me. No one could. It resulted in the destruction of my marriage.

Since becoming a Christian, I have seen that marriage rebuilt. I have learned some difficult principles that I have had to knead into my life. One principle is that relationships are not only important, they are essential. Through Christ's power we can be broken, merciful, sensitive individuals who not only *want* to have relationships with other people, but also *need* to have relationships in order to be servants of the Lord. I didn't realize it, but I need other people. God made each of us with a desire for relationships. As fathers, we all want to be close to our kids. But as men, we often don't know how to build those relationships.

A Goal of Being Fun

I don't have any younger brothers or sisters, and I have always avoided being around little children. I was a businessman who would get up and move to a new seat if a mother with a little child sat next to me on an airplane. My main goal was to keep so far from children that nothing of any liquid nature ever got on me! I used to pull out my handkerchief to pick up something off the floor that a little child had touched, since I did not want to contract anything from the germ units known as "little boys."

Needless to say, when Susy got pregnant, I was in for a great change. I decided I would try to change things by building relationships. Some friends of ours, June and Jackson Wingfield, were with us at a conference when June said, "Jackson is the highlight of our kids' day. When he comes home from work on Friday night, they start doing things together and it lasts all weekend. The kids *love* to be with their dad. To them, Dad is fun, exciting, and interesting." I couldn't believe my ears. It had never occurred to me to think of my father as being "fun." And it excited me that a father could be that way.

That day I set a goal of being "fun" with my kids. I decided not to be fun just on weekends, but on the weeknights, as well. I set out to be close to the kids and build relationships. The problem was, I had no idea what to do with babies. I knew how to throw baseballs and how to wrestle, but was clueless about having fun with little kids. So as I was praying about our new baby that Susy was carrying, I asked God to show me how I could get involved with the child. Realizing that babies spend most of their time sleeping, eating, and pooping, I knew that if I were not involved in those three areas, I would not spend much time with my children. So I tried to take on the whole diaper routine. I reasoned that if I was willing to take care of my puppies as a kid, and shovel dung out of the corral for the horse we owned, I ought to be able to care for my own flesh and blood.

So when our first child came along, I announced that Susy could have a night off each week and I would take care of the baby. Unfortunately, we experienced an emergency the very first evening Abigail and I spent together. Having heard that a child can be brain-damaged from having an exceedingly high fever, I became alarmed when I thought Abigail had started running a high fever. I went next door to see the doctor's wife, in order to borrow a thermometer for Abigail. As I was walking away from their back door, the neighbor yelled to me, "Hey, Phil, do you know how to use that thing?" I assured her I did, and got back inside my house before I realized the problem at hand. It occurred to me that you probably don't take a baby's temperature orally. Our first, Abigail, was born weighing ten pounds, and had always been a strong child. So I was completely stumped, wondering where I was supposed to put that thing without having her bite the end off. My look must have warned my daughter, because Abigail made it very clear to me that I was not going to come close to her with that thermometer.

Forty-five minutes later, after a wrestling match that ended with me putting my knee in the middle of her back in order to hold her down, I finally determined she had a normal temperature. We were both totally exhausted, and I kept wondering when her screams were going to bring the police, but I did learn one thing: Anybody, even a knuckle-head like me, can learn to take care of his children.

I next started getting involved in the process of bathing and feeding my daughter. Then I started reading to her, playing with her, and eventually having long conversations with her. Now, after many years of being involved in her life, Abigail will tell you that the highlight of her life through age 17 is going out with me for our one-on-one discipleship time together. Somehow, I learned to be fun. Years ago we began with CBMC's Operation Timothy material, which not only provided great spiritual fundamentals but also was a wonderful conversation-starter on a myriad of subjects.

Of course, being a father is never easy. What happens if your daughter comes home pregnant, and you feel as though your life and testimony have just been shattered? That's what happened to my friend Miles, whose 18-year-old daughter brought that news to him. He went through a period of remorse, self-blame, anger, bitterness, and discouragement before he recognized it's not how you start in this world, but

---

Build Self-esteem and Vision by Pointing Out the Gifts of Your Children

✦ Find ten different ways to encourage and compliment each child.

✦ Remind them of God's view of their uniqueness, value, and potential.

✦ Show interest by asking enough questions to gain their confidence.

✦ Describe how one of their good choices resulted in fruit in their life or someone else's life.

✦ Pass along the compliments you hear about them.

✦ Look for biblical principles they have demonstrated in their activities.

how you finish. Miles was determined to finish well. He decided to follow Christ's model of loving people even in the most unlovable situations. Miles forgave the father, forgave his daughter, and even asked his accountability group to pray for him to have strength and gentleness as he saw that baby growing in the belly of his unwed daughter.

The child came in the person of a bouncing boy named Jeremy. The prayer and submission that this new grandfather exercised in faith turned into a joyful desire to teach that little boy the ways of Jesus Christ. Beginning with the care of diapering, bathing, and even sustaining spit-up on his pin-striped business suit proved the beginning of raising that little boy to love God. Today Miles will tell you his greatest joy after Jesus, his wife, and his own children is that little grandchild. Jeremy's father abandoned him, but his grandfather accepted and loved him, and the two spend a lot of fun times together.

Family Fun Times

Relationship-building is essential for dads, but most of us do not come by that quality naturally, and so are easily dissuaded. The year before we began homeschooling, we had our older three in a Christian school. They started school in September and immediately began getting birthday invitations. I would come home from a busy week of law practice, fully expecting to have a wonderful weekend with my kids, only to realize that most of them had been invited to birthday parties at someone else's home. So I would take them to birthday parties and postpone my time. The next weekend the same thing would happen. Eventually I realized that birthday parties were destroying my opportunity for building relationships with my kids. Taking seriously Deuteronomy 6:4-7, I prayed about the situation and announced to Susy that we were going to cancel all birthday parties. In my house that was like saying we were going to cancel Christmas. After I explained myself, Susy and I reached an agreement where we would cut back on the number of birthday parties and outside activities.

Instead of hosting birthday parties with 30 kids (each of whom would in turn invite my kids to *their* parties), we started having family parties. We would invite two or three families with children to come to our home, so that we could spend a number of hours in parent-to-parent and child-to-child time, building in-depth relationships. After all, most of the birthday parties our kids went to were those rent-a-clown, tear-open-presents, throw-cake-at-one-another kind of events. A parent stressed out with work and other responsibilities would take all the kids to Chuck E. Cheese or hire a clown, balloons, and a face painter. I didn't feel that our kids were missing much in-depth time by skipping a few birthday parties like that. Our family parties also gave me a great opportunity to begin using some creativity with birthday parties at our house. We began to do new things with other families, and our neighbors began to say, "Wow, we love your 'old-fashioned' birthday parties, where we can really get together and talk." Most important of all, I finally achieved the margin of time on the weekends which allowed me to begin to succeed at building relationships with my kids.

There were several things I wanted to avoid with the activities of the kids, so I set up some guidelines. I didn't want to become just another "Disneyland dad" who invests in paid entertainment for the kids and sits in the stands. When the children were younger, I virtually never spent money on our outings. They didn't require professional help. We simply tried to keep the activities wholesome and outdoors, focusing as much as possible on teaching responsibility, work ethic, family enterprise, and fun. So instead of going to Stone Mountain just to walk around, we would take balloons and have water-balloon fights, or take food to feed the ducks, or build rifles to play guns as we walked down that huge mass of granite.

We found that downtown Atlanta was a great place to get outdoors. In every city I am convinced you can find a safe park to play in that allows a number of alternative games. Near our neighborhood, which was two miles from downtown Atlanta, we found a park with several acres of woods and grass, plus an active stream.

It was on one trip to what we christened "Stream Park" that Abigail began to dig in her heels. She was never eager to get dirty, and didn't even want to sit down in fresh grass. Her words were "I am not going to Stream Park, Dad." But after talking to my wife about it, I decided to require Abigail to go with us to the park. I reasoned that we all needed to be together as a family, and she reluctantly agreed. Abigail would stand by the creek as Paul and I got down in the water, dug holes, chased fish, and doused each other. After a while Abigail became interested and got into the act of playing with the water and the fish.

As each new child of ours came along, we would devise new things to do. We played word games, had races, created forts, and learned all sorts of things about animals, plants, and people. Along the way we discovered it is important not to be preoccupied with other things while you're trying to play with your children. Instead, I learned to ask questions.

This was particularly important when I would take the children out one at a time. One time when Matthew was about eight, we were going through one of our Operation Timothy discipleship series books, and I thought something was bothering him. "Matt," I asked him, "how are you doing?"

"Fine," came the reply.

"Do you have any problems?"

"Nope."

"Are you upset with Dad?"

"No, you're doing great."

"Well, what can I pray for you about?"

"Nothing."

At this point, I realized I had not really gotten down to the honest issues of life with my son, so I continued to probe. "Matthew, have I hurt your feelings lately?"

"No."

Although I could not specifically think of a time that I

had, I know that children's feelings are hurt easily, and I can sometimes say insensitive things. So I repeated, "Matt, have I *ever* hurt your feelings?"

At that point he responded, "Well, yes, Dad. . . . You hurt my feelings with the fence."

I asked him further about the fence, and he told me that when we were out doing one of our great fencing projects on our property, I had hurt his feelings. All the kids had been involved, digging the holes, setting the posts, mixing the concrete, stringing and nailing the wire, and using the winch to tighten the wire around the post. Along the way toward the end of the afternoon, we were pouring a key corner post. Matthew, losing focus on the task, ran across the concrete. Midway through the slop, I grabbed him to stop him from doing any further damage. As I stopped him, I also shook him inadvertently.

As we continued to talk about it, Matt said, "But I have forgiven you, Dad, so don't worry about it."

"Son," I told him, "I know you have forgiven me, but you still have some pain. I know that what I did was wrong. At the time I apologized to you and asked God to forgive me for grabbing you in that way. But if you're still hurting over it, I want to talk about it some more." Then we took some time to go back over the idea that I should not have been focused on the project or the quality of the concrete, but more on the relationship with my boy. I told him I was sorry I had hurt our relationship by getting angry, and I asked him again if he would forgive me. He readily said he would.

A couple of weeks later, I brought up the fence situation again, and he said, "Oh, that is completely forgotten, Dad. I forgave you." By my being honest and taking the time to communicate with him, we were able to strengthen our relationship.

Taking Time
When I am traveling, I try to make up for some of the lost time by calling our kids often and taking a few minutes to

talk to each of them. I don't just talk to the older ones in order to get the facts of who, what, where, when, why, and how, but I talk to the younger ones, too, and ask them about what they are doing. I try to tell them a couple of things that I am doing, so they can connect with my life. I also tell them that I am praying for them, and I encourage them to pray for me.

One of the greatest relationship-builders for us has been our Bible-study times, in which we use the CBMC Operation Timothy materials. Discipleship doesn't just happen because you are all around the dinner table or sleeping in the same house. Discipleship is something that is planned, and that takes an investment of time and energy. We do a lot of events as a family together in order to build our family/team relationships, and we do one-on-one discipleship using Operation Timothy in order to make us both spiritually and relationally strong.

I have wanted to avoid the mistake of being too content-focused, so I keep the biblical content to about ten percent of our time together. My goal is not to go through all the Bible stories in a year, but that our time together would be part of a lifetime process of discipleship. We spend a lot of time talking about the news of the day, plus the pain and challenge and wonderful times that come with growing up. We sometimes meet over a meal, and I try to make sure it is not a time when I am correcting them—not about manners, friends, schoolwork, or anything else. Our study time is really a time for building our relationship, a time of encouragement, and a time of affirmation and fun.

I try to find about five different ways to tell them how much I love and appreciate them. I want my kids to know I value not only what they are doing, but also who they are. It's important they understand I love them each tremendously. That's why I want to show them with both my words and my attention that I care for them today, and I care for their future.

Times together need to be times of vision. Remember, Jesus called Peter a rock long before he was ever rock-solid

in his walk as a disciple. I'm always trying to remind my
kids, "God has a great plan for you." Years ago I heard a
speaker say that fathers ought to tell their children that they
are loved even when they make a mistake. That advice res-
onated with me, for I remember growing up feeling that I
had to be perfect, and I could never reach perfection. So I
try to let my kids know, "I will love you even if you really
blow it. God loves you when you are good, and He loves
you when you are bad. In the same way, my love is not con-
tingent upon your performance." I try to describe for them
how we really do want to walk with the Lord, and often
share something sensitive or difficult in my life so that they
are praying for my day, my work, and my struggles. I usually try to tell them about any problems that I am having at
work, to instruct them in dealing with people.

One time, after listening to my conversation on the car
phone, my son Matthew said to me, "Dad, it seems like 90
percent of what you do is deal with people problems." That
gave me a great opportunity to talk to him about how the
family is the greatest training ground in the world for personnel management study. If we can't solve problems in our
families, we will have a hard time solving them in business.

Building Competency by Building Relationships
One of my goals in doing projects with my kids is not only
building relationships and having fun, but also building
competency. In our earlier book, *Unlimited Partnership*, Susy
and I make the case that everyone has intimacy needs:
acceptance, affection, appreciation, approval, attention,
encouragement, respect, comfort, support, and security.
Most people will have one dominant need, and one or two
other secondary needs. In other words, one person craves
affection, while another most wants approval. To offer
approval to a person craving affection won't help that individual. So getting to know your child's intimacy need is
crucial if you want to draw close.

Periodically I sit down and talk to my kids about these
ten intimacy needs, with questions like, "Which of these are

most important to you?" and "How am I doing at providing the things you need most?" I've received some astounding responses from the kids.

When I discussed this with my son Paul several years
ago, he told me, "I don't need as much hugging as Matt
does, but I sure do need your approval." When I asked him
how I could show him my approval, he told me, "One way
you give me approval is when you come down and look at
my fort—especially when you don't point out the ways that
I could have made it better." All he wants is to know that
his dad thinks he is competent. It is comments like that that
have made me humble, and I realize how far I am from
being a great dad. Matthew, on the other hand, is not so
much into projects as Paul is, but he really does appreciate
a lot of affection. Abigail, the oldest child in the family,
needs to know that her opinions count. She has a high
"respect" need. I have to be sure I am listening to her and
giving her opinions great weight.

Anna, our middle daughter, has the high need for security that many women do. In one of our Operation Timothy
meetings I asked her about fears, and told her about my
fears while I was growing up. She wanted to know about
the times I heard my mom and dad arguing. I was about
halfway through telling her about it when I realized Anna
must have heard Susy and me argue. In fact, her room is at
the head of the stairs, and there have been times when Susy
and I have argued downstairs and Anna has heard some of
those arguments. So I asked Anna if she had ever heard
Susy and me argue. She took a long time before admitting
that she had. Then I asked her how it made her feel. At first
she brushed off the questions with short answers, but as I
persisted and waited for her answer, she finally admitted
that, yes, she had some pain because of our arguments—
and some fear. She told me she would become afraid when
she heard us argue, and it gave me a great opportunity to
tell her how I understood that from my own childhood, and
how sorry I was I had ever argued with Susy. I explained to
Anna that when I argued, it was usually begun by my own

lack of trust, or job pressures at work, or a lack of patience, and sometimes by my desire to stand up for my own rights. Then I had to apologize to Anna and ask her to forgive me for not always being nice and gentle to her mother. That also gave me the opportunity to explain that Susy and I would never consider divorcing, but we would always be willing to resolve our differences. By taking the time to clarify the need and deal with it, Anna and I developed a much closer relationship.

Build "Insiders" with Your Children

Often the problems you are struggling with, the disappointments you feel, and the challenges you face are the very ones your children will also someday experience. By sharing these struggles honestly and confidentially, you will build an "insider" closeness to your son or daughter. Some hints:

+ Share the process. Don't just speak in terms of conclusions and results.
+ Admit the fear of making a bad decision, explain your options, and talk about what you do to make good decisions.
+ Encourage their feedback concerning what you have done. Our children know we aren't perfect—we're trying to train them to avoid our mistakes, not impress them with our perfection.
+ Share with them your pain in a variety of situations: upon learning that a colleague is leaving his wife, that a friend is facing a health crisis, or that you received bad news.
+ Don't be afraid to share some confidences with your children if they are mature enough to handle them. You can always change the names, dates, and places in order to protect the confidence.

Joshua is the one who always needs be heard, whether I like it or not. He once served notice on his twin sister, Anna, that he was "suing" her for breach of contract for failing to have the circus weekend in accordance with her posted notice. My wife and I were lawyers, so we decided to schedule oral arguments and a trial. Joined by another legal gladiator (his buddy Morgan), Josh and his able co-counsel began the case with a long opening statement, then offered an array of witnesses, which was followed by a parade of the defendant's witnesses. Anna was defended by her older brother Matthew, and the jury broke into hysterics when Joshua peered over the top of his notes and objected to his brother's constant interruption and badgering of witnesses. The defense motion for dismissal was denied by the judge (me—dressed up in my wedding tuxedo). Matthew presented the defense, pointing out the circus notice was not dated and therefore the contract technically had not gone unfulfilled. However, the defense's credibility was greatly undermined by the fact that the counsel for the defense had purchased tickets to the event for seven dollars!

The jury, as usual, came up with a split decision. Both parties went home amidst gales of laughter over the funny things that happened (but with the firm conviction that the judge had not fully appreciated the merit of their case). The entire affair was pretty typical of a lot of cases that Susy and I had experienced in the courtroom, and it was a great time of building competency in our children's lives by doing projects that complemented their giftedness as given by the Lord. It is important that we raise up our children in the Scriptures in accordance with the way in which they are guided and gifted by the Lord.

Last year, while my wife and I were speaking in Asia, I called and talked with everyone on the phone. When Paul got on, he immediately asked me, "Dad, how are you doing? Have you been patient with Mom?" It's funny that my then 14-year-old would be asking that sort of question, but Paul I are in an accountability relationship with each other. He needs me to check on him, and he feels a responsibility to check on me. We talk honestly about what we're doing, and I'm always mindful of the fact that if I fall into sin, I'm going to have to go back to my sons and explain it to them.

Each of the children is different, with different needs, but each desires to feel valued and competent. Find ways to meet their individual intimacy needs, and look for jobs that you can give each so that you'll have a reason for praising and encouraging them. Children want to feel competent and part of the family, and they especially want to hear their father tell them what a good job they're doing.

Socrates Was Right

One principle in building relationships is to follow the Socratic method of teaching: Ask questions and talk about answers. Law schools and business schools follow that practice, having instructors not so much convey answers as questions, allowing the answers to be derived from the students. That method teaches students how to think. Don't just spew out rote information or ask your kids to memorize stuff. That doesn't teach kids to think. It merely teaches them to regurgitate information.

We want our kids to think through problems and to work through their inner feelings and thoughts. By asking a lot of questions, you can find out how your kids are thinking. I try to stick to the what, where, when, who, why, and how questions, but that usually takes us into new territories of conversation. It is amazing what you can do in a discussion just by asking questions. I've found myself asking about homework and getting into a lengthy discussion on science and the Bible. We've started talking about sports and found ourselves suddenly discussing honesty and integrity. Small conversations can turn into great learning times if we look for ways to seize the instances of the day and move our children toward God.

The apostle Paul instructed the believers at Ephesus to "let no unwholesome word" come out of their mouths, but instead to use their conversation to build one another up (Ephesians 4:29). Too many conversations on television are negative and unwholesome. Many of the private conversations at school are aimed at criticizing and tearing others down. In that sort of world, fathers need to make a point of building their kids up. We need to set an example for our children of sharing praise, not just sounding negative. Paul went on to encourage the Colossians to "let your speech always be with grace, seasoned, as it were, with salt, so that you may know how you should respond to each person" (Colossians 4:6). That's great advice for dads, who can appear to their children as critical if they are always pointing out the weaknesses and foibles of others.

Asking questions is not just a way to get information, it is also a wonderful method for finding the positive in something. One time I came home from work, and Susy was a little disturbed that Abigail, about eight, had been disrespectful to an adult. A neighbor, Mrs. Carruthers, had reported that Abigail had argued with her and been rude. My wife asked me to talk to Abigail about the situation, so I began by simply asking for the facts. It seems that Abigail was at the Carruthers' house when her teenagers were playing some music our daughter knew we did not approve of. Abigail told Mrs. Carruthers that she did not think her parents would like for her to listen to that music, to which Mrs. Carruthers replied, "I'm sure it's okay. Don't worry about it." A few minutes later, Abigail confronted Mrs. Carruthers very directly and said, "If you don't turn off that music, I will have to call my mom and ask to go home."

Mrs. Carruthers was very offended. She talked to Susy and said that when we turn our kids over to them we needed to trust her as a godly woman to decide what music is acceptable and what music is not. Susy quickly took Mrs. Carruthers' defense as she talked about the situation with me. However, in talking to Abigail about the whole situation, we realized that Abigail had not only sought to walk righteously and to separate herself from something that we

did not think was right for her, but she also had been willing to take on the authority of a mother and subject herself
to criticism, perhaps discipline, in trying to keep the rules
we had given her. Abigail was willing to stand against peer
pressure from the kids listening to the music. So instead of
disciplining Abigail, I wanted to reward her for her willingness to stand up under pressure to try and do what she
believed was the right thing. I never would have found out
the truth if I had not asked a lot of who, what, where, when,
how, and why questions.

Using Scripture As a Tool

One principle of communication is that the Bible is a great
tool for "teaching, for reproof, for correction, and for training in righteousness" (2 Timothy 3:16). The more we can
expose our children to the truth of Scripture, the better-
equipped our kids will be for facing the world. Your children need to see you reading your Bible, not just watching
TV. They need to know you think about Scripture as you
bring it up in conversation, and then try to apply it to life
on a regular basis. If you'll read your Bible each morning,
you'll soon find yourself talking about it naturally with
your wife and children.

   Of course, it is important that we not force-feed Scripture. As a mid-life convert, I have always been somewhat
envious of the people who did not have the disastrous, sinful life that I did. Yet my pre-Christian days allowed me to
value the worth of God's Word. Some people who became
Christians early in life have told me that Scripture reading
and memorization just wasn't fun for them as they grew
up, though it became more enjoyable years later as they
developed a love for it. If you have struggled with spending time daily in God's Word, I urge you to develop an
accountability relationship with one of your kids. You'll
read, they'll read, and you'll both check with each other to
make sure you're keeping your word.

   In analyzing this with my kids, I was intent on not forcing the Bible on them. Instead, I spent a lot of time talking

about it and how it relates to our lives. Often I'll take one line of a psalm or proverb and ask them to put the verse into their own words. Sometimes we discuss what a particular passage means and how it relates to our lives. I try to draw my kids out, so that they're having to interact intellectually with the thoughts of God. Sometimes with the little kids we've had them draw pictures about the Scripture. The main thing we want to do is to try and show how Scripture is not only the Word of God, but also the pattern for our lives.

Too many of our Christian experiences in business, education, and government simply take our culture and try to glue the various aspects of life together with random Bible verses. We've found a great exception to this sort of thinking: the Bible-based homeschooling materials produced by Bill Gothard's Advanced Training Institute. It has allowed us to take a passage of Scripture, study its derivation, meaning, and context, then build principles of science, law, and history out of the principles found in the verse. For example, in the Sermon on the Mount, the Lord says in Matthew 5:13, "You are the salt of the earth." The Advanced Training Institute material describes how salt is an agent for raising the temperature of ice in the winter, cleansing a wound, and preserving meat. Taken in context, we can see how Christians have historically pursued exactly those same goals. We should desire to raise the temperature of joy in our communities, cleanse wounds with comfort and forgiveness, and preserve souls by sharing the salvation message. When you start talking about the Bible as a family, you begin making some wonderful spiritual discoveries.

At a conference recently, somebody asked my oldest daughter what difference it made to talk about Scripture so openly in our home. Abigail just looked at the person and said, "I can't tell you how many times I've had a problem or a decision to make, and I'll think back to something my parents have told me or something we've discussed from Scripture, and the answer is clear. Without our discussions, I wouldn't have God's wisdom for my life." We talked about her answer afterward, and she told me that when she had been at a Christian camp, a number of the guys admitted that they struggled with the thought of living up to the expectations and examples of their fathers. They didn't want to admit their weaknesses to their dads, and they were really hurting because they had all these questions they wanted to ask, but they felt like their dads were untouchable. Then my daughter told me that she was glad we had talked so much about the Bible and about life, because it had helped her understand that her father isn't perfect!

It's true. I'm not even close to being perfect. But it's okay for my children to know that, because they've got the perfect Word of God to guide them. By using the Bible regularly in our conversations, and by praying together through our struggles, we've worked to create strong relationships with each child. We are very grateful that our kids love us, and that they love the Lord. That's probably as close to perfection as I'll ever come.

Quotable Quotes

✦ *One Good Turn Deserves Another*: Several months after dear friends received our Christmas package to their family, which included two suction-dart crossbows for their sons (resulting in their younger daughter's blackened eye), the mom said, "I liked your Christmas presents so much that I've decided next year to give your kids truck air horns!"

✦ *A Great Lawyer Argues a Not-So-Great Case*: Having presented, with great persuasion, why the dealer of our video recorder should honor our expired warranty and repair the serious defect in our camera, which had persisted several times since he had previously repaired it, the man said to Susy, "Lady, this camera isn't broken again—you're out of tape!"

✦ *The Perils of a Mom Overworked and Under-recreated*: As Mom raced across the yard to respond to a child's cry, Joshua said, "Wow, Mom! I didn't know you could run."

✦ *Butchering and Cooking Our Own Chicken:* While being assaulted by both his sister (who was combing his hair) and his dad (who was tying his tie) in preparation for a special event, Matthew exclaimed, "Ouch—I'm getting plucked and strangled at the same time!"

✦ *The Perils of Encouraging Honesty*: Without the first thought that honesty may not always be the best policy, Abigail commented, "You know, Dad, it's really hard to pick sides when you and Mom have a disagreement, because she's too sensitive and you act like a two-year-old."

Study Questions

1. As you think back on your own childhood, what was your most fun moment?

2. What fun things would your kids like to do with you?

3. How can a father use Scripture in his everyday conversations with his children?

4. What would you say are your kids' greatest intimacy needs: acceptance, affection, appreciation, approval, attention, encouragement, respect, comfort, support, or security?

5. What sort of "baggage" did you bring into your marriage, and how does it affect your family relationships?

Parenting Is Modeling

*H*e who walks with the wise grows wise, but a companion of fools suffers harm (Proverbs 13:20
NIV).

We were headed out of town for St. Louis, and we were
late as usual. Leaving late for the long trip after a lengthy
holiday celebration means that large chunks of time will be
spent with me driving alone and the rest of the family
sleeping in the van. Often the driving conditions around
the holidays are pretty bad. Susy's parents live in St. Louis,
so we usually celebrate our own private Christmas at our
home in Chattanooga, then pack up the car for Missouri to
spend a fabulous time with the grandparents, aunts, uncles,
and cousins. This particular Christmas I had done well with
all of the stress of December projects and challenges at
work: setting up the Christmas tree, buying and wrapping
presents, putting toys together, covering my absence at
work, getting all our year-end activities wrapped up in the
office, and the like. But after all that and our family celebration on top of it, I was really tired.

My wife had also spent weeks getting ready for Christmas. After all the joys of unwrapping gifts and celebrating
together, it was time to get ready for the long haul on the
highway. We had finally gotten everything loaded into the
van and made it out of the driveway when we had to turn

around and go back to get the ice chest we had left on the kitchen floor. By this time I was really pressing hard to get going. It was starting to get dark. We loaded the ice chest, headed down the mountain as fast as I could push it, and were several miles from the house when Susy exclaimed, "Oh no, we forgot Susanna's crib! We'll have to go back!" She then asked me to turn around.

I don't know how you do with trips, but my goal on a long drive isn't to see sights or enjoy the ride. My goal is to get there as soon as possible. Turning around one more time was the last thing I wanted to do. So I lost grace completely with my wife. Although I did not say anything, my whole demeanor radiated anxiety and frustration. We went back and got the crib, threw it in the back, and headed down the road. *For the third time,* I thought to myself. My jaw was tight. My driving was deliberately rough. There was not a sound in the car.

We all want to trust God for our circumstances, to return love when we don't feel like it, to be godly and not fleshly when we hit obstacles, and to be willing to suffer for Christ when things get hard. However, none of those principles were on my mind as I went flying down the road. All I could think about was the insensitivity of my family in starting so late, leaving things behind, and interrupting our trip so many times. Now I was going to have to drive half the night to get to St. Louis, and I was exhausted before I had even started. But this night would turn out to be one of those great "teachable moments" that would leave a lasting impression on all of our kids.

As I turned down the road leaving Signal Mountain, I started to tell the kids and Susy how they could have done things better, and within a few seconds it turned into a lecture, and in a few more seconds I had left description and moved into berating. My tone was anything but godly. Realizing that I was not explaining but exclaiming, I suddenly stopped talking and started stewing. As I began running it all over in my mind, the thought occurred to me that maybe I wasn't setting a great example as a father. That thought stayed with me for the next few miles, and I decided I had better pray about my attitude and ask God for strength.

The Lord began impressing upon my mind that it is in the tough situations that my children need a model to follow. Anybody can set a good example when things are going right. What's needed is an example to follow when things are all going wrong. With that, I decided I had better be done lecturing my family. Then another thought popped into my head: I had already blown it. I had yelled at my kids, berated my wife, and shown everyone exactly how *not* to act in tough times. What was needed was something dramatic. So I pulled the car over to a rest stop the first chance I got.

Turning to my wife, I said, "Susy, I want you to know just how much I appreciate you for taking care of the kids and being a wonderful mother to our family, and a great wife to me. I realize I shouldn't be blaming you for everything that's gone wrong, nor should I be treating you with disrespect. Thank you for all the labor you've gone through to get ready for the trip, and all the hard work you put in making our Christmas morning special. It wasn't easy, and we all appreciate you." Then I turned to my kids and thanked them for all their diligence in packing and preparing for the trip. I also described how I was excited to see the grandparents, and what a privilege it was to be the husband and father of this family.

Now, before you start thinking I was being noble, you need to know something important: *That's not what I wanted to say.* I wanted to yell and scream and make everybody feel bad. I wanted my kids to act sorry and tell me I was right and they were wrong. The most natural thing for any man would have been to put everybody in their place. It was hard, but I made a decision that I wanted to be different. It was an act of obedience. The interesting thing is that after I had apologized, I felt better. Once I had chosen to turn my own attitude around, I had renewed energy. The family seemed to get along better. As I pulled the van back onto the highway, the mood in that vehicle felt completely different. When we act in obedience, feelings will follow.

Lately I've been thinking about how I can be a model for my kids. How can I set an example for them to follow, and not regret that my kids are doing exactly what I did? As I reflected upon it, the thought came that Jesus has set for us the perfect example. In Philippians 2:1-4, we read these words:

> If therefore there is any encouragement in Christ, if there is any consolation of love, if there is any fellowship of the Spirit, if any affection and compassion, make my joy complete by being of the same mind, maintaining the same love, united in spirit, intent on one purpose. Do nothing from selfishness or empty conceit, but with humility of mind let each of you regard one another as more important than himself; do not merely look out for your own personal interests, but also for the interests of others.

In other words, Christ has given us an example of selflessness. We are to follow His example.

As I focused on joyful, wonderful thoughts of encouragement, my whole demeanor changed. In speaking truth and acting in grace, my feelings followed my words and I actually felt better. My feelings were enhanced by the positive response from the kids, and Susy's soft touch as she said, "Phil, I love you." The kids began to smile and relax as they realized Dad was not going to blow up. The father's example sets the tone for the family.

You see, every father is a model. We model good and godly conduct, or we model worldly, sinful conduct. I have done plenty of both with my family. But it is critically important we realize that what we do and say will be multiplied in the lives of our kids either for good or for bad.

The Mission of Modeling
As parents we are models to our children, whether for good or bad. Parenting *is* modeling. Our children see us and follow our example, whether we like it or not. Men often say

they do not want to be the spiritual leaders of their home, but I always respond that they *are* the spiritual leaders of their home, whether they like it or not. His desire (or lack of it) has nothing to do with it. The dad is the spiritual leader because God planned it that way. The father either portrays a spirit of worldliness or a spirit of godliness. Either they are leaders for righteousness or examples of slothfulness. Either they are modeling Jesus Christ or mirroring sinful man. Make no mistake about it: We are all modeling *something*. We are all spiritual leaders of one kind or another.

One of the most important things we can do to provide a safe and secure environment for spiritual growth is to model forgiveness. Susy and I do not have many fights, but when we do we usually are not able to hide them from the children. Our kids seem to have radar when it comes to our interior emotions. Many parents think they are successfully hiding from their children the fact they are upset with one another, but nothing could be farther from the truth. Our children know us too well. They're aware of the fact that we are disagreeing with one another, even when we are trying to hide it.

That's why it is important not only to resolve the disagreement, but also to inform the children. We usually do this by getting the kids to come around the dining-room table and explaining to them what happened. I usually take the lead on that, describing to everyone what I did wrong and explaining to them *why* it was wrong. Often it's because I am focused on myself, or a problem at work has caused me to be less than patient with things that happen at home. Also, it is important to ask Susy to forgive me in the presence of those who observed the argument, so they can learn how to do that with each other, and, in the future, with their spouses or children.

I will never forget the Christmas my dad took me to E.J. Korvettes, the first discount store I had ever been in. Korvettes was located in New Rochelle, New York. When I was about 16 years of age, Dad and I were in a hurry to get something for Christmas, and we both went bursting through the front door. As we did, Dad bumped into a man carrying a large number of packages, and they were knocked out of his arms. But my father was in such a hurry that he just kept going. The man with the dropped packages turned and said with a snarl, "Merry Christmas!" I remember thinking we should have stopped to say we were sorry, but I was so embarrassed I was glad my dad kept going. We did our shopping and never mentioned it. We never discussed it. That memory is still vivid in my mind, as though it happened yesterday. That night my father was preoccupied and frustrated, probably struggling with the feeling of guilt for what he had done. But he never dealt with the situation, never apologized, and never talked with me about it. Today, more than 30 years later, it still bothers me to think about it.

As a father, I know that my kids are watching me. When I do things like bump somebody accidentally, I try to communicate with my kids what I have done wrong and what I could have done better. Sometimes I'll ask them to suggest how I could have better handled the situation. To be honest, there are times I don't like to listen to their ideas because they begin to tell me things that I know are true, but I don't like to hear. When I go out on dates with our kids, I try to model what I would expect their friends to be like. For example, with the boys I try to be careful not to talk about someone behind their back and to be respectful of other people. With our girls I try to open the door and show respect toward them. I always ask them what they want to eat, take pains to listen to them, and show them the respect I show Susy when we are on a date. I also try to sit in a position where I won't be distracted by others. Often I will let them sit in a corner facing the room, and I will face the wall so I will not be bothered by something else that might be going on in the restaurant. You see, I want my girls to be the focus of my attention, and I also want them to learn what a gentleman is like. That way, in future years, they'll recognize if the guy taking them out is a gentleman or not.

Dad, you're always modeling. Keep that in mind when you go to the store, when you're driving on the freeway, and when you're watching a game. Every situation is a chance for you to disciple your kids. When they're in the car with you, do they hear you criticize others, or be gracious to other drivers? When they're at the mall with you, do they see your desire to honor God with your money, or do they observe you handling it carelessly and selfishly? The example you set in the little things helps to shape the character of your children in the big things.

If your children see you address store clerks politely, they'll learn to be nice to strangers. On the other hand, if they see you be rude to employees and those hired to help you, they'll assume they only have to be polite to members of the family. I remember one time I received too much change at the cash register in a hardware store. It wasn't a lot of money, and it was a lot of trouble to go back, but I wanted to go back to please the Lord, and to model to our kids what a godly man does when someone makes a mistake that benefits him.

Demonstrating Diligence

One of the great needs for Christian husbands is to be diligent in work. I have some friends who are seeking to follow God, but they simply have a hard time getting out of bed in the morning and going to work. They come home and complain about their jobs or their employers or their customers or clients, and I wonder what sort of example they are offering their children. I often talk about challenges at work with all of the above, but I try to do it in a way that is respectful of those people, recognizing that God has placed me under an authority. I am to be a servant at my job, just as Jesus was a servant in His role. My kids need to see me get up and go to work, then come home without complaining and criticizing. After all, if we really believe the Lord has put us in our places of employment, to complain about the job is to criticize the Lord!

Sometimes I have found myself being very critical of those causing me problems, and I pass that criticism on to my family. When I do that, I have to go back and apologize

Teach Your Children to Work

✦ Explain to your kids the economic system of labor and wages.

✦ Don't just tell your children to work or be diligent, demonstrate it by modeling those principles in your own life and by showing them what to do on a particular task.

✦ It takes a long time to train a two-year-old how to put away his blanket—and just as long to train a 16-year-old how to change the oil in his car.

✦ Once a child has grasped what to do and why to do it, give him a reasonable time of practice before you seek to enforce the task by accountability.

✦ Don't expect what you don't inspect. Begin with simple accountability such as, "I'll check back later and see how you are doing."

✦ Both boys and girls can value from learning how to change a tire, sew on a button, clean the house, vacuum a rug, load a dishwasher, and repair a broken chair.

✦ To pay someone to read the Bible may never achieve the desired result of becoming more godly, but to give him a $100 reward for reading through the Bible in a year may be just the incentive he needs to read those three chapters a day instead of watching another movie.

for not offering the other side of the argument. I try to teach my kids the truth of Proverbs 18:17: "The first to plead his case seems just, until another comes and examines him." In other words, you need to hear both sides of the story. A management principle I live by is that people do what makes sense to them, so if there is a mistake, it's likely the individual did it because he or she thought it best. When

Dad is presenting a particular problem happening at work, he needs to be sure to communicate to his family that there are two sides to the story, that he knows he isn't always right, and that he still respects the other person.

One of the greatest things that happened to me was when my wife and children picked up on my morning routine. My greatest challenge is getting enough time with the Lord every morning, so I get up at an early hour to spend time with Him. Unfortunately, when the family starts to awaken they can often be a distraction to my desire to have the house quiet in order to study the Word, pray, meditate, and memorize Scripture. Many years ago it occurred to me that our kids ought to be doing the same thing that I am doing, but every time I suggested it, I felt like the authoritarian father imposing his schedule on the household. I quickly realized that if I continued to do that, I would end up with rebellious people.

Therefore, I decided at least for a while not to insist everyone do what I do. Instead, I simply tried to be a model in my morning devotions with the Lord. I would get up every morning and read my Bible, do some Bible study, pray through my prayer list, and work on memorizing verses. We start family devotions every morning I am in town at 7:30, and since I've already had my quiet time, I can share with them the insights the Lord has shown me from Scripture that morning. I'm afforded the opportunity to reveal to my children how exciting it is to be meditating on God's Word each day. I also share with them my particular method of Bible study, but I don't offer any commands that they should do it.

Within a few months of taking this approach, I found that my children started following my example. They would say things like, "Dad, we appreciate when you have had your quiet times, because you are a lot more fun to be with." My regular weekend joke is to tell my kids, "You know, I think I will skip my quiet time this Saturday and just play baseball." Remembering the unhappy result on the days when I've made that choice, the kids will respond,

"No, no, no! Dad, please have your quiet time. We can wait." Through my own Bible reading and prayer time I have been able to encourage my family to follow my example, pointing out that when they have their quiet time they are often more considerate of their brothers and sisters, and more attentive to what God would have them do that day.

For many years now, the older five children have done a daily quiet time out of pure habit because "that's what we do in our family." Susy and I have prayed that the Lord would make our conviction to study God's word that of the children's, but we know that is a work the Spirit must do in their own hearts. It has been exciting to see it start to happen in each of our older children, as the Lord has brought circumstances into their lives which prompted them to fall in love with the Scripture.

When Abigail was 14, she learned to study the Bible inductively during the two weeks of Kay Arthur's Teen Boot Camp. Kay imparted her deep love for the Scripture to Abigail, and she returned home a different person. Now, time in the Word flows out of her love for the Lord and her desire to learn from His Word. Paul's interest in the Scripture had certainly grown during our years of family Bible study, but his current commitment was sparked during his missionary trip to Africa. Matthew's determination and competitiveness to read the Bible in a year and earn a reward promised by a friend helped him keep his "nose in the Book" long enought to fall in love with the Scripture. Anna just completed reading the Bible through for the first time—it took her two years and we are thrilled. Now Josh has taken up the challenge. We continue to pray for that spark of inner conviction for the twins.

While we don't want to cause rebellion by insisting on our schedule, we have seen the value of setting up patterns, even though they are initially the parents convictions. Pray that the Holy Spirit will work in your child's life as only He can so that your convictions become your child's.

As increasing numbers in our family are having their quiet time in the morning, we've found we need to reduce the number of distractions in the home during that time. Christian radio and music is wonderful, but we found even that was distracting the children from their quiet times. Lately we turned off the radio for the early morning. We've established a schedule by which everyone gets up and does their quiet time, exercises, and chores in the morning, so we can begin the day refreshed and renewed.

Modeling with Our Mouths

I learned about the importance of modeling from the man who discipled me: Jim Lyon, a medical doctor who not only spent about three years taking me through Operation Timothy, but who also took me with him as he visited men and talked about their need for a Savior. I learned partly by his instruction, but mostly by his example. Just as Jesus took the 12 disciples with Him to minister, Jim took me to talk to men about Christ. Now I do the same thing, taking my kids on speaking trips with me, letting them talk to people about their walk with the Lord. These trips have afforded me a wonderful opportunity to discuss not only what we do to reach other people, but also to show them exactly how to do it.

I'll never forget taking the son of a friend with me on a two-day speaking trip to Florida. I spoke several times, gave my testimony, and did follow-up with some of the guests who came to the meetings. After one session, the young man came with me as we visited a lawyer who had checked on his card that he prayed to receive Christ. After some discussion with that lawyer in his office, I asked him if he would like to confirm that commitment by working through a small tract entitled "Steps to Peace with God." He told us he would love to do that, so we talked him through the tract. At that point, he admitted he was not a Christian and asked to pray to receive Christ, which we did together. After the meeting, my young friend and I left the office, went to our car, and as soon as we sat down he burst into tears. "I've never done anything like that before in my life," he told me. "I've always wanted to, but I've never helped lead anyone to the Lord. Thanks for sharing this experience with me."

It was one of those wonderful moments neither of us will ever forget. That day my friend's son learned more about evangelism and discipleship than he could have learned in a dozen evangelism classes. He learned how to lead someone to Christ by watching someone do it. Modeling is vital to the maturing process—that's why Jesus spent so much time modeling for His followers. If we can reveal to our children the ministry of Jesus Christ by the example of our mouths, we will impact their lives forever.

James 3:6 states that "the tongue is a fire." Too often in our culture that fire is burning out of control. Criticism and cynicism are epidemic in our culture. Talking trash and putting others down has become standard fare in our modern society. I have often found myself criticizing those around me and modeling the very things I don't want my kids to do. In our competitive world, too many guys are revealing a lack of godliness through their words. Dad, you don't like it when your kids get into squabbles and point out one another's weaknesses, but that is precisely the conduct we engender when we start yelling at the slow driver in the fast lane or begin complaining about lousy store clerks at the sporting-goods store.

A while back I was at the post office, which sometimes seems to specialize in teaching patience to the American public. On top of the long wait, one particular clerk appeared to be awfully surly with her customers, which slowed down the process even more. When my daughter and I finally got to the front of the line, the clerk suddenly closed her window, and everybody behind me raced to another line. Before I could think, I started to complain out loud about the inconvenience and ineffectiveness of the United States Postal Service. People were looking at me, steam coming out of my ears, when suddenly I caught the eye of my daughter. She was watching my every move, waiting to see how a mature man of God handles these sorts of little bumps in the road. I bit my tongue, walked

Unity and Discipline Repel Rebellion

✦ Be unified as parents in your discipline and discuss it with your children in advance.

✦ Always discuss the whys of discipline as well as the hows.

✦ Admit mistakes by saying, "I really could have done that better."

✦ If you discipline in anger, admit it, correct it, and ask forgiveness.

✦ Point out that some of your child's frustrations in dealing with his or her friends are due to a lack of proper discipline by the parents.

✦ Remember that our children are not as experienced in seeing the results of sin and the fruit of righteousness, so without lecturing, point out each in the lives of others.

outside, and said quietly to Anna, "Boy . . . it sure is frustrating to be treated like that." Those words started us on an in-depth conversation of how we treat others and how we would like to be treated. I didn't set the perfect example, but at least I tried to talk honestly about the situation, and admitted I hadn't been as patient as I should have been.

Often we tend to justify our own frustration with people, while in the next breath we criticize our kids for not handling tough times as well as we would like. It is scary but true: If I am impatient and critical with my kids, they will be impatient and critical with each other. I've learned that I need to wait before I complain, even though I've had a hard day at the office. The Bible says God hates grumbling and complaining, so I try to postpone commenting on a situation until I can handle it with emotional maturity, rather than turning it into a time of venting the frustrations of my day.

When things go wrong, we have to try and model a

positive attitude. As a father, this might be the hardest thing I face on a particular day. We live in an instant world, and there are many demands on us, so when we have to wait for something, we start complaining. The thing to keep in mind is that children aren't robots. We don't program them once with information, then expect them to handle all future situations perfectly. Children, even if they are Christians, are still sinners saved by grace, and they don't have the maturity yet to handle things as they ought. That's why God put a father into their lives, to show them how to keep a positive attitude when things go wrong.

Learn to confess your failings and ask for forgiveness when you blow it. Rather than making you smaller in their eyes, it will cause their respect for you to grow, for it helps your kids recognize that you don't think you are perfect. Often the most effective teaching moments are those when I have to relive a situation in which I've blown it, where my tongue got away from me, and now I need to go back and repair the damage done. I've found my children always want to listen and love me when I admit I've used my words in a negative way.

When I get ill-tempered with the kids because of circumstances going wrong, I try to tell them *what* went wrong, *why* I acted improperly, and *what the biblical principle* is that I broke. I always try to end by telling my kids that I hope they'll be more mature than I am when they grow up (because I don't want them doing the same thing with my grandchildren!).

If our children see that we are accountable to one another, that we love them, and that we are committed to being obedient to the Lord, they will be more likely to try and follow our example. And eventually we'll find our kids starting to do the right things for the right reasons, without any intervention or corrective discipline on our part.

Demonstrating Discipline

There are two crucial areas every father must reflect on when considering the example he reveals to his children: *his body* and *his money*. In a fast-food world, many of us are struggling with our weight. Just about everybody I know is on a diet. People who are overweight are on a diet to take pounds off, and people at the right weight are on a diet to keep from putting pounds on. You know, it's tough to talk with your children about the importance of self-discipline when you're 20 pounds overweight. You lose your integrity when your belly is hanging over your belt and you're trying to discuss the importance of sacrifice.

I spent 15 years in law practice, going into court each day, and only gained 15 pounds. Then I spent 15 months with CBMC, attending a bunch of conferences and dinners, and gained another 15 pounds! With 30 extra pounds and virtually no exercise, I was headed for some health challenges. My body didn't fit with my faith (to say nothing of it not fitting my clothes!). In order to be able to talk with my children about self-discipline, I started exercising. At first I began running—just a little bit, to try and get my heart going. Over the course of a year I worked up to actual distance running, and added push-ups and sit-ups every day to get in shape.

By sharing my struggle to lose weight with my kids, I was able to show them how a man develops discipline. Of course, I also became a living example of how hard it is to get in shape once you are out of shape. The funny thing is that each one of my children, particularly the older ones, have not only noted this challenge, but have also begun to be more regular in their exercise and more disciplined in their eating habits. Seeing their father work at it motivated them to make life-style changes.

Perhaps the area in which most fathers face their greatest struggle is in the disciplined use of finances. I'll criticize Susy for buying too many books for our homeschool, but then I'll go out and spend a hundred dollars on a tool I need for my shop. For some reason, when we earn the money, we have a tendency to feel it gives us the right to spend it on ourselves. I've got a buddy, Bill, who constantly scolds his wife about her "slothfulness" with money. But when it comes to his projects, money is no object—and he can't seem to grasp why his wife is always frustrated with finances. You see, the message Bill is sending to his wife and kids is that *his needs are more important than their needs.* He insists others use fiscal discipline, but he doesn't evidence any.

A father needs to honor the Lord with his money, then show his kids how his budget reflects the Lord's priorities. Too many dads keep their finances a secret, as though the kids shouldn't know what the parents are spending. But how will children learn the godly use of finances if their parents don't show them? Talk with your children about money, taxes, spending, tithing, and your overall priorities.

Oliver, a colleague of mine, became frustrated with his family's lack of appreciation for what things cost. He and his wife were concerned that their kids had no idea what it took to operate a family, so he reserved a conference room at the bank and got the bank manager to do him a favor. The manager brought to the conference table the entire annual salary Oliver had earned the previous year, in piles of 100-dollar bills. Over the next several hours, Oliver and his family doled out the money according to what they had spent the previous year. They allowed each child to act as the banker for various categories such as clothing, utilities, groceries, education, insurance, sporting events, vacations, the mortgage, and their Christian giving. As they counted out each pile of money for each budget requirement, the children got a firsthand demonstration of how much it costs to operate a family. They also were able to talk about the routine comforts and necessities that they had been taking for granted, and they had a wonderful discussion about how much money is paid to the government in taxes each year. That exercise completely changed the attitudes of his children. They developed a much greater understanding of the wise use of God's resources.

What do your spending habits reflect to your children? When we teach our children by our example that how we spend money doesn't matter, we abandon stewardship and short-circuit the teaching of self-discipline. On the other hand, modeling thriftiness doesn't mean we have to be cheap. Some dads are so thrifty they are simply no fun to be around. When a father goes overboard in one direction or the other, it often results in the children going to the opposite extreme. Even the way we talk about money can reflect a godly or worldly attitude. For example, when we are questioning a clerk about the price of a particular item, we can quickly give the inference that others are trying to cheat us. A man can convey suspicion and condemnation instead of thriftiness if he fails to use God's grace when discussing financial issues.

On the other hand, it is important we teach our children that not all items are created equal. Deceptive trade practices can sometimes fool us, so we need to teach our kids to be aware. For example, a friend of mine recently helped his son recognize the old "bait and switch"—the practice of advertising a low-priced item, then telling the customer it's sold out and selling them something more expensive. The boy was looking for a bicycle, and had seen just the right one advertised at a bike shop. But when they walked in, the salesman told them that bike had been sold, and immediately started pitching them on a much more expensive model. The boy was faced with the dilemma of having wasted a lot of time investigating the purchase and coming away empty-handed, or spending a lot more money than he wanted to. So the father encouraged him to wait, they went outside, and he educated his son in the subtleties of sales tricks. The dad was able to explain to his boy why we need to stick to a budget and trust God for the right item at the right price.

Giving is another area in which it can be a challenge to model godly character. Some parents keep their giving a secret, but if we want our children to learn how to give generously to God, we've got to make them part of the process. One of my friends has a great practice which his family goes through every Christmas in their year-end giving to charitable organizations. They tie envelopes, addressed to various Christian ministries, onto the Christmas tree. In the morning the children take the envelopes off the tree, stamp them, and send them to the ministries. That way the children know how much is given, and it is a real testimony to the parents' charitable hearts. The parents don't brag or make a big deal about the amount, but rather let the children enter into the spirit of giving.

A Positive Attitude

If you watch much television, see a few movies, or hang around a playground for a while, you can't help but notice the negativity rampant in our culture. Kids seem more negative than ever. What began with the rebellion of the fifties and sixties and grew into anger and cynicism with Watergate, has now grown into full-fledged pessimism and despair among young people. Music pounds out the message that the world is a bad place. Characters in the movies and television are filled with selfishness and self-loathing, and the real-life actors behind those characters are often involved in destructive personal behaviors. That sort of negativity has been pushed by the media, so that kids grow up thinking they've got to feign cynicism in order to appear mature.

To counteract that, a father has got to make sure his kids maintain a positive attitude. We need to regularly remind our kids that we love them, that they are valuable, that they belong in our families, and that we respect their abilities. The reason why children are joining gangs in record numbers is because the gangs fill a need the kids aren't getting at home: a place to belong. Study after study has shown children who feel loved and respected by their parents are far less likely to get involved in any sort of juvenile delinquency. That's why we work to make our children feel that they are part of the Downer "team." That's why we work on projects together, and help the children grow in their skills, and praise them when they do a good job. The feeling of competence assures a child of his or her self-worth, and bonds the child to the family.

Unfortunately, your kids are often in contact with other children who aren't getting that sort of encouragement at home, and who want to share their negativity with others. The apostle Paul warns us in 1 Corinthians 15:33 NIV, "Do not be misled: 'Bad company corrupts good character.'" That's one of the reasons we started homeschooling: so that we could have a greater role in shaping our children more than friends, teachers, or the television do. We wanted parents, not peers, to be the dominant force in their lives.

You may remember that a movie called *The Program* started a disturbing trend when it was released a few years ago. In the movie, college sports stars would prove their toughness by lying down on the dividing line of a highway. Unfortunately, young men across the country, many of them churchgoing kids from good homes, decided to imitate that behavior. The results were tragic. Several young men died when they were hit by cars on darkened roads across the country. What makes a young man need to prove himself to his buddies? A need for belonging, for having friends who respect him. A strong family can offer that sense of belonging and respect, so that the kids don't have to "prove" themselves through some kind of half-brained activity.

Some people have criticized our decision to home-school our children. Every homeschool parent hears the same argument: "Your kids won't get enough socialization!" Brother, that is one of the weakest arguments imaginable against schooling your kids at home. What is "socialization"? It's defined as the process that a person goes through to become part of society. I submit that a child learns to become part of society by spending time with adults, not children. For example, if you want your kids to learn table manners, you don't put them in a cafeteria with 50 other kids. You place them at a table with adults, so they can learn proper table etiquette. In God's plan, we learn from our parents and grandparents, the men and women with gray hair who are older and wiser. If a child spends all his time around children his own age, he'll stay forever a juvenile. Immaturity breeds immaturity. However, godly friends are also important to a child's maturing process.

I was visiting a fine Christian family recently, and the couple sat me down in the living room with their 15-year-old son while they were getting dinner ready. I tried striking up a conversation, but I noticed the young man didn't shake my hand, nor would he look me in the eyes.

"How are you doing?" I asked him.

"'kay," he replied, looking at his shoes.

"What have you been up to lately?"

"Nuthin'."

I tried again: "Well, what do you like to do with your free time?"

"I dunno," he mumbled, stifling a yawn. I don't think he knew how to communicate with an adult. He could only talk with other teens. That's what age segregation has done for us. It has taught people to worship their peers. At the same time, kids have learned to disrespect their parents and compete with their siblings. They often hate their brothers and sisters, and think their parents are out-of-it, so it's impossible to create a "team" of the family. The peer group runs the show, and the peer group has a negative attitude. For Dad to counteract that influence and help shape the character of his kids, he will have to reflect a positive attitude toward his family and the world.

Parenting is modeling. There's just no getting around the fact. We are examples to our kids, whether we like it or not. God set up the family that way, and He gave each child a desire for belonging, worth, and competence. A child wants leadership and a model to follow. The first place your kids look is at you. So ask yourself this question: When my children look at me, what do they see?

Quotable Quotes

✦ *Typo of the Year Once Again Goes to Dad*: My hand-written note to a faithful supporter omitted an apostrophe and the letters *n* and *t*. It read, "Thanks, Joe, we really *could* do the ministry without you."

✦ *Quick, Get Joshua to the Car*: To two dear friends who both had been born and raised in Colorado and described themselves as "natives," our son Joshua said, "That's funny. You don't look like natives."

✦ *The Realities of a Budget*: Matthew in his most analytical voice said, "I would much rather be *real* cold than only a little bit cold, because when I'm *real* cold, Mom will turn up the heat."

✦ *Creativity of Two Weary Travelers*: Lugging our suitcases through the Denver Airport while changing planes following the father/son retreat, Paul resourcefully suggested, "Hey, Dad, why don't we imitate a pregnant woman and jump on one of those electric carts?"

✦ *May God Guard All of You for Another Year*: After studying the passage in the Book of Isaiah where God is described as "the one who goes out before us and is our rear guard," Paul looked up midway through his closing prayer to inquire at the gales of laughter from the family after he had prayed, "God, please guard our rears."

Study Questions

1. How do you see yourself reflected in your children?

2. If you could pick one word, what word best describes the example you set for your children?

3. What are the three qualities you would most like your children to develop?

4. What are some things you could do to help foster those qualities?

5. When have you failed your kids? What did you learn from the experience?

6

Creating Memories

*T*rain up a child in the way he should go, even when
he is old he will not depart from it (Proverbs 22:6).

A father can use everyday events, even unpleasant everyday events, to build great memories. For example, a funeral
in the life of a family can be remembered as something very
painful, but also as a wonderful memory as a family gath-
ers together. It is important that those out-of-the-ordinary
days—funerals, weddings, births, vacations, visits from
friends—be captured as lifelong memories in the lives of
your children. Learning to create memories is one of the
most fun and most meaningful tasks you have as a father.

One of my most vivid memories is the time I attended
my cousin's wedding in New Jersey. I was 16 years old at
the time, and so that I would look right, I got to buy my first
sports jacket. It was a beautiful white dinner jacket, perfect
for the formal Princeton, New Jersey, wedding. However, at
that wedding I broke out in a severe attack of hives, so I
ended up looking like someone who just escaped from a
leper colony. But my embarrassment was overcome by the
fact that my parents didn't make me feel ugly. Instead, they
complimented me for my adult behavior and how good I
looked in my new white jacket. Maybe because I recognized the importance of the occasion, I remained on my

best behavior that weekend, and my folks noticed. In fact, the groom got involved in a fight with his best man at the swimming pool prior to the wedding, and my mom made a point of telling me that I had acted more mature than the groom and his attendants. I've still got a picture from that day (it shows me running after the car, a handful of rice flying at the window), and I don't think I ever looked more dapper. Every time I look at that picture I remember how my parents encouraged me that weekend. Sometimes a special occasion can be used to create a lasting memory.

Building Traditions

Nothing helps individuals feel like they belong to a group more than traditions. We come to know ourselves and our families as we tell the stories and relive the traditions of the past. Traditions lend depth and texture to our lives, giving us a sense of our place and helping us better understand ourselves. As the father in the home, *you* are the person most responsible for maintaining traditions in your family. Most guys tend to think of that as being the wife's job, expecting her to tell the stories and pull out the decorations on appropriate days. But your children look to you, as the man of the house, to share the history of the family and be the repository of knowledge.

Therefore, build traditions. If your family has stories about ancestors, tell them to your kids. Repeat them over and over, so the children begin to understand their history. If there are certain anniversaries or traditions that were important to your parents and grandparents, pass those along to your kids. Use them as an opportunity to discuss modern life, and look for those teachable moments when you can offer insight into your child's life. If you don't have traditions, start your own. Do Christmas the same way every year. Make a big deal over Thanksgiving, Valentine's Day, and Easter, and involve the children in activities you can repeat each year. Above all, use the opportunities to talk with your kids. The two keys to building traditions are to make them meaningful and make them fun.

Don't just have fireworks on the Fourth of July—talk about the founding of the country. Tell your children what happened, and why it was important. Use the opportunity to discuss our nation's history, and where the country is today. Don't be strictly negative when discussing the government, as some Christians appear, but talk about the role God played in the founding of our country. That way the holiday will be meaningful, but by doing the same thing each year it will also give the children a fun day to look forward to. In the same way, throughout the month of December you should talk about Christmas. Read the various Bible passages together. Explain how Santa Claus became a part of Christmas. Chat about the laws surrounding the public display of a crèche, and how the Supreme Court has shaped the way we celebrate Christmas. When friends of ours started discussing this, one of their children asked some questions about the Supreme Court, and it led to an exploration of the three branches of government and how those branches' roles have become blurred, with the Supreme Court becoming more legislative in recent years. It's amazing in what directions you'll go when you start talking about traditions and history. Ask your kids why things have happened and what the impact has been.

We have tried to make sure our kids have to think through things as we approach each holiday tradition. One of the most challenging projects we have had occurred one July, when we decided to take a look at the American Revolution in light of what Romans 13 says about authority and paying taxes. We considered what the colonists were involved with in the Boston Tea Party, discussed taxation without representation, and let the kids struggle through the issues. Were they right or wrong to withhold taxes? What about throwing the tea into the bay? Was there a violation of property rights? Was it destruction, stealing, or the birth of a nation that God wanted? Helping our children deal with some of these hard questions presented us with a wonderful opportunity to shape the perspectives of our kids.

Modeling Hospitality

Another way to create memories is to invite people to stay
with you in your home. Don't worry that your home isn't
perfect. You've got to decide that the life-style the Lord has
allowed you is the one He wants you to share with others.
Remember, Eleanor Roosevelt was known to serve hot dogs
on the White House lawn to visiting dignitaries! By opening up your home to other believers, you offer your children an opportunity not only to observe your godly
hospitality, but also to hear what the Lord is doing in the
lives of others from around the world. I once heard a pastor, a man raised in a poor neighborhood of New York City,
state that nothing shaped his life more than his father's
invitations to visiting missionaries. He grew up hearing
wonderful stories of how God was working miracles
around the globe, and decided at a young age he wanted to
be part of the most exciting career imaginable: serving our
great God.

We have a number of friends who come through town,
and it has been a very important part of our lives to have
board and staff members of CBMC stay with us and take
part in our family devotions. Typically, during that time we
will ask them to talk about a certain aspect of their lives, or
a particular pain, joy, principle, or aspect of Scripture, and
let our kids build memories from what we call "guest
speakers" at our family morning devotions.

Building memories by inviting people into your home
enables you to demonstrate generosity and godly character,
but also teaches your children how to be a practical help.
Kids need to learn to serve. They need to learn how to cook,
and mend, and clean, and wash the clothes and dishes.
They need to learn how to care for a pet, to take care of the
yard, and the responsibilities that come with being mature.
Unfortunately, many of us didn't grow up with responsibilities, so we struggle with knowing how to pass on the
notion of hard work to our children. My father expected my
mom to do everything around the house. I grew up not
knowing how to sew on a button or turn on a washing

machine. My mom had always taken care of me, and I guess I assumed she would take care of me in the Marine Corps. (Unfortunately, the drill instructor said she couldn't come stay with us, and I would have to learn how to do a lot of things by myself. It was a rude awakening.) A godly father has to learn the lesson that he didn't marry his mother. The husband is called to serve his wife, to protect her from overwork, and to be the leader. If he works at the office all day, then comes home and figures he has earned the right to be served, he is going to constantly be disappointed, and a terrible model for his children.

We've noticed that many men in our society don't see themselves as servants. They come home exhausted and expect their wives to wait on them, even if the wife has a job. But Jesus calls us to be servant leaders, caring for the needs of those around us. Having kids creates an even greater servant responsibility, because the father ought to be serving his children as well as his wife. In order to start taking on more of a servant's role, I wanted to start doing something to help my boys see that Dad takes part in the duties of hospitality—cleaning and kitchen duties—and that those aren't just "women's roles." I have no culinary expertise, but I wanted to do something that would have a high impact, so I decided I would make it a tradition to cook the Thanksgiving and Christmas turkeys. One important lesson I learned: *It's not that big of a deal*. If you can hold down a job, you can learn to cook a turkey.

Purchase a big turkey, and a day or two before cooking, let it thaw in your refrigerator. Get up early, take it out of the fridge, read the instructions on the package and wash out the insides, being careful to get the giblets out. Remember that there are two cavities, in the top and bottom. Buy yourself a box of Pepperidge Farm dressing and stuff that bird. Cover it with butter on the outside and close up both cavities with either turkey pins or a needle and cotton string and stick the whole thing in the oven. Next, get yourself a good gravy recipe. I asked my mother for a gravy recipe, added a few things, and now it's known as the

"Tri-City Bazooka Gravy Special." It's a big joke around the Downer household that Dad is making his Bazooka gravy, and it has become one of the great hits of the holiday. (I have promised to reveal my secret recipe to my kids only if they marry a godly spouse!) So twice a year I cook the turkey, give my wife a break, and put a lot of mileage on the family car taking trips to the supermarket. All my children are involved, and it has become a treasured tradition.

It has also become a time when we all sort of hover around the oven and wait for the bird to be ready. My handling the kitchen gives Susy time to do other holiday things, and it gives me a way to demonstrate service to my family. It also builds a memory of Dad in the kitchen, dirtying just about every pot he can find to try and serve his family. And best of all, it makes it much easier to get everybody working together on the dishes after the meal!

I remember reading James Dobson's story about eating Chinese food every Christmas Eve. It doesn't make any sense that an American family of northern European heritage has Chinese food on Christmas Eve, but that doesn't matter. What matters is that they have developed a tradition, which gives the children something to look forward to and reminds them that they belong to a family.

In Susy's family, all of the children get a can of black olives in their Christmas stocking. Again, I don't know what black olives have to do with Christmas, but it's not the meaning so much as the tradition that makes it important. Having traditions based around little things like that really builds memories. Susy's family has developed Christmas family traditions to the level of a fine art form. Susy's parents, two sisters, brother, spouses, and children (25 of us in all) gather each year in St. Louis for a week sometime around Christmas and New Year's for what we call "the Great Underwear Exchange." The men always play paddleball one day and have lunch at Dooley's. The women always have lunch at the Olive Garden. In the evening of whatever day is designated as "Olschner Christmas," Susy's mom, Rena, reads about an hour-long Christmas letter recounting the highlights of the year of all the family members. It is amazing how much we have already forgotten in just 12 months, and what a treasure that letter is after 25 years of letters.

New Year's Eve finds Susy's brother, Tom, organizing the Olympics for the kids. He divides them into teams with designated country names, and younger and older children balancing each team. Then he sets out an obstacle course in the house. The bell rings, the stopwatch begins. The first child runs up the steps, jumps over the couch, wiggles under two coffee tables (six-foot-four-inch Andy had a special exemption to go around them this year), piles up ten blocks without toppling them, then pounds all ten pegs through a child's toy workbench with a hammer, assembles a simple puzzle, jumps on a mini-trampoline the number of times that equals his or her age, then crawls over the maze of pillows and rings a bell to stop the clock. Each child gets the best time of two tries. Everyone from the 2-year-olds to the 18-year-olds wouldn't miss it!

Creating Projects Together

Work on projects with your kids. Find out what they like to do and spend time doing it. If they like science, buy a chemistry set and do some experiments. Build a model rocket and send it into space. Teach them to play baseball. Paint pictures, then go to an art museum and explore various kinds of art. Have everybody learn to plunk out a melody on an instrument, then take them all to a concert. Instead of watching TV, sit down and watch old home movies or look through your scrapbooks, photo albums, and wedding pictures. Kids love looking at albums and seeing what you looked like in high school. It builds memories, and it also models family, holiness, and righteous activity, instead of plunking them down in front of everything that is wrong with our society.

Be sure and give your kids plenty of opportunities to dream up their own projects. One of the memory-builders we have in our home has been the building of Paul's tree houses. Our mechanically minded son built tree houses in every corner of our yard—one was even a two-story tree house. Much to my chagrin, he wanted to run water and electricity to it. After several days of prayer and persuasiveness, I finally talked him out of sinking a conduit into the ground and convinced him of the wisdom of having a 300-foot extension cord and three 100-foot hoses strung from tree to tree to get water and power to his tree house. I'll never forget building that tree house. We worked for weeks, planning it out, gathering the pieces, and constructing each portion. My willingness to build it went a long way toward his willingness to help me with my projects. As a result of the great bonding we developed, it has spread to the other kids, too.

When I first became a dad, I used to stumble home from my law practice feeling exhausted, with a hammering in my head from the courtroom challenge. There were many nights when I could barely move. Fortunately, my kids were small then. I would start rug games like "roly-poly," in which I would lie on my back and lift them with my legs, flipping and catching them. It was roughhousing, but at least it allowed me to lie flat on my back while doing it. We would also play "horsy" or "fly," in which I would pretend to sleep, the kids would tickle my forehead or nose, and I would smack the fly. If I smacked them three times, they lost. Often, I smacked my nose and yelled (to their delight). I admit that I was often so tired I couldn't do anything but lie on the floor, so that was a game I devised in order to let me lie down and snooze between slaps.

One of the things I learned is that some of my projects simply made things tougher on Susy. I thought I was ministering to my family when I loaded everybody into the van to take them to the park. But the reality was that my wife would spend hours buying juice boxes and hot dogs, packing up the stuff, and making sure we all had shoes that didn't get ruined in the stream. She would get everybody ready, pack us up, and send us out the door. Then I would take them to run in the woods, dig holes, and have adventures. In other words, *she* did all the work, and *I* got all the glory. After a couple hours, I would return with the kids all wet and smelly, and Susy would have to spend another two hours getting everybody and their stuff clean. Of course, she never complained. As a matter of fact, I remember her regularly saying, "Phil, this is great. Thanks for getting involved with our kids." But eventually I realized I was taking advantage of the situation.

That prompted me to change our system. I wanted to teach our kids lessons about discipline and orderliness, so I used a lesson I learned in the Corps: *Delegate!* On Saturday morning, I would say, "Okay, men, fall in!" Everybody would come running, giggling, and lining up like soldiers. "Here's what we're going to do, men," I would say, and then Abigail would chime in with the words, "And women!"

"We're going to Stream Park today."

"Yeah!" they would all shout.

"But this time everybody is going to help out. Abigail, you get the juice boxes and the Oreos. Paul, get the tools, shovels, and ropes. Anna and Josh, you get the inner tubes and the bug spray. Matthew, grab the ice, the coolers and the plastic bags. Okay, dismissed."

With a shout, all of them would go running around, then they would come back and say, "What were we supposed to do?" So I would go back through it again, teaching them to take verbal instructions, follow through quickly, and work together as a team. It brought us together, so that we could laugh with one another and build memories.

But besides building memories, projects can also build frustration. One day we were building a fence in the backyard, and Paul was turning the crank to tighten up the wire. All of the kids had been helping dig holes, place posts, and string the wire, and we were on the very last post. "Okay, Paul," I said, "one more crank ought to do it." It was a big roll of wire, 50 feet long, all unwound, strung tightly between the posts. Paul was about ten, but he was working hard to turn the crank.

> **Build a Safe Relationship**
>
> ✦ Avoid always having an agenda when you sit and talk with your children.
>
> ✦ Try to spend some time "hanging out" with them, even if it's while doing something else.
>
> ✦ Don't just "hang out"—have good face-to-face quality time on a date regularly.
>
> ✦ Don't talk negatively about your spouse with your children.
>
> ✦ Don't criticize their friends or their behavior without asking a lot of questions and building a rapport first.

"Dad," he said, giving it a tug, "I think that's tight enough."

"No," I assured him, "give it one more crank."

"Dad, I really think it's tight enough."

"No, give it one more crank," I insisted.

"Are you sure? I think it's tight enough."

"Paul, I'll tell you when it's tight enough. Now give it another turn."

So Paul cranked it, the winch broke, and with a *grooooosh!* all that wire recoiled back up in a roll as it raced down the hill. A whole three hours' worth of work wasted. As you can imagine, I was angry. I stood there with a red face, eyeballs bulging, and veins popping out in my neck.

I knew if I said anything—anything at all—it would be the wrong thing, and I would blow the afternoon. As I stood there with my emotions raging, my kids went silent, afraid of the coming storm. Abigail, who was 12, showed great wisdom and looked the other way. So did Paul, who at 10 recognized that discretion is the better part of valor when Dad is about to blow it. Matthew, 8, eagerly waited to see who was going to get it. Anna, who was 6, decided she was not going to be the first to speak. But her twin brother,

Joshua, our great teller of truths, blurted out in a loud voice, "Yep, Dad, Paul was right! It was tight enough!"

Joshua's hopeless indiscretion (and the obvious accuracy of his analysis) resulted in all of us exploding in laughter, thus saving the day. We didn't get much done on the fence that day, but we sure had fun laughing about Joshua's willingness to step into the den of lions.

Building Team Spirit

Learning to control my temper when things go wrong, and to keep my sense of humor when children fail to act like adults, has done a lot toward building team spirit. When the kids aren't afraid of getting barked at every time there is a minor slipup, they develop a confidence which sparks the entire family. The world is filled with messages telling our kids that their hair isn't shiny enough, their teeth aren't white enough, and their face isn't beautiful enough. But as fathers, we can overcome that negativity by being encouraging and working through the small failures. Remember, every child wants to succeed. Sometimes they just need better instruction. A healthy relationship with their father will make them much more ready to listen when that instruction comes.

I see a lot of people pick up their sons and daughters and take them to sports practices, then expect the coaches to teach their children how to play. That's really discouraging, because children want to learn from their heroes: their fathers. I don't think most team sports really *teach* the sport, so much as offer games to those who can already play. Most of the kids doing well in sports have a mom or dad out there throwing the ball with them. We decided to postpone sports for Abigail and Paul for a number of years. Though they were not on a team, I was out there in the yard throwing the ball with them, building our relationship, and teaching them how to stop ground balls. More than just coaching my kids, I taught them how to play sports, and they picked up on my commitment. Your kids will be good at what you are committed to teaching them.

Baseball has really been fun for our family. It doesn't take a lot of height or weight, and because we practiced with them at home, the children have done pretty well with it. We started out with the basic skills: how to catch a fly ball, stop a grounder, and put the wood on the ball at the plate. If you send your children to their first season of baseball and they don't know how to catch, it's usually not going to be a very encouraging time. So spend some time working on the fundamentals with them. I'll admit that was hard for me. Playing catch with a kid who can't throw is not my idea of relaxation after working all week. It took some time and diligence on my part to teach them how to catch and throw. I blew it sometimes and became impatient. But over time they developed the skills and I grew up, so it was a growing experience for all of us.

Not every child is going to be talented at sports, so look for something else he or she is good at. But sooner or later every kid is going to have a chance to play with other kids at some team games, so look for a sport at which your child can excel. It might be soccer, or swimming, or golf, or tennis. Friends of ours with a child who had motor-skills problems got involved with a Christian martial-arts group, and their daughter had the time to develop at her own pace, eventually becoming a black belt in her sport. Team sports also force your child to learn things like teamwork and patience with others. We want to build teamwork in our family, and the team cannot be built if the members do not have a stake in what happens to the team. So look for ways to get your family involved in decisions and cheering for each other.

Family vacations can be a great team-building time if you sit down together, analyze your resources, your time availability, the time of year, and the interests of your family, then agree to create a vacation that will meet the needs and interests of everyone. Along the way make sure Dad is not so big a scrooge that he fails to spend enough money to really have some fun. I don't think we have to play miniature golf every day or spend a pile of money on race cars every night, but at the same time, we don't have to be so tight that nobody feels they can buy a Coke for fear of spending an extra dollar or two.

Music is a wonderful tool for teaching truth and keeping a positive spirit in the home. We have wonderful praise music that we like to play. Our youngest child, Susanna, loves dancing to this praise music. To be completely honest, I felt very silly joining in, but when the kids raised up their arms and said, "Dance, Daddy! Dance, Daddy!" it just melted my heart . . . so I became the Nureyev of the neighborhood (but only with the shades pulled down!).

A Part of the Process

One thing I've learned about creating memories is that we've got to use special days to our advantage. When my grandparents died, my dad flew home to attend the services. I never heard anything more about the funeral. I never even heard much about what had happened to them. It was just a mysterious weekend to me, with my dad gone for a few days and my grandparents gone forever. Had I been let in on the process, I could have learned a great deal about life and death, and perhaps could have drawn closer to my father. Instead, the subject was considered taboo. Nobody ever talked with me about their deaths, and I was left to wonder what had taken place, and how everyone felt about it.

Dads can learn to use even these hard times to strengthen the family. In times of loss, particularly the loss of someone who is not an immediate family member, we can establish a wonderful training time for our kids. It gives us a chance to talk about death, eternity, and how we cope with the feeling of loss. Our family has been through a number of funerals with family, friends, and relatives, and we've discussed with the kids some of the related spiritual truths, then took them through some decision-making as to what kind of funeral to have and what to do with the remains. We really try to make the children a part of the proceedings and then let them express their needs, their hurt, and their pain. It has become a great time of building memories.

Of course, it is more fun to build memories around joyful things such as weddings and special events. One of the things my sister did at her child's wedding was to give each of our kids a cheap camera so they could take pictures. The kids ran around and took pictures of the kitchen, the sky, and the dog next door. They had a ball taking photos. They probably wasted $20 worth of film, but they will never forget when one of my sister's kids got married. Sometimes building memories takes a little investment.

Another great thing about photographs is that it allows children to become part of the memory-making process. Let your son or daughter get an album and put all their photographs in it. Abigail has done a great job of building albums for our family to display the pictures that we've taken at important events. Part of building memories is not to let things just happen, but to try and capture the moment, then spend some time intentionally talking through what happened. Be intentional about creating memories. The what, where, when, how, who, and why questions are important if we're going to make sure everybody understands what is happening and why it is significant. It is also important to have traditions surrounding as many special times as possible—every holiday, every wedding, every funeral.

I take each of my children on dates, and try to make them a part of that process as well. We go to McDonald's and eat hamburgers, and we talk about decisions or situations they are facing. I try to listen to their questions and concerns, and encourage them just to talk and tell me stories. That way I find out how they are doing, and how they are getting along with their brothers and sisters. I also find out what type of pain they are having in their life. The only important principle I have for dating your kids is *don't take them to see paid entertainment.* That's not building relationships—it's usually just chaos. Try to find things in your community that are incredibly exciting, and times when the two of you can just be alone and talk. That way you have a

Let Your Kids Hear You Say Nice Things About Your Wife

✦ "Susy, thanks for your hard work getting dinner ready. You're a great wife."

✦ "Boy, I've been dealing with a friend struggling in his marriage, and I'm so thankful for your mother."

✦ "How did I get so lucky to convince your mom to marry me?"

✦ "You know, kids, your mom is really God's greatest gift to me after Jesus."

✦ "Boys, you just need to pray to the Lord that He will give you a wonderful, godly wife like He has given me."

connection, and you're strengthened in your role as a father. Again, if you discipline without a relationship, it comes across as legalism. And eventually that results in bitterness. But if you discipline from the standpoint of a relationship, and your kids see your love and your heart, you build disciples.

Have a goal of offering substantially more encouragement than advice, so that they will remember the praise more than the criticism. We tell our children how smart they are, how wonderful they are, how grateful we are to be their parents, and what a privilege it is to have them in our family. I tell my sons that they are handsome, and my daughters that they are beautiful. If they believe that, if they grow up feeling really good about themselves, the rewards will come later. If a girl grows up knowing that she is pretty because her daddy always told her she is, then her head won't be turned the first time some boy mutters some sweet words. It won't be news to her; she'll already know about her beauty, and she'll have a deep desire to please both her family and the Lord.

Family Times

One of the most fun things family members can do together is to explore their heritage. It creates wonderful memories, and offers unlimited possibilities for establishing new traditions. My editor, collaborator, and dear friend, Chip Mac-Gregor, comes from a Scottish family, and knows a lot of great Scottish stuff about bagpipes, drums, famous Scotsmen, and Highland games. In Oregon, where he lives, there were a lot of Scottish immigrants, so when his kids were little he would take them to the local version of the Highland games. Apparently it rains a lot in Scotland, just as it does in Oregon, so the people became great at thinking up games while sitting around inside. For example, the shot put and caber toss were initiated in Scotland, so they let everyone give it a try at the games. Women have a "frying-pan toss," where they attempt to see if they can plunk their husband with the pan from across the room, so at the Highland games they set up a dummy and have little frying pans so the girls can practice! Chip's girls thought it was great. They also tried their hand at Highland dancing, got to beat a drum, and even blew on a bagpipe. His kids have enjoyed hearing about Scottish history (he is a descendant of Rob Roy), which you don't hear about much in this country. The unique heritage of Chip's family helped him establish some new Scottish traditions with his kids. If you are of Dutch or Italian or French ancestry, learning the language, exploring the food, and taking a look at some of the history can be educational and fun.

Use your vacations as times for learning history. Who was involved with your part of the world? If you live in Pennsylvania, explore the Amish. Go to shops where the Amish build furniture and ask them about their faith, their traditions, and their families. It can build lasting memories that the kids will never forget. It may look silly for the Amish to be riding in carriages, but when you stop and talk to them about why they are doing it, you start to understand their biblical point of view of trying to stay separate from the modern culture. That offers tremendous discussion possibilities about how we are supposed to be righteous and not involve ourselves in the world, but also how we are supposed to "become all things to all men" (1 Corinthians 9:22). How those two principles complement and collide can make some wonderful discussion-starters. Talking about how we need to make individual decisions provides a great teaching time. Who immigrated to your area, and what can you learn from their history?

One of the things we've tried to do over the years is take our kids on special trips. I remember speaking in the capital city of a certain state, and taking Joshua, who was then five. I had worked with Joshua to sit still during devotions, so I thought he would probably sit still during the hour-long breakfast where I shared my testimony. Also, I told him that I would mention him during my talk, so he was listening intently to find out what I was going to say about him. So there I was at the head table, with about a thousand people in the room, and Joshua was waiting to see what I was going to say. The emcee introduced Joshua and told him to get up on the chair and wave, and to my absolute shock Joshua got up on the chair and waved to everybody in the crowd. (I am glad the guy didn't tell him to deliver the message, because Joshua probably would have done that, too!)

After the meeting a friend of mine and I were going to do follow-up with some of the men who had attended. On the top of this guy's list was a man's name I did not know, but my friend was absolutely thrilled.

"Do you know who he is?"

"No."

"He is the attorney general of our state! He is the third-highest elected official. We've got to go see him first."

"Great!" I said. Then my friend looked at my son.

"What are you going to do with Joshua?"

"Well," I responded, "I'm going to take him with me."

He couldn't believe I would take a five-year-old to see an attorney general. But I insisted, so we went over to the capitol building and found the man's office. We walked in unannounced—two men and a five-year-old boy—and asked to see the attorney general. His secretary asked us to wait, then referred us to his personal aide, who asked us questions about the breakfast. Eventually the attorney general must have heard that there were two guys in suits and a little boy who wanted to talk to him, so out of curiosity he poked his nose out.

We started to talk to him, thanked him for his tremendous service to the state, and he invited us into his chambers. After about 20 minutes, I asked him if he had ever come to the point where he considered having a personal relationship with Jesus Christ. He admitted he was very interested, so we walked him through "Steps to Peace with God." At the end of that, he prayed to receive Christ. That is an event Joshua will never forget. He went with Dad, talked to one of the highest-ranking men in that state, and watched him meet Jesus Christ.

Fathers, take your kids to work if at all possible. Let them see what you do, and how a godly man responds to people at his job. You'll find it's a great way to build memories. Let your children see what your world of work is like, and they will better understand and appreciate all you do. I'm making a special effort to let my kids see what I do and how I do it. At work I try to look for opportunities that my kids can be part of. At my home I hire someone to do the difficult projects, but I do the simple projects with the children. Now the kids have surpassed me in their ability to do handiwork around the house. It's provided us with some wonderful memories.

Shared Spiritual Experiences

One final way of building memories with kids is to share a spiritual experience. I said to my son Paul, "There is a new Christian movement started called Promise Keepers. I have some meetings with some of the men involved with it in Boulder, Colorado. Would you like to go with me?" Of course he agreed, so he and I flew to Colorado to discuss using some of the CBMC materials at their conferences. Neither one of us will ever forget being in a stadium with 50,000 men, singing to the Lord, praying, and praising God together. One of my friends took a picture of us in the stadium crowd, and Paul has that photo hanging on his wall with a little note from me that says I will never forget being there with him.

Another important memory for us has been going to Colorado Springs to visit the Navigator headquarters, Glen Eyrie. We have all been to Dawson Trotman's grave, and my kids know all about him. We decided to build a memory that would be ongoing, so we went to the side of the mountain, scaled the steep hill above the grave site, and found a rock we named "Downer rock." The rock has four points to it, one for each of the Downer males. Every year we have gone back to visit, we've gotten around that rock, each of us have held onto a point of it, and we've prayed for one another. We pray that each man would honor the Lord in thought, word, and deed, that we would be faithful to our wives (if God brings each boy a wife), that we would not bring discredit to the gospel of Jesus Christ or to our family, and that we would stick together as brothers in Christ to help one another walk the narrow road for Jesus. After a couple years of that, I realized we needed to do something similar with our daughters, so we have taken our girls out there too, and have decided on a place where we have prayed for one another together. Our goal is to make sure the Lord is the center of our family, not just a sidelight. We pray for one another regularly, and hold each other accountable in prayer.

We have also created our own bar mitzvah. At Christmas, when a boy or girl has turned 13, the family officially declares them "adults." The boy or girl will go out with the men or women for a secret time together. Only the adults know what we do. It has proven to be an unforgettable time. It is our time to usher them into adulthood—the time when they recognize they are no longer little children, but adults. At the close, we all pray a prayer of commitment for one another.

I think the greatest memories for a family are the ones that are ongoing—the simple ones we continue to share together. The greatest memories are probably our dates, once-a-week times with one another where we get together, eat a cheeseburger, sit on a rock, and talk. Those are the times I like best. They are simple, quick, cheap, and I can do them on a regular basis. Yet they probably have the most profound impact of anything I'll ever do in life. I want to leave my children with memories—memories that will enrich their lives, shape their character, and move them toward Jesus Christ. When I leave this world, I don't care if anyone talks about my legal career or my administrative ability with CBMC. What I want to leave are spiritually reproducing Christians from my work, neighborhood, and country, but especially from my own family. What I want most is for people to look at my six children and say, "Phil Downer left a godly heritage. His kids are walking with the Lord— partly because of the memories he built into them, and now they are winning and discipling others in the faith." That's the ultimate joy of a father's heart.

Quotable Quotes

✦ *Typo of the Year:* A very minor lack of follow-through resulted in Anna's *a* looking more like a *u*, so that on a day when I had struggled through the aftermath of a disastrous financial decision, I received Anna's birthday card with the greeting, "Dear Dud."

✦ *An Encouragement or Something:* Having lectured Joshua daily on the importance of hanging up his clothes, on the afternoon of a particularly vociferous morning reminder, Joshua caught his mother's rising eyebrows as she noticed a pile of clothes still in the middle of the floor. He quickly said to her, "Mom, I want to tell you something I think will encourage you. You see that pile of clothes in my room? It's not the same one you told me to put away this morning!"

Quotable Quotes cont.

✦ *Sealed With a Kiss*: Following a discussion on germs, Joshua took the lesson to the extreme and now refuses to even share a soda with anyone in the family. Abigail, who has the reputation for not even betting a cent, made a token bet regarding Joshua's latest health-conscious pronouncement. She bet him five dollars that he would let caution fly to the wind and kiss his wife on the lips on his wedding day. Joshua accepted the bet! Since then two other members of the family have made the same bet with Joshua. If you would like to get in on this windfall, you can reach him at our home number.

✦ *The Experienced Traveler, Part One:* Immediately after my lecture to my daughter Abigail on how to be sure her gear was together, I realized I had forgotten my passport for our trip to Jamaica. I will forever be indebted to Susy, who swallowed her pride to make a predawn race down the mountain and into the airport with hair in curlers, nightgown hanging from under her coat, in an effort to get the "experienced traveler" his passport.

✦ *The Experienced Traveler, Part Two:* Having weathered the embarrassment of the forgotten passport, I was well on my way to recovery when I realized I had brought my red tie . . . and *only* my red tie for the entire trip—which included speeches, meetings, and a banquet! Loving the further gaffe by the "experienced traveler," Abigail gushed with enthusiasm in a singsong voice that could always be heard yards away each time I wore it, "Oh, Daaaad, I just loooove your tie; that red one is my very favorite!"

Study Questions

1. When have you felt closest to each of your children?

2. What family traditions do you have?

3. How could you use hospitality to help your children mature?

4. What sort of creative projects would you like to try with your kids?

5. How did you come to know Jesus Christ as your personal Savior? How old were your children when you told them that story?

Part Three:

How to Be a Hero

A father has to recognize that the home is a great training center. The family is a basic ministry unit, like a "squadron" in the army of God. When I recognized that truth, it revolutionized my life. Because it is true, we make an effort to cause things to happen in our home that make it a training ground for the kids and a ministry to others. After all, we are called *soldiers* for Christ—we are in His army, serving the true King. God's men have always been of a warrior nature. There is a little hero in each of us, and it is evidenced in every soccer match or softball game you attend. In the same way, the desire to do something that really counts for God is present in the heart of every believer. That warrior mentality in men and that desire to be courageous can be played out in ministry as well as it can in sports. Our world is not looking for platitudes, but for people of character. Imagine, in this world of obstinate, rebellious youth, the influence of a strong, competent, capable young man or woman of God. I've found that other parents will often listen to godly teenagers because they so obviously stand out in a generation that is falling away from truth. One of my goals as a father is to build warriors—young men and women who fiercely love God and will fight for Him.

I try to remind my kids that God intends for His people to be warriors for the cause of Christ. Several times we have had a severe infestation of hornets in our shed—sometimes six or seven large nests. I've tried to use those times to train my kids to think like warriors. We've had fun with the hornets. Instead of calling the exterminator, we went to the store and bought "Yellow Jacket Eradicator," which shoots a stream of poison about 15 to 20 feet in the air. Then we designed a battle plan. We would send one team to shoot the hornets at a distance, and the other team to cover them. Then one team member would go in and knock out the nests, while the other team members covered. It was like a strategic military exercise. It took planning and courage to face those bees. Later, we would talk about how God's strategy is a lot different from the strategies of man. In fact, there were times when God's battle plans seemed like total nonsense to biblically untrained people. For instance, in the battle of Jericho, God instructed His army to do something that appeared completely worthless, but it led directly to the defeat of the city.

Likewise, God's battle plan in our communities can sometimes seem like absolute nonsense. The very idea of losing your life before you can gain it appears crazy at first glance. The notion of serving someone and dying to yourself in order that you might invite them to receive Christ and have new life won't make sense to a non-Christian. But those are the plans God creates to help us accomplish His purposes. God's ways are often a paradox to our way of thinking. Yet as we help our kids start thinking strategically like soldiers and warriors, they not only become more courageous, but they also begin to think strategically about being part of God's team, and about obeying Him in all things.

7

Teaching Kids on
Ordinary Days

L isten, O my people, to my instruction; incline your ears to the words of my mouth. I will open my mouth in a parable; I will utter dark sayings of old, which we have heard and known, and our fathers have told us. We will not conceal them from their children, but tell to the generation to come the praises of the LORD, and His strength and His wondrous works that He has done (Psalm 78:1-4).

I was driving along the freeway, my four-year-old son strapped into his car seat and looking quietly at a book as he rode behind me. It was a rainy day in Tennessee, and the guy in front of me had apparently never seen wet stuff on the road before. He was puttering along at 40 miles an hour in a 55 zone. Try as I might, I couldn't get around him, and I was hustling to get to my meeting on time. After a few moments of increasing frustration, I finally slapped my steering wheel in disgust, shook my fist at him, and shouted, "Come on, buddy!"

It wasn't 30 seconds later that my son, whom I'd thought wasn't paying any attention, slapped the little toy steering wheel on his car seat, shook his tiny fist at the guy, and shouted in his small voice, "C'mon, buddeee!"

It suddenly occurred to me that I had just discipled my son to be a road warrior.

I slowed down, smiled, and said to my son, "You know, I guess my attitude isn't very good. How does Jesus say we should treat people who treat us badly?" With those words, we started a wonderful conversation, talking about why we are supposed to be nice to people, and what our attitude should be toward those who are our enemies. I confessed my sin to my little boy, and he helped me pray for forgiveness. I even admitted that the problem was that I had left the house late, which caused me to be in such a rush that I failed to treat the other driver with respect. By the time we arrived at my appointment, my perspective had changed from angrily shouting at other drivers to happily announcing, "See what God has done!" It's amazing what you can learn from watching your four-year-old.

The Teachable Moment

Years ago a teacher came up with the notion of the "teachable moment"—that is, those special times the Lord allows in which we find ourselves in a situation where we can offer our children a real-world education. For example, our six children don't miss anything. They have an insatiable appetite for input. Our three teenagers are constantly asking questions about the future, work, marriage, family, and ministry. We've found that the best guidance is to ask more questions than we answer and listen more than we speak. We've really struggled with making sure we hand over decision-making authority at the right times, because our children haven't tasted the sting of sin that Susy and I have experienced. Our kids haven't walked with friends who have come down with lung cancer from smoking, AIDS from fornication, bankruptcy from slothfulness, or the sick feeling from bearing the loss of friends who don't know Christ. We want is to introduce them to people who are walking in righteousness, but at the same time we want to introduce them to the *consequences* of sin.

If you are not communicating with your teenager about

the trials, temptation, pain, risks, failures and opportunities of your life, you aren't fully using the teachable moments God has given you. We need to be helping our kids learn what it means to live as Christians in an unchristian world. We can do this by giving them five or six people to interview who are over the age of 60 and "finishing well." By taking your kids with you to ministry meetings, involving them in evangelism and discipleship, you can show them how to make an impact on the world. Your sons need to learn practical steps that will help them avoid the traps of visual pornography in the newspaper and on television. Your daughters need to learn the importance of purity, and the love that can only be found in knowing God. That will keep you from having the conversation where your daughter looks at you and says, "Dad, I'm sorry, but I'm pregnant."

Get away from the lure of the television or the latest action movie, stop tinkering with your investments and overworking yourself to gain security that you can only gain through Christ, and involve yourself with your young child teenager before it's too late. We all have a narrow window through which we can impact the next generation. There is nothing in the world like being in the latter part of life and seeing your children walk with God. As I talk to men who are now in their 70s and 80s, they aren't debating whether they should have worked longer, or made better investments, or closed one more deal. They are watching the lives of their children and grandchildren, to see if they are making an eternal impact on this world for Jesus Christ. Seize the teachable moments of every day with each child.

The woman who came up with the concept of teachable moments was an educator who argued that rather than focusing on a schedule—"We are going to teach kids this at this time"—we would be better off focusing on the circumstances of our lives. She argued that, as educators, we need to be aware when the opportune time comes along to teach something that is not on the schedule. For parents, the principle is best expressed as, "Be sensitive." Keep your antennae out. Be aware of moments when you can talk about one of those things which you had planned to cover later. You don't have to be in a classroom to talk about geology. If you're driving around and notice some interesting rock formations, use that as the starting place for the geology lesson! Be aware that at any time you might come across an opportunity to talk about an important issue or principle you find valuable and want your kids to learn.

We were in a shopping mall with our children recently, when suddenly there was a big commotion and a police officer arrested a boy for shoplifting. A security officer was helping the cop put the kid in handcuffs, and all the while he's crying, "I've never done anything like this before!" and "I'm sorry!" He was sorry, but that didn't make a bit of difference to the policeman. He simply arrested the kid for breaking the law. It was an uncomfortable situation, and it would have been easy for us to let the situation go undiscussed. But all our kids were interested in the wild goings-on, so it allowed us to talk as a family about honesty, coveting, and God providing for our needs. We used the moment as a teaching opportunity.

In most families, kids are so busy they don't have time to do much of anything but school and homework. Unfortunately, we have observed that one of the things that is missing from young people today is that they often don't learn to work. I've been a stickler for insisting from the time the kids were little that they learn to work. We have friends whose children do very few chores. In fact, just a few weeks ago at one of the kid's games, a friend who has three boys, ages 7, 9, and 12, said to us, "I would cook more, but it is just such a pain to clean up for the whole family."

I said, "You mean your children don't help clean up the kitchen?"

"Well, they bring their dishes to the sink."

"Why don't you have them help you clean up the kitchen?" I asked incredulously.

"Well, I don't think they would do a very good job. Do your kids do that?"

"They not only clean up the kitchen, they clean the whole house."

"Clean the house!" She looked at us as though she had never heard of such a crazy idea. I didn't have the nerve to tell her the rest. Our kids have to keep house. That means they learn to clean, learn to pick up after themselves, and learn to fix things. We've assigned cabinets, drawers, and toilets that each child has responsibility for. Now, trust me, there are many days when you could walk in our home and find things in disarray. We all get out of the habit at times, and then we have to set aside a block of time to get everything straight and start over. Ours is not a perfect system, but the kids have learned to work, and when they have families someday, the wives will know how to keep a good house because they've been trained to do it, and the husbands will know how to help their wives.

The Key to Success

Capitalizing on teachable moments really takes a lot of patience and energy, but it's a key to successful parenting. Typically, my inclination is to continue with my activity and ignore inquiries by my kids. However, our children are always asking questions about how things work and why they work. It's absolutely amazing how a few simple questions can lead to a huge amount of discussion and information. For example, the youngest kids are always questioning me about the fire department: "Why do we have a volunteer fire department? What's it like to race to a fire?" It is not something I want to spend a lot of time talking about, to be honest. I don't *care* about the fire department, unless my house is burning. But my kids are interested, so I've become the "fire department expert." As I started talking about the volunteer fire department and how one serves, they wanted to know if it is as effective as a regular fire department. We talked about how our town has some full-time people who remain with the trucks, why they have volunteers join them, and what different types of trucks they use in fighting fires. We got into a whole discussion on fires and how fast they can burn, and even visited a firehouse to see the difference between a tanker truck and a ladder truck.

I told my children about my friend, who came in from a boating trip carrying a battery in one hand and a gas can in the other. It is exactly what I have done on many occasions, and I have never thought of the risk in doing this. My friend came into his garage—a grown, educated, competent, healthy, able man—put down the battery, then placed the gas can on top of the battery. I asked the kids what happened, and they didn't know. Then I described how the battery has a "plus" pole and a "minus" pole, and how it is a storage vehicle for electricity. When you put those two together, electricity escapes. That electricity caused a shock, and a spark landed on the gas can.

"What do you think happened next?" I asked the kids.

"The gas can caught on fire!" they shouted.

"Right. And what should they have done?"

"They should have called the fire department."

"But he didn't call the fire department. He tried to put the fire out. Then the fire got a little too much for him." I asked them again, "What should he have done?"

"He should have called the fire department."

"Well, he didn't. Instead, he went and got the hose. When he came back the whole garage was on fire. He tried to put it out with the hose, but by this time it had spread to the walls. So he called his wife, and they both tried to put it out. It still didn't work. He finally called the fire department, but by the time they got there, much of the house had burned to the ground."

Then I said to them, "Turn around and look at the house. Imagine it was gone, replaced by a steaming heap of ashes. Everything inside was ruined. Nothing survived the fire." The kids sobered at the thought of losing everything—their toys, their clothes, their memories . . . and we had a great lesson on batteries, gasoline, sparks, and calling the fire department. I was forever grateful for my friend, who was honest enough to share his mistake with me. It turned into a great teachable moment for my kids.

We also had a chance to talk about insurance, and why our insurance is higher than if we lived in a place that had a full-time fire department and fire hydrants (neither of which we have). The volunteer fire department has tanker trucks, so we pay higher insurance.

"So, Dad," my youngest son asked, "what's insurance?"

"Insurance is protection against a common risk. We all share some common risks, so we contribute to a company that spreads that risk by taking a little bit of money from everybody to cover the cost of someone who has a big loss." I described the whole insurance process to my family, including who sells it and how much it costs. That led us into a budget discussion, and how much it costs to operate a whole household. But it takes patience and energy on the part of Dad. He's got to be willing to go through all the questions, explaining the important little details so his kids learn the things they need to mature.

Staying Focused on the Lord

Several principles are involved in taking an ordinary day or event and making it a teachable moment. First of all, as parents we need to *stay focused on God*. Moms and dads need to be walking in the Holy Spirit, seeing our circumstances as tailor-made gifts from God, allowing us to be in the laboratory of life in which He is conforming us and shaping us into the image of His Son. We can take very frustrating or mundane moments and see God at work if we are focused on Him. If we are focused on ourselves, every situation we face is just another problem, another roadblock or flat tire on the highway of life. If we keep our focus on God, we know that nothing happens which is an accident. Nothing occurs to us outside of God's control, so there must be a reason for the circumstances in which we find ourselves, and we can use those to our children's advantage.

I remember driving to a conference in the middle of the night. We were on a very narrow bridge, and I blew a rear tire. I could only get about a foot off the road, but I pulled over and got out. I needed somebody to help me. The twins were too young and Susanna was just a baby, but I had to have someone hold the light. My temptation was to wake up Paul, my oldest son, who is very mechanical and confident, and has helped me before. But as I thought about it for one brief moment, I realized that I was trying to encourage Matthew to rise to the occasion and be a leader also.

I had realized after a lot of prayer that I typically gave the hard stuff to Paul, since he was the oldest boy. So instead, I got Matthew up, held him close, and said, "Matt, I really need your help. This is urgent, and if you make a mistake we could all get hurt. I need you to hold the light while I get under the car and jack it up." It was not a made-up job. There was no way to do the work without someone holding up a light, so I got Matthew under the car, showed him where to lie down, and he held the light as I worked the jack. Cars were whizzing by right next to us, just a couple of feet away. It was a moment of excitement, fear, trust, and a lot of responsibility. Matt was never the same after that—he really delivered. I complimented him by saying, "Boy, under fire, you are a great guy to have in the foxhole next to me."

It was a memorable teachable moment that could otherwise have been very disturbing—especially when I realized our spare was flat! I had the car jacked up and the tire off, so we called the AAA towing service to come finish the job for us. Matt and I decided we had better ride back to the service center with him so we could pick out a tire, and as we were going with him, I started to share Christ with the driver. I asked him where he was in his walk with God. I'll never forget the moment, because my son was listening wide-eyed as I was talking about my faith with a guy who was driving a tow truck on the graveyard shift. In fact, the driver looked at me and said, "I'm a Christian—that's why I'm doing this. You don't think that I would have them get me up in the middle of the night for an eight-dollar tow call, do ya? I am doing this because I am 'born again,' and it gives me an opportunity to help people and talk about my faith!" What started as a scary time became a wonderfully enriching hour for Matt to be with his dad, doing the hard work, leading the family, and meeting a brother in the Lord who, like us, sees the circumstances of life as providing opportunities to share Christ.

Revealing Your Weakness

A second thing we can do to capitalize on teachable moments is to *admit we are not perfect*. No father is perfect, and sometimes it isn't our strengths that teach our kids, but our weaknesses. We were headed back from Pennsylvania one time, when we learned that two of our golden retrievers had been poisoned. It was a major tragedy in the life of a family who had invested a lot of love in those two animals. When we got home, we found not only that the two dogs had been poisoned, but also that we had had rats in the house! There was rat dung in virtually every room of the house—up the stairs, down the halls, and in all the rooms. We have fields around our house, so it is not uncommon for rats to come into an occupied house when it gets very hot in the summer. So on top of the trauma of two dead dogs, we had a major infestation of rodents—and that wasn't the end of the bad surprises!

An entire wall of shelving had collapsed in our storage area, knocking canned food all over the floor. Walking into our home that night was awful. It was as though evil forces had been in that house while we had been gone. Those three events—the dogs, the rats, and the shelves—gave each one of us a sense of vulnerability, violation, and fear. I also felt much anger, and a desire for revenge over the dogs' deaths. It was a tragic moment, and I was steaming mad, but my own weakness turned out to be one of the more positive teachable moments that we have ever had.

The loss of the dogs was painful, but over the years we have asked the Lord to give our kids all the experiences necessary to prepare them for the lives He has for them. We want to be available to coach them through some of the tragedies and difficulties people go through in life. We prayed about the dogs and tried to get the perspective of thanking Him for the days we had enjoyed them. We thanked God for the privilege of having raised those lovable pups to adult dogs. We also prayed that we would find in our hearts the ability to forgive whoever did it.

The only way we can forgive anyone is to realize that we are forgiven, and realizing that we are forgiven, we have to conclude that we all deserve the cross. We deserve death for our thoughts, words, and deeds, and the Lord has taken that from us in His grace. In response, we need to return that grace—that undeserved merit and favor—to those around us, even to dog-killers.

It was a very difficult time, but we discussed the fact that there were many people going through much more difficult circumstances. We walked through it together and shared one another's feelings. We read Scripture and talked about the biblical principles of forgiveness and grace. We prayed together and discussed it as a family. Susy and I checked on the kids daily about how they were feeling over the loss. It was a time the Lord used to greatly mature our kids. Frankly, I had to admit my anger to the kids. As we went around the table at devotions the next morning, we found that everyone in the family had grief, and most of us also had anger. However, I was the only one who had a deep sense of revenge. I was picturing myself arriving home a little bit earlier, catching a stranger throwing poison over our fence, and rescuing the dogs before doing in the culprit. I was visualizing my vengeance, and had to confess that to the kids and explain to them where those feelings came from. It was an absolutely sinful response, and one that would bring tremendous pain if I continued to harbor such thoughts. I told my kids if I continued to dwell on that sort of visual image, it would bring much more than just pain. A man can get consumed with his anger and bitterness, so that it strangles his relationship with God and damages his relationships with people. My charge as a Christian was to pray for that person who had poisoned the dogs.

That experience gave us a chance to visit the account in Scripture of a man who stood for God in a great way, but who suffered from living in the flesh. Samson was a man whom God used, but he was a man who never overcame the flesh. Each member of our family has their own struggles with that. Some of the kids struggle with their temper, or resentment, or standing on their rights, or wanting what they don't have, or giving in to fleshly desires. Of course, I struggle with those, too. So I admitted as much to my family. It was a great opportunity to talk about Samson and revenge, and what his struggles led to.

One of the specific things we talked about was how Samson took revenge on the Philistines who had manipulated his wife against him. When Samson set out to destroy the Philistines, he said in Judges 15:7, "Since you act like this, I will surely take revenge on you, but after that I will quit." I related to the children how Samson thought he could be vengeful for a while, then simply let it go. But revenge doesn't work like that. When we reap vengeance on someone by retaliating, we may *want* to quit, but it doesn't end with that one act. The other person spends his energies getting even with you, and it escalates until you both are destroyed, just as in the life of Samson.

We talked for a long time about that awful day of coming home to disaster. We buried the dogs, set traps for rats, and cleaned up the house and storage area. For days we found ourselves talking through our feelings and temptations. As I shared openly with my kids, I found that by revealing my weakness, it created teachable moments. It gave us a time to talk about getting hold of impetuous desires and moving toward maturity in Christ.

Turn Off the Tube

A third thing we can do to maximize teachable moments is to *stop watching television*. Whenever I talk with fathers about the importance of using teachable moments, I have some guys say that they just "never can find the time" to talk with their kids. My response is usually to ask a question: "In the last week, how many hours have you spent watching television?" Many dads can't find time to talk about life with their sons and daughters, but they can still find time to catch the news, the game, and their favorite sit-com.

The TV set can be the greatest enemy we face in our culture. It kills conversation, isolates us, and fills up our time with useless activity. Many years ago we made a decision to pretty much turn the TV off. We do watch select Olympic games, political convention activities, and America's team (the Dallas Cowboys), but for the most part the tube stays off. (Some of my friends have pointed out that the Cowboy team members are not the pristine, righteous fellows they used to be under the Landry leadership. The implication seems to be that no good Christian should be a fan of the Dallas Cowboys. But I've pointed out that our family's support of the Cowboys is purely an evangelistic effort!) Turning off the television has given us all kinds of time in the evening. There is time to read books to one another, to play board games, to wrestle, to talk about things, to read the Bible and pray together—all the things families claim they no longer have time for!

Developing conversation is one of the greatest skills we can share with our children. As they talk with adults, children develop speaking and conversational skills they can use for the rest of their lives. We've found that trips in the car where everyone is talking amicably are much smoother and more relaxing than those when we just sit in silence. I'll never forget the day we had all loaded into our van, heading to baseball practice, when it started pouring down rain. I didn't know what to do. Here we had all the kids, and they were ready to go. The temptation was to go home and sit in front of the ball game on television. But I have found that it's nearly always better to find something to do other than sit in front of the TV. So I prayed, "What should I do, God, that would teach something of value to my family?" Then I had an idea.

"Let's suppose someone just gave us $2000. What would we do with it? What do we need?" The kids started to think, and that got them going on the conversation. It was interesting that our kids really could not come up with any needs. I guess one advantage of not watching television is that our kids are not subject to the tremendous commercial promotion for consumption that is created by some of the greatest minds in advertising, enticing them to find things they think they need. Since we're generally outside the influence of commercial advertising, our kids really couldn't come up with any actual "needs."

Eventually one of them suggested he needed a longer baseball bat. Another thought he could use a larger glove, and another a new bike. So for the $2000, we thought we would get Mom a gift, and that we would purchase a new bike, a ball glove, and baseball bat. Out of the imaginary $2000, we spent about $200 and had the rest left over.

Then I asked, "What shall we do with the other $1800?" We decided that we ought to save 25 percent of it and give the rest away. We spent the next 30 minutes in the car

---

Developing a Peaceful Home

+ Create a basic schedule with respect to going to bed, getting up, eating meals, and doing homework.
+ Have some basic rules with regard to lights, locks, dishes, and cleaning.
+ Play godly, melodious music, particularly during the children's formative years.
+ Limit time in front of the television.
+ Tune in your local Christian radio station.
+ Schedule frequent family dinners that are unrushed and uninterrupted.
+ Establish family devotions which are not boring, and include a lot of discussion and relationship-building.
+ Regularly schedule family fun nights either outside the home or around the dining-room table, with games, puzzles, and storytelling.

excited about how we would give away the remaining
$1400. We talked about different ministries, CBMC staff
members whom we wanted to support, Moody Bible Institute, international ministries we appreciated, and a new
ministry of Focus on the Family that ministers to children
and families. We had fun giving away imaginary money
and talking about our values.

When we finished, just as if I had perfectly timed it, we
arrived in the parking lot of the largest mall in the state of
Tennessee. I said to the kids, "Okay, let's go take a look in
the mall and find that bike! Let's assume we still have
$2000." So we hit the mall, and the first place we saw was a
men's shop. I noticed the most beautiful shirt and sports
jacket on sale. We spent some imaginary money buying
that. Then we walked by the Laura Ashley shop, and the
girls found two dresses that they just couldn't live without.
We went by an electronic shop and dropped another $300
on stuff that really excited the boys, though it was all stuff
they found they really needed only *after* they had seen it.
Then we went to other shops, eventually winding up at the
bicycle shop to see how much the bike was that we said we
needed.

By the time we got to the bicycle shop, we had already
spent the imaginary $2000 on things we didn't even know
we needed until we saw them. We priced the bike, but at
that point we didn't have any money left to spend on it! So
as we got back to the van and looked at our list, it was
amazing to see the lights go on in the children's heads. On
the way over, they had only had a couple of needs. They
had saved some of the money and given the bulk of it away
to Christian ministries. But once in the mall, we forgot all
about the needs of ministries and began thinking about all
the things we would like for ourselves. It was a rainy-day
lesson that we all appreciated—including dear old dad.
Conversation turned a drizzly day into a productive time—
a teachable moment that was fun and instructive for everyone in the family. Had we watched more TV, I doubt we
would have learned anything.

Learning to Be Crazy

A fourth thing we can do is to *be a little crazy once in a while.* As fathers, we need to learn to be somewhat unpredictable. Don't do everything the same. Occasionally throw in something fun for no reason. My friend Chip MacGregor occasionally takes his children for a "pajama ride." As soon as everybody is in bed, with the covers up and the lights off, he and his wife yell, "Pajama ride!" and herd everyone into their car. They drive to the local Dairy Queen, buy Blizzards for everyone, and get a chance to laugh and talk about the things that are important.

I remember one time I got home and the kids, especially the boys, were being bad. They were being rambunctious and not following Susy's instructions. They were quibbling, fighting, and being unruly. So I marched the boys into their room, got the big paddle from the closet, and assumed the stance as though I were going to give them a big spanking. But then, with Susy's permission, I diverted from my previous idea. I had them bend over, slapped the bed with the paddle, and said, "Now scream." They looked at me with great surprise, so I repeated, "Scream." Those boys started to scream for all they were worth, so I slapped the bed six or eight times and kept yelling at them, "I can't hear you! Scream!" My boys were in there screaming their heads off, and I was beating the bed with the paddle, and everyone got the biggest laugh out of it. They really appreciated the grace, and it turned their attitudes around. Sometimes we've got to do things differently to shake life up a bit.

On another occasion, however, I went the other way. I came home and found the boys had been just plain unruly and undisciplined with Susy, who was pregnant at the time and at the point of being totally exhausted. It was really unkind and ungodly of the boys to take such advantage of their mother, so I took them upstairs to the bedroom and had them do countless sit-ups, push-ups, squat-thrusts, and "mixing chilies." ("Mixing chilies," a skill I learned in the Marine Corps, is when you take a can of refried beans in one hand, and a can of Mexican picante sauce in the other—

soup cans work just as well—extend your arms straight out from your shoulders, and then make circles with your arms while holding onto the cans. After about three or four minutes, your arms feel like they're going to fall off.) I got them to the point of total exhaustion and tears, then said, "Boys, this is about how tired your mother is when she gets up in the morning and is eight months pregnant at the age of 42." They got the point. We didn't have any flare-ups for days after that particular teachable moment.

Sometimes people will say that Susy and I deserve some kind of commendation for homeschooling six children, especially Susy for the time she spends preparing and instructing each of the kids. My answer is always the same: "We are not the only ones homeschooling. Every Christian is homeschooling." We are all bound by the dictates of chapter 6 of Deuteronomy to teach our children about the Lord as we sit in our house, walk by the way, go to sleep, and get up. The only difference is that some people have made the decision to subcontract various aspects of their kids' education to others. That may work for some people and some topics, but I don't think we can afford to turn over to schoolteachers such important lessons as development of character and a Christian worldview. Nor do I think we ought to turn over that process to CBS or NBC. Instead, we need to focus on how we can use our time effectively, seeking out those teachable moments in which we can relate our values to our children in unique ways.

We're in This Together

When the world-famous corporate consultants McKenzie and Company walk into a business to evaluate vision, systems, financial governance, employee morale, and product development for a company, they can quickly evaluate how well the CEO is performing his or her function, and generally offer some principles of guidance for improving the organization. In the same way, God has given us as parents a great deal of wisdom in how best to lead our families. We need to follow His principles as best we can, recognizing our weakness and need for Him, and seeing our task as an opportunity rather than an obligation. We need to seize those moments of failure as teachable moments, and decide to move forward in a way that allows us to positively impact the next generation.

Susy and I often pray that we would be equipped as soldiers, ready to face the battles that will come against us as a family. There seems to be endless conflict in families these days over such important issues as radio volume and phone usage. (I just talked with a mother who became exasperated when one of her children got mad at his brother because "he was breathing my air"!) Our individual differences create natural conflicts in a marriage. My wife and I share a love for many things, but we are reminded each day how different we are and how we can both look at a situation and see very different dangers. We are different people with different gifts, but God wants us to use them in oneness to complement each another for a great purpose.

Of course, if Susy and I are that different, imagine how varied our eight-member family is! Abigail, now 17, grew up the center of attention, with tremendous involvement from two parents early in their Christian years; whereas Susanna, who just turned 5, has grown up in a noisy and active family of eight, with more mature parents and all those older siblings. They're bound to be different. Paul, our oldest son, had a lot of "firsts" in our family: first boy, first one in sports, first one to outgrow his dad. He'll always be the "older brother." Matthew and Joshua, who are 13 and 11, respectively, at any given moment are fluctuating from best friends to bitter competitors. Anna is the only laid-back individual in a family of strong-willed personalities. She is tender, merciful, and more inclined to be quiet than to express her opinions in a conversation.

With all those differences, one of the keys to resolving conflict in our home is to recognize that these differences are a great opportunity to grow in Christ. Second, they are an opportunity to learn how to deal with conflict. Third, they are a chance to learn how to get along with your future spouse, because your brothers and sisters will probably be much more like you than the person you marry. Fourth, conflicts bring people together in sharing mutual needs, pains, and challenges. They offer a great opportunity to share differences with other members of the family and help them become spiritual reproducers. So one vital step that must be taken by the father is the explanation of how these differences exist and work together for God's plan.

I will never forget the first time I sat down to talk to the family about the different giftedness of the family members. On this particular morning, Matthew was driving everyone crazy with his noise, his teasing, and the attention span of a hyperactive puppy. He was jumping from point to point, conversation to conversation, and distraction to distraction—doing everything besides what he was supposed to be doing. Matthew is someone who can move from topic to topic with the ease and swiftness of a honeybee going from flower to flower. His silliness absolutely drives Abigail crazy, does Susy in, and bugs Josh, who finds his brother's dominance and teasing to be confrontational. That causes trouble and strife between Matthew and Josh, which in turn brings Anna to her twin brother's defense. This sweet little girl turns into a mama lion when somebody attacks her twin. All of this is greatly amusing to our youngest, Susanna, and she constantly enjoys the entertainment and activity in our home. For me—the father who likes orderly, constructive activities—it creates tension. So on that fateful day when we first started talking about gifts, and Matthew was driving everybody nuts, I asked my eldest daughter what type of man she thought the girls in our family should marry. Abigail responded, "Someone like you, Dad."

I was a bit surprised. "Why me?"

"Because you're fun and interesting, always willing to take on a new challenge, you enjoy being with people, you like home projects, and you are willing to share your emotions, good or bad, with the family so that we can be a part of your life."

Then I asked a killer question: "Okay, who in this family is *most like me?*"

Everyone stopped and looked at Matthew. With big eyes, Abigail said, "You've got to be kidding. You mean *Matthew?*"

"That's right!" I said, then went on to describe how Matthew's quality for being able to handle a lot of things at the same time probably means he will be leading a lot of different people. His sensitivity to the emotions in the room, when properly honed by the Lord, will give him tremendous insight into team building, leadership, and effectiveness in any kind of endeavor. His keen mind in asking questions and his ability to defend each and every action that he does mean someday we will probably be paying for his advice on critical matters of culture, the community, and the church. I explained that when Matthew learns better timing with his corny jokes and teasing, he will become a fun-loving, delightful person to be with. He simply has not yet grown to the point of honing all of those skills.

Joshua, I explained, is the same way. His ability to argue and defend may result in his being the next great orator to defend the gospel, or an attorney protecting the rights of Christians throughout the land, or a congressman pushing through legislation that will guarantee the freedom of expression and religion in our country.

As I looked around the table at all the stunned faces, I noticed the women were especially shocked to learn that they were actually a part of God's plan to hone these gifts in the lives of two young men who could literally change the world. A constant reminder that I give my children is that the greatest impact they may have on their generation will be helping to disciple and direct their brothers and sisters. In other words, we are all part of the team. We are all warriors. We, as a family, are the most effective ministry team on earth.

You Can Do It

I was speaking at a conference a while back, when somebody asked me if I would list the things I thought were most important for teaching children. As I thought through all the ordinary days we spend with our kids, five things came to mind immediately.

First, *look for ways*. Keep your eyes open for the teachable moments in life. I find that when I'm trying to find things, the opportunities are abundant. When my mind is elsewhere, it seems like I never have the chance to teach my kids anything. Look for ways you can teach your kids the things you feel are important.

Second, *look for needs*. What do your kids need to learn? What are the areas in which they need to grow? When my children needed to learn about hard work, I started seeking out opportunities where they had to work hard. I had them watch some guys working in the fields. I put them to work in our own field, shoveling and hoeing and planting things in the hot sun so that they would appreciate a hard day's work. Whatever your kids need, seek ways to accommodate their learning.

Third, *look for interests*. What do your kids like? If you've got a daughter who likes cooking, then give her the chance to feed her interest. Buy her a cookbook and create something special together. Take her to a fancy restaurant and arrange for her to meet the chef. Ask her to be in charge of dinner one night a week. By taking the initiative, you can foster an incredible number of teachable moments.

Fourth, *look for connecting points*. That is, find ways to involve your children in your life. How could you include them in your job? What do you do regularly that your kids could learn from? Take your son to work with you for a half day. Bring him along when you visit the hardware store. Don't just watch the game on television—explain it to him in words he can understand. Seek ways to involve your children in your everyday life, in order to expose them to your maturity.

Fifth, *look for opportunities to minister*. Nothing develops a heart for people like the example of service. Reveal the love of God to your children by asking them to serve meals at the Salvation Army mission one night. Take them into the inner city and have them help you repaint a graffiti-covered church. Invite a missionary to stay in your home while in town. All of these create teachable moments in which your children learn to serve others, not just themselves. As they observe your love and dedication to God, they'll experience the greatest of all teachable moments: the moment at which they decide that serving Jesus Christ is the best thing they can do.

Quotable Quotes

✦ *The Vanity Award Goes to . . . :* Noticing the frequent-flyer bags under my eyes, I caked on the "new lotion" I found in the bathroom cabinet, fully expecting a fresher, more youthful look in the morning. Unfortunately, I had mistakenly applied Susy's new, industrial-strength antiseptic soft soap in lieu of lotion. The resulting huge, puffy bags under each eye, riddled with crater-cracking lines, made it look like I had been hit by a bus.

✦ *Land Speed Record Crushed by a Lower Level of Efficiency:* In her busy days of classwork, ball games, and provisions for the family, Susy continually looks for ways to get more done in a shorter space of time. One Saturday we all were amazed at how quickly she raced up the mountain from her favorite grocery store, which requires more travel time but rewards the budget. Before we could celebrate her breaking all records in her early arrival home, it was pointed out that she had forgotten her groceries. Turns out in all that racing she had left them in the baskets—down the mountain, at the grocery store, at the curb.

✦ *Children Excel at Great Achievements*: Unable to contain his great achievement, Matthew blurted out, "Hey, Dad, I set the world's record, eating 22 red-hot sunflower seeds without getting sick—yet!"

✦ *Let's Get One Thing Straight: I'm in Charge*: In our annual snow storm football game, Dad, wearing out from lumbering up and down the field, recites again the out-of-bounds rule for the game: "Okay, everyone, out of bounds *is where I say it is.*"

Study Questions

1. What teachable moments have you come across this past week?

2. What would your kids learn from you if they spent a day with you at work?

3. How many hours did you spend watching television this week? How many hours did you spend doing something active with your children?

4. What skills, attitudes, and information that you have would you like to pass on to your children?

5. As you reflect on your kids, how is each one unique? What could you do to foster each one's gifts?

8

Let's Do It Together

A fool rejects his father's discipline, but he who regards reproof is prudent (Proverbs 15:5).

He who gives attention to the word shall find good, and blessed is he who trusts in the LORD (Proverbs 16:20).

In the movie *Sense and Sensibility,* one of the young ladies in a family develops a terrible illness. While she is lying in bed, the gentleman who secretly loves her paces the hallways, anxious to help. The doctor goes in and out, the nurse scurries around him, but the man can only stand and wait. I love the character, for not only does he act with grace and dignity to people, but he also feels a need to keep himself busy. Waiting won't do. Eventually, in desperation, the guy cries out to the nurse, "Give me something to do!" When offered the mission of fetching the young lady's mother, he races out the door and grabs his horse, pleased that he can finally offer something of value.

I can relate to that character. In my experience, men have a tendency to fall into two categories: *people guys* or *project guys.* Either we like people and don't care much for projects, or we love working and projects and find people to be somewhat of an interruption to our goals. *People guys* find it hard to delve into instruction books, tools, and equipment for projects on the weekend, preferring to do something with others. *Project guys* want to disappear into the garage on Saturday morning and not show up again until Sunday night. We have a variety of gifts in the Downer family, so we have certain people who gravitate toward each pole.

My problem with projects is that the ones I really enjoy, I enjoy doing alone. I can achieve my goals best when I don't have to deal with anybody else. The projects I don't know how to do I don't want to learn. Having worked a long and difficult week, the last thing I need is to expend the emotional energy to figure out instruction manuals for some new machinery. However, I've found that overcoming these obstacles and dealing with my natural inclinations is a great training ground for my kids. It is through the tough projects that I'm able to teach my children tremendous principles of godliness and maturity.

For example, I used to have a quiet time five times a week—until I had kids, and realized that one of my most challenging days was Saturdays. Dealing with the different personalities of my kids and the demands of being a dad was hard, so I figured I had better start getting into the Word on the weekend. My Saturday devotions became the most important quiet time in my week because it was the time I wanted to be patient, godly, sincere, and sensitive to my kids. I wanted to do something constructive that would build our relationship and bring fruit into their lives through time with me. So I started doing devotions on Saturdays. Then I noticed that my attitude wasn't always the greatest on Sundays. We would be getting ready for church, planning to go enter the house of God in order to worship Him, and I would find myself tired and crabby with my family. So I made the decision to start having my quiet time on Sundays, too. The discipline of doing that has changed my life.

Now I'm trying to build that same sort of discipline into my children's lives, keeping in mind that self-discipline doesn't come naturally to kids. They observe how I spend time with God, are able to see how important the Lord really is in my life, and it has helped them take their spiritual lives very seriously. Our oldest son gets up every morning to jog, exercise, and spend time in the Word. He is developing the discipline that he'll need if he is to be successful later in life. There are meetings that I've missed and conferences that I've turned down because I was with my family. It may have hurt my professional advancement, but I'll never regret a single moment I spent with my family. When I do things with them, it shapes them. In a small way, I'm helping to prepare the next generation of Christian leaders.

One of the greatest training processes I have experienced was the United States Marine Corps, where they first show you what to do, then they make you do it yourself. By employing that process, I have tried to teach our kids principles that they will use in life. For example, getting up early on Saturday morning, I started out cooking pancakes, bacon, and eggs. This quickly became a great activity, around which we had fun and a lot of good discussions. But then I realized I could teach the kids how to make good bacon and flip the pancakes. We established a great time gathering around the skillet, talking and, of course, enjoying the customary juggling of eggs and the spills that go along with that.

Again, after my Vietnam days, digging holes every night, fighting in the jungles, and sleeping in the dirt of South Vietnam, the last thing I would ever want to do is go camping. I hate to ever get too far away from a shower or a toilet, and the idea of going out and sleeping under the stars on hard ground had really lost most of its glamour for me. However, in raising kids, if we don't sometimes go beyond our comfort zone and do things we do not want to do, we are going to lose them to television and the neighborhood activities which are more exciting than Dad. It was my goal to build principles into their lives, and I knew it would require something different, where we were all together. So I picked just the thing: camping. Susy was also hesitant because at that time the twins were two, we had a four-, six-, and eight-year-old, and on top of that, one of the neighborhood boys was spending the night with us. She said, "Are you sure you want to take six kids camping?"

"Remember all the crazy things we did in high school?" I responded. "Remember staying up all night working on the float for homecoming? Remember all the crazy things we did in college: all-night sporting events, midnight movies, and outings with friends? Well, all the energy and vision we used in that craziness of college, I can use in raising our kids. So I'm taking them all camping."

I got home, packed the car, and we went off to the campsite with two goals in mind: First, I wanted to have food. My goal was not to have clean food, or even healthy food, but just to *have* food. It didn't have to be an orderly campsite, but I figured if we could get everybody bedded down and zipped up in sleeping bags for some period of sleep, and be able to feed them when they awoke, we would be okay. I just wanted to bring them all back alive. One thing I've learned is that if I have too many goals with kids, I take my eyes off the relationship and start focusing on performance. So I simply told them I wanted to have fun and not let anybody die or be left behind. They seemed to think those were reasonable goals.

At the same time, I had my own inner goal: not to lose my temper. It would be easy for me to get mad about something going wrong, and I really wanted this first camping experience to be great. So the pancakes burned when I flipped them on the side of the stove and they caught on fire, but I just blew it off. When we tipped over the drinking water, I didn't worry about it. We wanted to go to the best camping site, on the end of the peninsula, so I carried most of the equipment through the woods and out onto a piece of land about 15 feet wide, jutting into the middle of a lake. It was the best campsite in the whole campground. However, once there, Josh tripped and fell headlong into a log, severely bruising his lips and teeth. I counted his teeth with my fingers, and despite all the blood it felt like they were probably all there. I didn't get upset. Although his upper and lower lips were swelling up like balloons, there were no serious gashes. I looked at all the equipment I had carried to the campsite and decided we were not going home.

The fact is, we had a great time. We cooked and ate until we could not eat any more. The kids cooked, and we burned most of the stuff. We went fishing in the raft, spent two nights camping, and one night even entertained ourselves with the local wildlife. Matthew, who was then four, began screaming. "Dad, Dad, come here! You've got to see this!"

"What is it?" I cried, expecting the worst.

"We trained these frogs!"

"Uh . . . could you run that one by me again?"

"It's true, Dad. Come see. We trained the frogs."

The night before, much to the chagrin of Abigail, that peninsula became *filled* with frogs. We caught about 30 of them and put them in a bucket overnight. As the kids were playing with the frogs, they noticed something special: If they tossed a frog into the lake, it would turn and head back toward them. So they said they had "trained the frogs." I went over and watched the kids picking up these dirty little frogs. Matt yelled, "Hey, Dad, watch this!" Then he picked up a frog, threw him out into the middle of the lake, and we all watched it swim back toward shore. It was the funniest thing I had ever seen. "See, Dad," Matt told me. "I think it must be a homing frog!" I laughed until I cried, watching these little kids "train" the homing frogs. It was great!

Now when I was growing up, we always tore up tents playing in them. I wanted to make sure that the kids did not play aimlessly in the tents and tear up the new equipment, so I made a rule that I wanted the kids to sleep when they were in the tents and do nothing else. I decided to stipulate that everyone had to stay up until ten o'clock. The kids were actually barred from the tents and from sleeping until then, on the theory that I would wear them out, and they would long to go to sleep. At first the kids thought it was great that they could stay up late.

That night we loaded up our packs and went on a "search-and-destroy" mission, attacking a few other campgrounds with our squirt guns. We were making our way back to camp at about eight o'clock, just dragging with exhaustion, and the children were asking me, "Dad, can we *please* go to bed?"

"Nope," I said. "No, you can't go until ten o'clock." At about 9:30, they were begging to go to sleep, so I said, "Okay, you can go to bed if you promise to go right to sleep." Those little kids crawled into the sack and went to sleep, and I got eight great hours of shut-eye before I heard the first stirring the next morning. Like I said, it was a great time.

We got home in one piece. I almost blew it at the end, though. I had gotten through the two days pretty well, until we were at the campsite toilet. Joshua, who was two, walked in. I turned my back on him just long enough for him to wash his hands in what he thought was the bathroom sink. Actually, it was a commode hanging on the wall in a men's bathroom, full of urine. I almost lost it. Some words quickly came to my lips, but I shut them off and suggested Joshua wash his hands carefully before grabbing any red-whip candies. His only other mishap was poison ivy behind both ears, which caused an allergic reaction, so both of his ears were swelled up and were sticking out 90 degrees from his head when we pulled into the driveway. I can't imagine what Susy must have thought when she got her first look at us. Here we were, unshowered, with Joshua's lips swollen nearly to the size of hot dogs and his ears sticking straight out. Susy looked down and screamed, "What happened to Joshua?" I said, "Look, he's alive, all right? We went camping, and he's alive! This calls for a celebration."

Since that time we have done a lot of camping. After a while the kids got so proficient at it that I could call on Friday afternoon and say, "Okay, load the car," and by the time I was home, everything would be ready. They knew where the sleeping bags were. Abigail would make the shopping list. We would all pile into the van, stop at the grocery store on the way out of town, then go camping. I learned by delegating that we could go camping without all the effort that I used to expend. At the same time we could have fun putting the camp together, learning orderliness, leadership, management, and principles of teaching and supervising.

I'm no camping expert, but you would never know that by talking with my children. Just by spending time with them, I became the guru of camping wisdom.

The Role of Sports

After camping we got into sports. We found that the area of sports was a great training ground, but also one that was ripe for overcompetitiveness. There is a lot of risk that you will get too busy and not have time for family activities, so we had to limit the sports that we took part in. Although all of our kids enjoyed soccer, they were not particularly gifted at it, so we decided to give up soccer in order to focus more on baseball, softball, and wrestling for the boys.

Sports have become a trap for some families. They feel a need to get involved in every sport, and they end up running themselves ragged trying to get every child to every practice. We decided that wasn't a schedule that would work for us, so each of the kids could pick one sport, and we tried to have the children enjoy the same sport at the same time. That way sports became something we did as a family, drawing us together rather than pulling us apart. One of the funny projects that started out horribly but turned out great occurred when the boys started wrestling. I travel a great deal in the winter months, so the kids and I do not have as much time together during that part of the year. Susy decided to have the boys take up wrestling. All of them were excited about it, and Susy came home and announced, "Phil, the boys are going to wrestle. It is very inexpensive, and they practice at the junior high right down the street. There are only six tournaments. How tough could it be?"

I went down to the first practice and came home with the shocking news that we had failed to inquire about some key issues in regard to the wrestling team. First of all, I informed Susy that wrestling was not like baseball, in which everybody plays at the same time. A wrestling match is like a swimming meet, where you have different heats for different weight classes and competitors. In wrestling, tournaments often start on Friday night and are not finished

Building a Team

+ Assign tasks to each child, teach how to do them, and hold him or her accountable.

+ The mother isn't the maid and cook—*everybody* helps in the household chores.

+ The tasks the kids learn will be useful to them the rest of their lives.

+ Make it a matter of family policy that every member of the family reports anything that is broken, out of order, or missing.

+ If you messed it up, you need to clean it up; if you broke it, you need to get it fixed or let someone know who can have it fixed; and if you open it, you need to close it.

+ Mom deserves a day off every week.

+ Dad isn't immune from helping with the house.

until midnight Saturday. Also, this little wrestling team we joined is a part of the Tri-State Wrestling League, so we went to tournaments all over Georgia, Tennessee, and Alabama—sometimes driving two or three hours to get to a tournament.

We were pretty overwhelmed and disgusted by the whole thing at first. We asked God to show us what to do. Surprisingly, we felt led to stay involved. Wrestling turned out to be a wonderful learning experience in self-control, discipline, diet, and individuality. Also, wrestling was a very humbling sport, where on any given day you could get your bell rung. We found that there were very few bullies who wrestle, because losing was a inevitable for everyone.

The wrestling tournaments afforded a great opportunity for me to load up the car and go off with the boys. Abigail and Anna often came along and read their books. Susy usually stayed at home with Susanna and prepared the next week's lesson. We went to different places around the Tri-State area, and wrestled and got to know other families. We really had a great time together, and it became a time for me to support the boys in what I would consider one of the most difficult sports ever. As the oldest Olympic sport, I can see why wrestling has been so popular throughout history. The only downside is that the boys are so big now, so I can't beat them as often when we all start wrestling on the living-room floor!

Principles for Projects

After camping and sports, I have continued to try to find projects that would challenge us as a family, as Christians, and as a team. A couple years ago, when Susy mentioned that she wanted me to consider putting a banister and rails on the porch, I was surprised to find that was exactly what God wanted us to do for a project. Over the years we have enjoyed working in the shop, but most of our work has been pretty rudimentary—model boats and planes, book-shelves, and those sorts of small projects that can be easily done around the home. But this was something far greater: an actual building project that people would be looking at whenever they visited the house.

One principle I learned early is that projects should be something we can learn *together*. A project is not simply Dad telling Junior what to do, then leaving him to do it himself while Dad catches the afternoon Braves game on television. A project is something we work on as a team, with Dad supervising and sharing his knowledge as appropriate. Second, it should be something *challenging* that Dad isn't necessarily an expert at, so the kids can see him struggle and have to study the instructions, too. Third, the project should involve *delegation*, so that you are delegating to each of the children a part of the project. This is probably the most difficult of the principles to implement, because it is hard to keep everybody involved. It usually requires me to do some reading with the older ones, while the younger kids do some other type of activity so they are not sitting around bored while we try to figure out the instructions.

The goal of doing a project is to *get everyone working on it together*. At first it takes twice as long to have the kids involved with a project. But just as I showed with the camping example, if you take the time to teach the kids and get them involved in the preparation, the result is great training for the children and a tremendous reduction in preparation time and cleanup. That's why I always tell fathers, "You must delegate or die." Too often parents fail to delegate, then continue to do what the kids can do. The parents fail to go ahead and do more sophisticated aspects of projects that would enrich the family, so no one gets as much out of the project as they would like. The older kids should teach the younger children the basic skills. It is important that the older kids not only take on the role of being involved, but also take on the role of being *leaders*.

Like many men, I am extremely task-oriented, and I'm usually looking for results. Organizations need results-oriented people, so in my career I always tried to be the leader by getting things done. The problem is, I often found myself looking at the bodies of wounded soldiers I had run over during my day. This is a problem I have had in my marriage, my law practice, my ministry, and life in general. You know, if God were goal-oriented, He would have just given us a list of 2000 rules. That seems like it would have been great—all we would have to do is memorize the rules and go on with life. There would be no need for growth in Christ. But the Lord tried that in the Old Testament, and it didn't work. Men like rules, but they cannot live up to God's standards. Therefore, He has replaced the "rules" with a relationship. Fathers, we need to teach our children that goals are important, but we must make sure we're after God's goals and not our own. We must be willing to plan, but let the Lord order our steps. The process and the people are just as important as the outcome.

I get myself in trouble when I set deadlines for jobs, or "quality measurements," which result in extra pressure on my children and make their jobs tense, boring, or no fun. But when I am controlled by the Holy Spirit, open to His interruptions, and looking for the teachable moments, He uses me to shape the spiritual life of my children. The goal is not just the completion of a task, but the construction of character.

Typically, there are times when I get irritable and perhaps become critical of the children. I try to follow Ephesians 4:29 in all aspects of what I am doing: "Let no unwholesome word proceed from your mouth, but only such a word as is good for edification according to the need of the moment, that it may give grace to those who hear." It is important that I remember one aspect of that verse: *"according to the need of the moment."* For example, sometimes it is very irritating when one of the kids continually asks me a question. Instead of snapping, I can teach that at the particularly tedious moment of assembling a new lathe machine, it is important for him or her to show understanding and kindness to me and be sensitive enough to wait until a more opportune time before asking me what to do. Now I love doing projects with my kids. It gets us learning and working together, and I don't know of anything else that can bring a group of people as close.

The Practice of Projects

It is important to teach kids to *practice things*. For example, while doing a carpentry project, although there is nothing to be hammered and nailed, it really can be a great benefit if you take a pile of wood and have the younger kids nail pieces of wood together and simply *practice* hammering. One of the early projects we did together was to lay heart-pine flooring in three rooms of our house. That project included cutting wood to fit, which Paul and I did primarily (Paul was eight), and all of us did the fitting of the wood, gluing the underside of it to the floor, then nailing the wood to the floor using square nails. I still love to look at some of the wood that has six or eight dents around the nail where the kids did the nailing. That was a spiritual success for me, because it was the time the Lord got me to stop my perfectionist ways and realize that those dents around that nail are a "red badge of courage." Truly our children took part in that project as little kids, but they learned how to operate a hammer.

Don't misunderstand me: We don't want to encourage work that is less than excellent. We all want to do great work for the Lord. But sometimes potentially excellent work requires backing off our standard of performance now in order to let our kids learn how to do things that they have never done before.

After the flooring projects and some of the toy boat and shelving projects, I was challenged by the porch project. My first response to Susy was a bit critical, because I did not feel I wanted to spend any money putting up porch rails and balusters. After all, the porch was there to shed water. The fact that it had four ugly posts with no railing did not bother me at all, but of course it bothered her. Trying to understand what God wanted, I prayed about it for several weeks and realized there was a great opportunity to help Susy with something important to her. She really wanted a new porch, and it would bless her life as well as bless the family if we worked together on the project while we built family values.

She had saved for many months out of her household funds to do the porch, and I figured that if we bought the spindles, brackets, balusters, and railings, we would spend about all she had saved and still only have half of it completed. However, if we did the work ourselves, we could save enough money to pay for all the machinery necessary to do all the work needed in our shop. So we investigated all the tools we would need. That in itself was a great project for the kids. To look at the tools, evaluate what we could do, shop the prices, read the reports on which were best, and get counsel from different places on pricing and procedures was a great project for all of us. The fact that I had never done it demonstrated to them, through my mistakes and going down dead ends that sometimes "trial and error" is necessary to figure out what you really want to do.

This entire project was something I needed to continually pray about in my quiet times because taking on a project like this with no mechanical or carpentry aptitude was a huge challenge for me. I found that, by nature some of my kids have a much greater aptitude for this type of work than I do, and there have been many times that they have figured out the solution to our problem in advance of my figuring it out.

The Porch Project

We first bought a lathe and read an instruction book on how to put it together. Actually, Paul put it together, and at 13 became a whiz in the mechanical area. Now 15, he has done a tremendous job of learning how to make all kinds of sophisticated carpentry items. After many weekends, we turned over 140 spindles out of raw wood using the lathe, with each one of the older five children, ages 9 to 15 at the time, doing the cutting. It has been fun to see the results of our hard work. Of course, if we paid each other by the hour for the amount of time involved, this would have been a losing project. But in working together as a team, it has brought tremendous benefits to our family. We also made brackets for the upper corners of the porch using the scroll saw to cut out gingerbread designs that included spool and ball fabrication. We even bought one-inch balls into which Anna and Josh cut holes with the drill press.

Realizing that we did not have the funds to buy a lot of the equipment needed, such as the band saw, drill press, and radial arm saw, one of our great answers to prayer was in finding a lot of this machinery used. Susy said, "We need to pray that we can find someone like a widow who is selling off some of her husband's shop equipment." So we began to pray. Within about 30 days that is exactly what we read in our local newspaper. A widow was selling her husband's shop, which included many of the power tools we needed. Because of the good price, we even bought some equipment for which we saw no present need. Before the project was complete, however, we used virtually everything we had bought.

We have now finished painting and installing all of the brackets, balusters, and spindles which has been very difficult but tremendously rewarding. The children learned many life principles from this project. First of all, in cutting a spindle, when the lathe is going at 2000 rpms, and you begin cutting on it with a chisel, after about five minutes you really see the pattern of the original model spindle. It appears that you are close to being done, but then when you turn off the machine and take a closer look at it, you realize that it looks absolutely horrible. You must then use a finer chisel, and then finally the rough, medium, and light sandpaper. Even after doing all of that, you then realize that you still have to take a very sharp chisel to cut out some of the details, such as the grooves and crevices.

What a great example this has been for our children to realize how God is molding us. In our early years of being a Christian, God takes away large chunks with a big chisel. At a high rate of speed we look pretty good until you take a closer look and realize that a great deal of rough, medium, and fine sanding will be necessary, only to be followed by the Lord taking a very sharp chisel and gouging away at the areas of our life that still do not look like the model of Jesus Christ.

The Scripture says that "love covers a multitude of sins," but we learned that paint exposes a multitude of sins. When you paint a primer on wood, all the grain pops up and the kids realized that sanding was really necessary. One thing we decided early: This would be a project showing that the children have been involved. No two spindles look alike. All of the spindles and brackets have been painted, but some still look a little rough and not very attractive because we did not sand them sufficiently. They are on the porch alongside the smooth spindles and brackets. Our goal is to refine our children's lives, not to have a perfect porch.

Learning How to Shop and Solve Problems

One time I sent Susy off to her sister's house for a much-needed rest, and I took a week off work and had what I called "Downer Boot Camp." Though I pray my kids will never have to go to war, I learned many things in the Marine Corps that I would like to pass on to my children. Many of the skills I learned were of great value. So about five years ago, when the kids were 12, 10, 8, and the twins 6, I sent Susy off to her sister's with our six-month-old Susanna, and we had boot camp.

The kids were really excited. They put together ragtag uniforms and created some rifles out of wooden sticks. We even had "close-order drill" out in the driveway, and we did "PT" (physical training) up and down the street. I had an old Smoky the Bear hat with a chin strap, so I felt almost like a drill instructor! Dressed in fatigues, the children marched in the driveway, with me running backward and barking cadences as the kids ran in step.

We woke up every morning to reveille (I had it on an old 33 rpm record album). I taught them the importance of working together as a unit. We then had one day when we went to the grocery store. We divided the store into different aisles for different members of the team, and I taught them where basic items were. The goal was to be able to pull up to the grocery store, swing open the door, have the kids go get the ten items they were supposed to get, meet at the checkout counter, load the basket, check out, and get it done quickly. I taught them how to cook some simple meals at night, and then we went on a bivouac.

The bivouac involved various assignments. One of the assignments was to free the dogs, which we pretended had been taken captive by the enemy. The kids had to pick a team leader. They picked Paul because he knows every inch of our backyard with its forest and stream. Using the blackboard, I showed them where the enemy was, and they devised a plan of where to go. I said they could take me along with them, but I could not speak or give instructions. So I just went along without saying anything.

It was amazing to watch them devise a plan. They freed the dogs, and then ran to freedom. It was an exciting game, but we also learned a lot. First of all, ever since Paul was a little boy, he had struggled with fear of the dark. It was amazing how he was not afraid at all in the darkness during the rescue. I think Paul found it amazing how well he could see. That was the night he lost forever any fear of being out in the dark. Second, Abigail, a very feminine girl who hates bugs, found that in the disciplined "war setting" she forgot all about the fact that she was climbing through spider webs and plants laden with ticks and bugs. She realized that if she could be focused on the objectives, then the bugs would be relatively harmless.

During boot camp week, I took away their watches so they never knew when they were going to bed or when they were getting up. One night I let them go to sleep, and then in about ten minutes I awakened them and said we were going on a bivouac. We marched around the neighborhood and the yard in assault positions, learning how to follow instructions and so forth. They loved it! Another night I let them go to bed early because they were so tired. I let them sleep for about an hour and woke them up. It was pouring down rain. I lined them up in the family room and said, "In war, you don't stop because of the weather conditions."

I told them about the time in Vietnam when I arrived at my unit and met Ralph Crosley, who was the machine-gun team leader of our company mission. The second night it was pouring down rain as monsoon season began. The water was literally over our ankles. I had assumed we would not have to go out because of the rain. Right? Wrong! War goes on in the rain.

This particular night I lined them up in the living room, told them that story, and said we were going to go out and assault an enemy position. Just about the time they really started to squirm about going out in the cold rain, I turned on the TV and we watched the all-star game! They roared with laughter and relief. One of the principles I wanted to teach was that we could have fun while we learned discipline. As dads, we need to show unexpected grace in the midst of challenging projects. We need to keep it not only challenging, but also fun and interesting for everyone involved.

During the day we worked on different projects, rode on the Alpine slide, went swimming, played baseball, and had a lot of fun. But we had an overriding sense that we were in training to learn how to help Mom. One of the things we did was organize the children's closets, the can cupboard, and the commissary area where we store the things we buy in quantity. When Susy came home we had things in pretty good orderliness, as well as all of us committed to keeping the house straight.

Learning from Projects

Susy's father is an electrical engineer, and during a visit from her parents, Susy asked her dad to do a science day on electricity. He explained how electricity works, in the most basic terms possible, and then set up experiments to demonstrate what he had explained. Most of us have parents, siblings, or close friends who have expertise in an area we want our children to learn about. Don't hesitate to "ride the coattails" of someone close to you for a project. Just don't make a practice of it or forget that your goal is to build your relationship with your children.

One of the projects that I will never forget was started by a couple having trouble with one of their sons. He was a lousy student and all he wanted to do was play baseball. They used to have to go into his room and turn off the radio or TV because he was watching baseball and not studying for school. They took Johnny out of school and home-schooled him for a year. Instead of forcing him to quit baseball, they *used* baseball and his interest in baseball, understanding they needed to raise a child according to his bent. They used baseball as a teaching focus. So they bought season tickets and went to every game they could.

The father was shocked when he was encouraged to do this. He was supposed to take his son to every game instead of keeping him in school? But he took the advice, they started getting involved in baseball, and after a few games he said to his son, "Do you know how to figure a player's batting average?" They began to calculate and record teams' batting averages. They figured out the measurements of the field. They delved into physics as they figured out the trajectory of the ball. They also studied how the weather conditions, the humidity, and altitude impacted the distance of the ball. They looked at how the balls and bats were made.

They began to read historical novels about baseball greats like Babe Ruth. They found that some of these sports figure's lives were interrupted by events such as World War I and World War II, so they diverted to side studies of these two periods of history. This previously poor, disinterested reader became an insatiable reader and a self-starting student. After one year, this lousy student turned into someone who was interested in and saw meaning in math, physics, science, history, reading, and writing, and also was still a great baseball fan.

What's the Perfect Project?

If you need a list of project ideas, consider these things that we have tried:

1. Go to the hardware store and get a piece of 1'x 8' pine. Take it home, cut it up, and make boats. This is not just for boys, because girls love it, too. All the kids will like displaying their creativity. Then find a creek and test the boats out!

2. Buy a cheap paint set and do an art project. Go to the park and try to paint a picture of a tree or a garden of flowers. This can be really hard for men, because as they look back they do not feel they have anything to show for their work. That is, they have not produced much of any "worth." But you can't always measure or sell worth. Just because you don't create great art doesn't mean you have wasted a lot of time. As you start to talk to your kids, you are building relationships, teaching them things, and it will prove to be some of the most valuable time you can ever have.

3. Work with them to develop order in their personal living space. In the Marine Corps we were all issued a certain number of T-shirts, socks, and fatigues, which we stamped, folded, and neatly put in our footlocker, precisely as dictated by the Marine drill instructors breathing down our necks. We had one towel we used that was folded neatly at the end of our rack, and our responsibility was to take care of our stuff. It was amazing that the Marines first had to teach us how to take care of ourselves and our own health needs before they could ever teach us to be combat warriors. The same is true in the Christian life. If we don't teach our children to take care of themselves and their stuff, it's unlikely they will be available to spend time with God and reach a lost and dying world for Him.

4. Take the kids to buy a sport jacket and get involved in shopping adventures. My idea of shopping is going to the closest place available, closing my eyes, and paying for what I need. The Lord has really had to teach me how to manage my money. As a result, I've become a lot more frugal. But Susy is a naturally gifted person at finding the best price and the best product, so she has helped me remind the kids that they have to be willing to wait to find the right product at the right price.

5. Do nice things for the neighbors such as helping them build a sandbox. It doesn't really matter how big or small the project is. The important thing is to have a mission, plan it out, and then work as a team to complete it. There are many projects that can be really beneficial to others.

6. Find ways to minister. Go to a nursing home and ask the director if someone needs some "adopted" grandchildren. A few weeks ago Susy brought flowers home from a luncheon. She decided to take Susanna to the local retirement home and asked the people in charge who would most enjoy the flowers. Susanna's eyes were as big as silver dollars when she saw a woman's face light up as she received

flowers from total strangers. That woman loved talking to our youngest, and Susanna saw the value in giving away time and gifts to people who are lonely and in need. It was a memory she and her mother will never forget.

7. Work at the church helping with the property or cleaning the vacant lot next door.

8. Buy a computer and learn how to operate it.

9. Be involved in supporting the sports team by selling candy bars and snacks.

10. Practice with your kids. Be interested in their piano practice by letting them audition for you. Practice sports in the backyard. Put up a backstop in the backyard for basketball. Assemble a pitch-back where they can practice their ball throwing.

It doesn't take a genius to come up with a half-dozen projects you can do with your kids. All it takes is some desire on your part, and a willingness to look around and see what needs to be done.

Quotable Quotes

✦ *The Honest Truth:* While talking to a member of the board of directors at the CBMC men's conference, Josh blurted out, "Don't tell anybody, but I've worn these socks for five days!"

✦ *No Sacrifice Too Great:* Dismissing Anna's upset stomach as merely associated with the rough flight into Denver, we all proceeded to a lovely dinner with friends at their beautiful country club. Suddenly, Anna left her chair and headed toward Susy, with a look on her face which said, "I'm going to throw up." Standing up to redirect Anna, my wife guided her away from the table, toward a corner of the room, attempting to lessen the impact of the certain dinner-time disaster. Her eyes searching for an appropriate container, the only possibilities were Susy's purse or the expensive Oriental carpet. Facing a difficult decision, Mom chose the self-sacrificing option—her purse, which contained her checkbook, organizer, and calendar!

✦ *On the Other Hand:* When he found out that his watch was in the purse which was doubling for a barf bag, Matt exclaimed, "Oh, Mom, you gotta boil it!"

✦ *Supply-Side Economics:* At the same conference, Anna's business was found to have an unbeatable profit margin when it was discovered that she was *selling* the candy placed on the conference tables to the guests. "Candy! Only a penny a piece!" Noticing one participant's hesitation, she added, "But if you can't afford it, you can have some for free!"

Study Questions

1. Are you a *people* guy or a *project* guy? How does it show in your fathering?

2. What kind of projects did you do with your dad? What do you *wish* you had done with him?

3. When does everyone in your family work together?

4. What are three projects you could begin doing with your children?

5. Why is it important for a father to lovingly allow his kids to fail?

9

Spiritual Training 101

or He established a testimony in Jacob, and appointed a law in Israel, which He commanded our fathers, that they should teach them to their children, that the generation to come might know, even the children yet to be born, that they may arise and tell them to their children, that they should put their confidence in God, and not forget the works of God, but keep His commandments, and not be like their fathers, a stubborn and rebellious generation, a generation that did not prepare its heart, and whose spirit was not faithful to God (Psalm 78:5-8).

Children, like retirement plans, cars, and a man's health, work on a very simple principle: "Invest now or pay later." Fathers must take ownership for the discipling of their children. Failing to do so will lead to disaster. We all need people to help us raise our families: local churches, pastors, youth-group leaders, teachers, and coaches are an integral part, but they cannot replace the God-ordained role of the father. Unfortunately, many of us have been duped into thinking that the financial concerns of the home take priority over its spiritual concerns.

Having a dad go to work faithfully and take care of the family's financial security is a key to every successful home, but if we take care of the finances without taking care of the faith, we've failed our families. Our children really don't need all the extra bedrooms, appliances, and clothes that our overworking can provide. They need time with Dad that overworking steals.

Most dads feel like a success at the office but a failure at home. We've been trained for years to be competent in our careers, but very little training has been given to any of us to feel competent in training our children. So we do what is easiest, or what we think will give us the most immediate outcome of success. We overwork, then we delegate to others the most important job we can have: the spiritual training of our children. God gives us our businesses, and He also gives us our children. We don't expect to sit on the sidelines and watch Him operate our businesses without any input from us, so we shouldn't expect to sit around and wait for somebody else to take responsibility for discipling our kids.

When I was starting out in law practice with just a handful of other men, we began to catch the vision of building new law offices in other states. We didn't send the least-experienced people to explore the idea, nor delegate to them the great responsibility of the future of our practice. Instead, we expected the most-experienced people to take the lead in the important decisions. As leader of CBMC, I send experienced people to start new ministry efforts because their experience and knowledge can reproduce what we want in our ministry. The same is true in our family. We should not delegate to strangers what we know and care most about. Other people can do my job, but nobody else can be father to my children.

We men tend to delegate the things that are hard. I learned a long time ago in business and ministry that the hard things reap the greatest results, so I should take control of them. When I delegate the hard things, I'm stuck with the results. So I was the one who (somewhat begrudgingly) stood in the backyard and taught our kids how to catch a baseball when, frankly, I would much rather have been doing something else. But as the years have gone by, I've found my most exciting moments are watching my children play on the field. Those sports activities have fostered relationships that have resulted in many people coming to know Jesus Christ.

Many of us feel inept at developing our children spiritually because we are not developing spiritually ourselves. Membership in a Bible-believing church, accountability with Bible-believing friends, a daily quiet time, and becoming part of active evangelism and discipleship teams are all steps that can help us move down the road toward spiritual maturity. Too often the father who teaches Sunday school and serves as a deacon is too busy to spiritually train his own children, so he takes the course of least resistance and subcontracts that activity out to third parties.

Parents often choose to subcontract to a Sunday school teacher or youth pastor for several hours a week the responsibilities of the spiritual development of their children. While a good Sunday school class and a godly pastor are essential in spiritual training, any one of those individuals would be the first to say that they are not competent to be responsible for 100 percent of a young person's spiritual training. Our family has been blessed with excellent pastors and teachers over the years, but Susy and I maintain not only the responsibility for teaching the principles of our faith to our children, but also the responsibility to see that they are implemented in their daily lives.

I have already mentioned how modeling is essential in spiritual training, and that includes sacrificing sleep for the Scriptures, sports programs for Bible memorization, and personal hobbies for spiritual discipleship of others. Too often we ask our children to "do as we say, not as we do." It's a mistake to ask our children to do something we ourselves are not willing to commit to. Our righteousness (or lack thereof) is passed on to our children as we live together in the home.

Years ago, before we ever had children, we were encouraged to pray for them by Ted and Edith DeMoss. Ted was my predecessor as president of CBMC, and we heard him say at a conference one time that he and Edith began praying for their future children on the first night of their honeymoon. They prayed every night that they would have children who would come to know Jesus Christ. Susy and I were so impressed at that thought that we began to make that our prayer also. We felt it was especially needed when the children were little. Of course, now that we have teenagers, it is important for our children to hear us call their name to the Lord. We don't just pray simple, rote prayers, but we pray with emotion and deep feeling that they will be godly and obey the Lord, that they will love the Scriptures and tell others the Good News and devote their lives to making disciples. We pray that they will be patient and wait for the man or woman that God has for them. We pray that they will keep themselves pure for that time. We pray for their future spouses, if God should give them each one. Right now, those persons are children or young adults somewhere, and we pray for the purity of those persons, and their protection, and their heart for the Lord. We also pray for their future children. We pray that the next generation will be godly and walk with the Lord.

Spiritual Humility

One area that men struggle with is humility. The best teacher is one who can share his mistakes and struggles. Just the other day, I was telling the kids some simple things about mistakes I had made. We had been working in the shop, and Paul had left the paint uncovered while we went to apply it on the spindles. I said, "Paul, you better go and cover up that paint, so no one will fall into it and knock it over. By the way, do you know how I know that?"

"Yea," he replied, "because it happened to you one time, right?"

"That's right," I admitted. "I once left off the cover, and a dog got his paws in the paint. You've never seen such a mess!" Everyone laughed, but they also learned from my mistake. That is something I have tried to teach the children over the years. The things that have gone wrong in my life can warn them so they have the advantage of not having to suffer the same consequences. Through my weakness, my children can learn a lesson. I can honestly say to them, "It happened to me, so learn from my mistake and you won't have to go through the pain I went through." You've got to admit, that is a lot better than just giving the kids a list of do's and don'ts, as though we have automatically gained superior knowledge over them just because we're older.

I can talk with my kids about memorizing verses, but the most effective way to encourage them to learn verses is to hand them *my* verses, written on my 3"x 5" cards, and ask them to quiz me on the verses I am trying to learn. As I stumble over them and have to rememorize and review them, not only do they see that I struggle with my memory work, but they also see how important it is to me to struggle through the process of memorizing Scripture. Inevitably, as they help me learn the verse, they also learn the verse. Most importantly, they are learning that there is no shortcut to obedience. Memorization, just as other godly endeavors, takes hard work.

Again, in spiritual training, the Socratic approach is greatly effective. For example, after church try asking your kids what they thought of the sermon. Don't quiz them about all the points, but ask them open-ended questions: "What did you think? What did you like? What did you not like? What really hit home? What could have been done differently?" It is amazing how this encourages attention and retention during the sermon. In the morning during family devotions, I sometimes ask the kids what they got out of their quiet times. It is interesting and encouraging to see, as we go around the table, how each of us got a different lesson from our quiet times. Over the last two or three months, some of the most insightful comments have come from our twins, Joshua and Anna. They are increasingly getting tremendous insights out of their time with the Lord.

Meeting Godly Families
One of the greatest assets to spiritual training is having your kids involved with other families who are godly. Susy and I had the wonderful opportunity to accept an offer from friends to spend a week alone on Maui in their condominium

(suffering for Jesus). Essential in going, of course, would be finding suitable accommodations for our children. Two godly families offered to take three each for the entire ten-day period. During that time our kids got to see how other families operate and teach spiritual truths. They came back with a lot of good ideas. One of the families spent a lot of time just reading through Proverbs line by line and asking questions. They would say, "What does that mean, and what does it mean to you?" I realized I had not done that in Proverbs for too long, and it got me back on track doing it myself.

Also, our kids saw how different fathers teach devotions. Both of these families take spiritual training very seriously when they have family time together. Their devotions are done a little differently than ours, so the kids got some great ideas on other ways to do things. One of the families used devotional study guides that the kids really found interesting. The other family just taught directly from the Scriptures, which was tremendously meaningful to the children.

One of the greatest advantages our kids received from staying with these families was that they were spiritually challenged not only by the parents but also by the kids. They saw how other godly children work out things like strife and jealousy. It encouraged our children to be better about doing that themselves. Also, when your kids are around other godly parents, they will be challenged by things that perhaps are better said by other people.

Spiritually Creative
Do something creative by which your children can really learn about the things of God. I'll never forget when Abigail was six and Paul was four. I would be doing my quiet time and just wrapping up my prayer, when the kids would get up and go into the kitchen. I would hear the box of cereal being opened and then cereal being sprinkled into the bowl. Then I would hear a tape pop into the tape player and a story would come on. The kids would listen to 30 minutes of a dramatic series dealing with Paul's shipwreck or perhaps Pentecost or a story about a famous Christian mis-

sionary who was fighting off evil to share Christ with tribes in Africa. One fictional story was about a boy who was diligent in his work of sweeping the floor at the bank, so he was given the job as a night security guard. Having turned in money mistakenly left under the teller's desk, he was promoted again to a day job. As the sequence goes, he became president of the bank. This story taught how diligence and honesty pay off in business.

One of the most phenomenal spiritual training tools we have come across is the 150-tape Christian series produced by Your Story Hour. Seventy or so of the tapes are dramatized Bible stories, and the balance are a variety of stories taken from history, literature, and everyday life, which illustrate scriptural principles that are demonstrated by dramatic stories. We have taken them on vacation, first listening to them in the car and then listening to them every afternoon around the pool. Also, before our kids were old enough to read, these tapes substituted for their quiet time.

In your quiet time in the morning, ask the Lord to bring to your mind spiritual application for the things that happen in your day, the good and the bad. Help your child learn to think as a Christian thinks. They can do this when they are really little, and the sooner they start, the easier it will be. I would encourage you emphasize Christian biographies. The choice of heroes today, even by Christians, is tragic. They tend to be either pampered professional sports stars or entertainment celebrities. There are some fine people in those arenas, but there are many great men and women in history who have walked with God, and we have much to learn from them. Look for books, movies, and tape series on these true heroes of the faith so your children can model them.

Memorizing the Scriptures has really helped us, because I've had a chance to share with my children creative and practical applications of God's Word. For example, when I've been grumbling, I am violating Philippians 2:14, that states, "Do all things without grumbling or disputing." By memorizing verses together and transparently sharing how I have failed to meet them, I'm revealing a model for my children as they struggle with the Christian life. I've tried to help my kids understand that anytime they memorize something, God wants to make sure they learn it not only intellectually, but experientially.

Not long ago I failed completely with my kids, snapping at them in impatience and being rude to my wife. I had to go back and make it right, which meant confessing to my kids that I had blown it again, and telling them I was sincerely sorry for my sharp tongue and insensitivity to their needs and feelings. I then asked one of the kids to recite Philippians 1:6: "For I am confident of this very thing, that He who began a good work in you will perfect it until the day of Christ Jesus." God is not finished with me as a father, and my kids understand that. Too often my tongue steers my ship into storms and disasters. Sometimes I get worn out and discouraged, and it influences my relationships. What a joy it is at those times to have my children share the truth of Paul: "Be anxious for nothing, but in everything by prayer and supplication with thanksgiving let your requests be made known to God. And the peace of God, which surpasses all comprehension, shall guard your hearts and your minds in Christ Jesus" (Philippians 4:6,7).

After they recite this passage, I ask them what it means, and we talk about it. Usually each of us has to confess something, then we pray through the truth of that verse. As we pray that God would change our attitudes, I can see the disputes and conflict melt out of the life of my family. But it must begin with Dad modeling the way. If we merely bark verses at our kids, we will cause rebellion and disdain for the Bible. If we talk one thing and do something else, we will be hypocritical and provoke our children. By focusing my family on the Scriptures, God's principles are being spread throughout their lives and being used in everyday matters the family faces.

Stories and Music
Another tool for spiritual training is the Moody "Stories of Great Christians" tape series. The Moody Bible Institute has

cataloged the Christian leaders of the ages—such as Jonathan Edwards, Gladys Aylward, and David Brainerd—and has described their lives in full dramatic series which are exciting.

Becoming a Christian at the age of 30, I had wasted thousands of hours lying in front of the television and filling my mind with trash and destructive thoughts. I particularly encourage families to listen to Christian radio—not mindless rock music, but the programs and stories that can fill their minds with wholesome truth. When you're cooking dinner, when you have a break, when the family is all together, turn on your local Christian radio and listen to the great preachers of our time. Don't miss the Chuck Colson commentary, or Larry Burkett talking about money—it's amazing how listening to Moody Radio Network has been one of the most effective teaching tools in our family.

Our children are products of a variety of mature inputs. The more influences that are Christ-centered, the more our children are going to be change agents for the Lord in their generation.

Just as television sometimes brings into our home a steady stream of robbery, murder, prostitution, hedonism, and out-of-control consumerism, Christian radio can bring into your home godly teaching from some of the great teachers of our day like Kay Arthur and Joe Stowell. Walk Thru the Bible has a terrific series for all age groups to gain discipline in reading the Bible and to learn great insights on a daily basis, and Bruce Wilkinson's videos on how to raise "first-chair" Christians is a not-to-be-missed opportunity for every family. Of course, any time you can catch David Jeremiah, Chuck Swindoll, or Steve Brown on the radio, you should do so.

Our kids have learned much about the issues of the world from listening to mature Christians on the radio. They don't think anything about it; that's entertainment for them because they grew up with it. Beautiful, melodious Christian music is a blessing in the home, so be careful of the music you select. It should bring peace and joy to the home and have a calming effect on everyone. You will train your children's taste by the music and entertainment you provide in the home. But it's going to take your turning off Dennis Rodman and the latest exploits of Madonna, and turning on Kay Arthur and Joe Stowell for your kids to get the idea that these things people great wisdom to share with us. It also gives you common ground on which to base discussions with your family.

Training Through Devotions

When I go home to be with the Lord, I know He's going to ask me some tough questions. Long before queries on business and the bank account, and before He gets to the orderliness of my garage, the Lord is going to ask some questions about our kids. God wrote the Bible as an operations manual, gave it to me as a father, and wants me to put its principles into practice. Of course, I'm really challenged by that. The fact is, I've failed a lot. One of my biggest problems is that I want to do my own things, rather than what the Lord wants me to do. Sometimes I'm just not controlled by the Holy Spirit. When I am under pressure, trying to get to work, and burdened with my day, I need the Lord. "These words which I command you today *shall be on your heart,*" it says in Deuteronomy. That means I've got to begin each day, early in the morning, taking the time to put His Word into my heart. When I fail to do that, it becomes immediately obvious to everyone in my family. Susanna will innocently spill something, and all of a sudden I'll get irritable. Things don't go my way, and I'll start snapping at people. The temptation is to insist on having things my way or to quit. I'm not qualified to be a dad. I don't have adequate training for the job. But once you've got a wife and kids, you can't simply abandon the role of father. You can try, but as long as you have children, you'll always be a dad. In order to find any measure of success, I've found the one thing I must do is allow the Spirit to work in me each morning.

So one rule we have around our house is that we do devotions every morning. If I'm alive and I'm home, we do devotions. The kids know that it's a priority for us—they've learned our commitment to Scripture.

With teens in the house, we've often heard the complaint, "We can't come—we were up late last night." But I figured they made a choice to stay up late, and now they've got to live with the consequences of their choice. God's Word isn't going to be ignored just because somebody made a lousy choice. "Let's get going," I'll tell them. "Get down here and join us for devotions." The Bible is the key to life, so in my view, this is life or death.

The other day we were packing to go on a trip. We had to be on the road two weeks, were running late, and everybody started heading for the car. Suddenly I held them up with the words, "Let's do devotions."

My wife just looked at me. "Now?"

"Yep. Unless we have someone who'll tell God we don't have time for devotions." There's just not anything more important to me. It's amazing the things that crop up in our lives to keep us from time with Him: vacations, job needs, activities, relatives visiting, stresses. If we do all those things and neglect the Lord, we've failed as fathers. I have a friend who is in full-time ministry, and his son has been thrown out of school. He's been on drugs, been involved in Satan worship, and has given his parents no end of grief. "Phil," my friend told me the other day, "I wish I'd spent every day teaching that boy the Bible. If I'd spent more time in the Word with him, rather than racing off to work in 'the ministry,' I have a feeling things would have been different." I know a lot of men who regret having neglected their families; I've never met the man who regretted spending too much time with his family.

Dad, how are you passing on truth to your family? Are you any fun to be with? I was with a group of pastors recently discussing what family practices had an impact on them growing up. Not a single one mentioned family devotions. When I asked why, they all replied, "Because it wasn't any fun." So we've tried to look for ways we can encourage our kids to know God that are also fun and interesting. Instead of trying to cover an entire chapter of the Bible, we'll often look for a nugget and then talk about the nugget. When our children were younger, we would sometimes act out the story so that the kids could really understand the principles. For instance, we chained each other together in the dining room after reading about Paul living in chains. I once chained my sons Paul and Matt to one another, then asked Paul to pretend he was the "apostle Paul" and share the gospel with the "guard" he was chained to. Now my boys have a picture of what really happened, and they had fun doing it. We've acted out Jesus healing people, raising Lazarus from the dead, Daniel surviving the lions (you'll never guess who the lion was!), and Noah taking care of all those animals on his ark.

If you want to impact your children, get them into the Word. The dad has got to lead—he can't wait around for his wife to do it. He can't sit around moping because he never did it in the past. He's just got to stand up, pick up his Bible, and decide to start sharing it with his children today! If you can start doing that, your influence on your kids' lives will multiply.

Developing Their Minds

+ Analyze and discuss the current events of the day.
+ Ask the question, "What would Jesus do?"
+ Read great books out loud to your children.
+ Order the age-appropriate level of "God's World" newsletter for children.
+ Listen to story tapes, Bible stories, and character-building stories.
+ Read biographies together.
+ Ask your kids, "How do you think that works?"

Making Devotions Fun

The Bible isn't boring, so time in the Word needs to be fun. When my son Matthew was younger, he admitted the main reason he liked Bible study was because the family was together and everybody tried to make it fun. We love the fellowship with each other, and it really starts the day off right because we started it together.

Of course, to many people the prospect of digging their way through Scripture is akin to eating their way through an elephant. However, in my vast experience concerning elephants, I've found the best way is to take really small bites. So start your family devotional time with something small and simple. Decide to spend ten minutes reading a little Scripture, talking it through, then saying a prayer together, and see what happens. Our family's devotion time began that way, but has really grown over the years. One of my biggest problems in the morning now is to stop our devotional time because it's just so exciting! We'll be getting into a big discussion, and suddenly I realize I've got to go to work. We get going and talking, and it is just a ton of fun. It's hard to shut it off so that I can head to the office. If you come and stay at our house, you will be at devotions. The chairman of the board came and I said, "Charlie, whatever you want to do before breakfast is up to you. Breakfast is at 7:00, but devotions are at 7:30, and everybody will need to be there. *Everybody* comes to devotions." He joined us, and we had a wonderful time.

Try not to take too much time. Some fathers have tried and failed at family devotions, so they don't want to expose themselves to another failure. But consider what we do in our family time together, and see if you can find what works for your own family. Let's say we Downers are studying the Book of Isaiah. I might find something in particular that really excited me about a chapter, and I will take that and try to find an application in my life, have the children read the Scripture, and then try and apply it to their own lives in some manner. Other times we'll get into a deep discussion on a subject, spend some time praying, or even sing some songs. The activities you do aren't as important as the fact that everybody in the family focuses on the Lord together each morning.

Let me give you an example of what a family devotional time looks like. First, we'll open with prayer. "Who would like to open up with prayer? Matthew?" And Matthew might say, "Dear Jesus, I thank You for today, and I pray that Dad would have wisdom on what to say and how to say it. In Jesus' name I pray, Amen."

Then we'll do a short study: "Okay, we're looking at Romans 5:10 this morning. Who would like to read that verse? Okay, Paul. 'For if while we were enemies, we were reconciled to God through the death of His Son, much more, having been reconciled, we shall be saved by His life.' As I looked at that verse this morning in my quiet time, I just had to consider some of the things in my life. We are told that 'while we were enemies, we were reconciled to God through the death of His Son.' " Then I might go into how I'm struggling with something at work and have realized that I'm acting very much as the old man and not the new man. Then I'll remind the kids that I've been saved by His life, and *all* of me has been saved, and I'll ask the children how I should be living in light of God's grace. I might ask something like, "What do you think of this verse? Does anybody have a comment about it? An illustration?"

Then my daughter Abigail will chime in: "That makes me think of the fact that we were enemies of Christ. We were in sin, away from the Lord, and could not go to heaven because God could not be around sin."

Trying to bring everyone into the discussion, I'll ask something like, "Does anybody under 11 want to tell us what an enemy is? Anna?" And I'll get a response that says, "Well, enemies are people who will hurt you if you're not nice to them and if you haven't said you're sorry to them. Sometimes an enemy can be someone who has hurt your feelings and you've never forgiven them."

Then I'll ask, "What does Jesus say about our enemies? What are we supposed to do with our enemies?" "We're supposed to love them." "So we can win our enemies by love. How can we win the people around us who don't know Jesus? Are we supposed to fight with them?" "We can love them."

The conversation goes on like that, with kids offering verses and ideas for our discussion. This isn't solely a teaching time, but a shared learning time—a time to think through ideas, events, and people. What we do is try to spend some time talking about issues. This is not a time to talk about the biggest failure of anyone. We want to make it a fun time, an encouraging time for all. This is the time where Dad retakes the family. He renews his leadership, becoming involved in family life, and encouraging every member.

It's also the time when I try to set up what we're going to do next week. "Okay, we're getting ready for a camping trip, so who's in charge of this and who's in charge of that?" or, "It's Good News Club day, kids, so tell me who is leading each part today." Susy and I will cover some of the responsibilities of the day, making sure everybody knows what's on the agenda: "We've got a big day today. Let's pray for it." We want to be positive, informative, and encouraging, and if anybody has done anything worthy of note, this is the time we want to talk about it as a family.

We also use this time to make note of special successes. For example, one morning we talked about Paul, who had stood up to peer pressure by refusing to climb on the roof the previous day. Susy and I told him how much we appreciated his leadership. "Paul, would you describe for us what you were thinking?" we'll ask, and we'll get the younger kids to follow his example. We try to take one point and somehow make it real. Just remember all the crazy things that you did growing up, and all the nutty things you did to get attention, and you'll soon figure out what your kids are facing.

Sometimes we'll do something silly, just to keep it interesting. For example, there are times when I have said, "Well, we have a guest speaker today. His name is Dr.

Fromberry. He is an expert who has come from a faraway land called Tomb Lake, and he's here as a part of a conference. Dr. Fromberry has some things in his bag he wants to show you." Then I'll walk out of the room and return all dressed up, pretending to be this silly professor:

"Good to see you guys. Hey listen, we're really going to learn today. Now, where does truth come from?" "The Bible." "Well, that's true, but it also comes from some other places. I'm involved in a little ministry that needs a lot of support right now. So I am going to teach you some truths today. If you really believe it in your heart, it's true, right? I mean, if you believe something with all your heart, it's true, right? It doesn't matter what you believe, as long as you believe it with all your heart, right?"

"No!" Matt said.

"What do you mean? What's this?" I said.

"An apple," Matt said.

"Yes! And what's that?" I said.

"An egg," Anna said.

"Right! An apple and an egg. How would you like to see an egg become an apple? You would like to see that? I believe that I can make that egg into an apple, but first I need some help to support the four starving children back home. Everybody get their money—I mean their prayers—ready. Okay, one more time: Everybody, what's this?"

"An apple!"

"And what's that?"

"An egg."

"Here we go, everybody ready? If you really believe it strongly enough, it doesn't matter what you believe as long as you believe with all your heart. Are you ready for this? Okay, then I believe this egg is an apple, and that apple is an egg. I believe it with all my heart! Now let's pray silently. Amen. So here it is, an apple! A bright-red apple. It may look like an egg, but I've just changed it into an apple! Like I told you, it doesn't matter what you believe, as long as you believe with all your heart. Isn't that right? Who is to tell me what an apple is? If I call it an apple, it's an apple."

And then, just as if on cue, Anna called my bluff and said, *"Okay, take a bite out of the apple!"*

I looked at her, made several excuses, but then the kids started repeating her demands: "If that's really an apple, take a bite out of it!"

As I crunched the egg with all my might, it splattered all over my face and shirt and part of the table. I thought Susy was going to faint from disbelief, and the children were howling with laughter as they beat the table, fell on the floor, and pointed at the silly doctor. They really couldn't believe I had done such a stupid thing.

Now I know it sounds messy and perhaps childish, but my children have never forgotten the point that it's not how sincerely you believe, rather it's what you believe that matters. Just because someone believes they can live with two women in harmony, doesn't mean that they will be able to do it and that it will lead to happiness. Just because someone believes he can love his wife and watch pornography on the Internet doesn't mean he will live a life of purity for the Lord. We must use practical demonstrations to show our kids that truth doesn't change—even if it takes making a mess on the dining-room table.

We don't often do stuff like that, but it can be helpful for teaching principles in a fun way. The key concept is keeping a healthy relationship with your kids. Keep them on your team. I've talked to people who have teenagers, and everybody says the same thing: "You've got to keep the relationship." If you have someone who's not interested in Bible study, you need to keep the relationship going and try to find common ground, to share the Scriptures with him or her in a relevant way (the Living Proof video series provides excellent training in the building of relationships).

Righteous Relationships
There is a little sign on my desk that says, "The relationship is more important than proving you are right." We can't

compromise God's truth, but we are commanded by God to love sinners. I think there are times when we need to stick with those we love as we would with the guy next door who is walking away from God. Stick with them and love them right where they are.

I've got to be careful that I don't build expectations for our children, and when they get outside my expectations, cut them off. I don't think you can lather on Bible study to teenagers who are just not ready for it. Keep in mind that we were married five years when we came to Christ and had five years of going to various Christian conferences before Abigail was born. So we were maturing Christians five years before our first child was born. This was a tremendous advantage. Most of the people I'm working with in ministry have come to Christ in mid-life, and they have children who are substantially matured. By the time a child is five, a lot of personality is already formed. So you could be playing catch-up there.

If you have children of different ages, you'll find the difference between the spiritual receptivity of the big kids and little kids diminishes over time. We've had people say, "How do they sit still?" By practice. We have learned the value of discipline in devotions. We do it in a loving way, but from the time our kids could sit at the table, we have told them to sit still. When they start wiggling and looking all around, we say, "Please look at me. Keep your hands on the table." They have learned from the time they were about three to sit there and listen. The little ones can't participate as much, but we'll ask them a little question—something that's on their level. It may not have much to do with Bible study, but it should be something they feel they can contribute.

When the twins were young, I didn't feel they were participating that much intellectually, academically, or spiritually in what we were saying. But suddenly we saw a tremendous leap in understanding, particularly in their understanding of the Scriptures and being able to make comments on it. I realized that for those years when I thought they weren't listening or getting much out of it, they were absorbing an enormous amount. Then when they developed both the confidence to hold their own in a discussion with the older children and the ability to verbalize their thoughts, they began to participate. There is no keeping them quiet now!

I think initially it's fine to have small children coloring or doing something similar if it's absolutely necessary just to keep them at the table. Then gradually wean them away from that to be around the table, really paying attention and giving whoever is speaking their attention. Children are much smarter and better able to understand spiritually than we give them credit for.

One of the most common questions we're asked is, "What about the morning time? It's so busy. Did you start out right away doing devotions every morning, or did you gradually move into it from a couple times a week?" My answer: Start twice a week. I travel a lot, so I'm gone half the time. Right away, I know Susy will have to lead the devotionals at times, or I ask one of the children to lead while I'm gone. That is empowerment, and will require teaching them how to do it.

For years I used to be the first in my law office and one of the last to leave. That was also my schedule with CBMC the first few years. I finally became convinced that I needed to give up the security I was gaining from that. If you know more and are working harder than anybody else, you have an element of control, and I realized that I needed to throttle back on my control. Now I'm in the office at 9:00, which in the first five or six months was horrible. I would pull into the driveway of the parking lot, and everybody was there, and I felt guilty. I began the day feeling like I was behind. It took a long time to overcome that feeling. One thing I do is I try to get prepared for the day at home by clearing up the paperwork, so when I get to the office, I'm ready to go with people.

I've had to discipline myself and say that if I'm going to spend time with my kids while they get up, or sit down, or walk by the way. The morning is the only time we seem to be able to control. We decided we're just going to get up however early is necessary to accomplish our goal, because we are at war, and the enemy wants our children.

It has taken years to develop a schedule that works, but I've finally disciplined myself to rise early, spend an hour in Bible study and Scripture memory, then go for a run. My boys run with me, so they also have to rise early for Bible reading and memory work. We start our family devotions at 7:30, and go for an hour. My biggest challenge is to get out the door by 8:30 so the kids can start school with Susy. It amazes me how time flies as we cover an array of topics.

When you're starting off, you're not only dealing with something new for the children, but you're also dealing with something new for yourself. The hard part is learning the discipline to do it. It's like reading the Bible. When you say you're going to read it every day, and then you miss a day, you heap so much guilt on yourself because you didn't do it that you miss the whole point. It doesn't matter what's happened before, you just need to start again, and if you miss once in awhile, so be it. If it only works to do Bible reading three days a week, well that's three days a week more than you were doing it before. Maybe that's what you need to do to get your family into devotions. The key is to offer your morning to the Lord, to be consistent, and to keep each other accountable, not getting discouraged if one morning doesn't go well or if you have one of those days when everyone just sits there and looks at you.

There were times we had been busy the night before, stayed up late, and Susy wouldn't want to get the children up—after all, she was the one who would have to be with crabby kids all day. But then we decided that was something we ought to think through the night before. So we would get them up regardless of the previous night's events. Devotions are preparation for war, and we don't give up preparation just because we're too tired for fighting one day. I've found that the morning is the best time, because it sets the course of the day. I would encourage everybody to try to do it then. If you cannot schedule family devotions early, because you have to be at work early, schedule it at night. The important thing is that you *do* it.

There are times when we've gotten out of the habit, since I've been out of town a lot, and we just couldn't seem to get everyone in sync. But then we would say, "You know, things just aren't right. We haven't been doing devotions." So we would start again.

Spiritual Resources

Consider some devotional books which can help you plan your family devotional time. Chip MacGregor's *Family Discipleship Handbook* is very good. So is Carolyn Williford's *Devotions for Families That Can't Sit Still.* Our children were particularly influenced by "Brokenness," a video tape from Nancy Leigh DeMoss. Again, it doesn't take a genius or curriculum writer to create this stuff. It just takes a willingness to do something constructive. Often parents will complain, "I couldn't come up with these kinds of ideas." But most of our devotional time is simply talking about the Bible. Ask the Lord to help you be creative and come up with ideas, and you'll be amazed at the things He will give you, even if you're a typically noncreative person. If that's a desire of your heart, He can help you make it fun.

Remember, there is great value in reading a verse and sitting silently while all the kids think about it and try to figure it out. Let them develop their intellectual and their spiritual muscles by wrestling with the Scripture. Even little children can do that. But you have to give everybody a chance to struggle and to fail to be successful.

Finally, we end our time of family devotions with prayer requests. Everyone can share whatever is on his or her heart, and we make sure that everybody is praying, though we don't insist they all pray out loud every day. Raising godly children is a challenge, but when a family has explored God's Word and prayed together, it sets the tone for the day. So we pray individually, then go around and make sure everyone spends time talking with the Lord and upholding the family in prayer. Sharing family devotions in order to develop the spiritual lives of our children is one of the most rewarding and enriching things a father can do. Be willing to take the risk, step out, and begin doing it in your own family.*

---

*To talk to some ministries mentioned in this chapter, you can call:
Bill Gothard's *Advanced Training Institute* at (630) 323-2842
Child Evangelism Fellowship at (800) 300-4033
Moody Bible Institute's *Stories of Great Christians* at (800) 626-1244
Your Story Hour cassette tapes at (800) 987-7879
Nancy Leigh DeMoss, Life Action Ministries, (800) 321-1538

Quotable Quotes

✦ *Preparing for That SAT:* Abigail was thrilled with the new calculator she received. It had every imaginable button, function, and process to help her get ready for SAT test day—the only problem was she couldn't turn it off. She finally had to take the batteries out!

✦ *The Best Idea, the Worst Idea:* Having finally caught a pesky raccoon on its journey out the cat door one Sunday morning, Dad and the boys skinned it (to the disgust of all female members of the household) before heading to church. Unfortunately, Paul made the mistake of seeking out the local taxidermist before the service and, within his mother's hearing, exclaiming, "It's great! I've got the skull and skin in Mom's refrigerator!"

Quotable Quotes (cont.)

✦ *Generational Insensitivity*: After bracing for another barrage of complaints from the 14-year-old neighbor who fell during the touch football game, Matthew, then 11, leaned over to his little brother, Josh, who was 9, and with a look of disgust said, "Teenagers!"

✦ *Big Mouth Gets Skunked*: While in line for a Subway sandwich with Matthew at the Salt Lake City airport, the customer just ahead complained to the server that he had mistakenly put cheese on the meatball sandwich, then shoved it back toward the counter and impatiently stomped off. Seeking to demonstrate my great businessman's skill of negotiation, I quickly said, "Hey, I'll take that sandwich . . . if you'll give it to me for half price!" Missing the smile on the attendant's face, I quickly paid half fare and proudly walked to the table, expecting Matthew to compliment me on my business acumen. However, upon inquiring, "How do you think that went?" Matthew replied, "That was great, Dad. But if you had kept quiet, he was going to give you the sandwich for nothing!"

✦ *The Experienced Traveler Gets the Facts*: Concerned that we had put the kids through a little too much travel to various conferences during the year, Susy was somewhat hesitant to announce the next week-long trip to Abigail, who simply responded, "Okay, hot or cold, and how many days?"

Study Questions

1. What helps you maintain your own private quiet time?

2. What influences help foster a spiritual climate in your home?

3. How could you create a family devotional time about Noah's ark and make it fun?

4. Why is having a ministry an essential part of spiritual growth?

5. What kind of ministry could your family develop?

Part Four:

Father of the Year

There aren't many organizations that give out "father of the year" awards. Instead, like in our walk with Christ, we'll have to wait to see Him face-to-face before we are rewarded for our faithfulness. That makes the task of fathering much harder, but it also makes it more important. In a world that values instant gratification, it requires patience and endurance to be a good dad. Maybe that's why soldiers for Christ are necessary, but few and far between.

During one of Paul's baseball seasons, a number of players on the team made fun of him because he was home-schooled. To be honest, Paul was one of the better players on the team, and was clearly the biggest young man on the squad. I thought those ridiculing boys were biting off more than they could chew. Paul shared the problem with me, and I prayed with him that he would not lose his temper and that he would maintain a good witness. As we talked, I realized that one boy in particular, Martin, was a pest, and someone I felt Paul could easily squash if he lost his temper. After much prayer, Paul continued to withstand the temptation to clobber Martin, though I saw Martin not only ridicule my son, but even throw things in his face. What's a dad to do when he sees his son up against the enemy? Should I protect him? Should I save him? I decided to wait it out, to see how my boy would respond.

Eventually, in the dugout between innings, Paul

realized he had become a soldier. One time, after Martin had dumped a hat full of sand on top of Paul's head as he sat on the bench waiting for the next inning, I noticed my son talking to himself. When I asked Paul what he was saying, he admitted, "I was just praying like mad that I could forgive Martin and not just strangle him."

"And did it work?" I asked.

"Well, I just looked at him, and pretty soon the other team members jumped on him and said, 'Hey, leave Paul alone. Cut it out! Quit being so childish!'"

It was interesting how the other team members came to his defense when Paul did not defend himself. He felt a deep sense of relief as he saw how the Lord had provided a way of escape from his temptation to strangle Martin. Paul got a key hit in that game, then went on to become one of the all-stars for that team. As the season progressed, Paul discovered that Martin came from a broken home. In the stands, his mom and dad would sit apart from each other and yell instructions at him, sometimes with differing advice. He was obviously a child who had been through a lot of trauma, but Paul realized this and developed a heart for him. Eventually, he earned the opportunity to talk to Martin about Christ. I didn't have to save my son—Christ already had. Paul became a much better soldier for the Lord because of that difficult season.

Being a soldier means we are willing to suffer for the cause. Our children are going to grow up in a time when they are going to face persecution unlike our generation has known. If they are peer-dependent, weak-kneed, or shallow in faith, they are simply not going to be able to withstand the temptations of the world or the wiles of the enemy. I may not ever win "father of the year," but I found out that summer that at least I've been able to pass along my faith to my son. It is soldiers we are after, and it takes a lifetime to build men and women whose faith can stand strong against great opposition. This last section of the book will help you learn how to build soldiers.

10

Wisdom in the Big Decisions

M y son, do not forget my teaching, but let your heart keep my commandments; for length of days and years of life, and peace they will add to you. Do not let kindness and truth leave you; bind them around your neck, write them on the tablet of your heart. So you will find favor and good repute in the sight of God and man. Trust in the LORD with all your heart, and do not lean on your own understanding. In all your ways acknowledge Him, and He will make your paths straight (Proverbs 3:1-6).

I remember reading a sad story a number of years ago about some American autoworkers who had lost their jobs. While it was unfortunate that they were out of work, that wasn't what made the story sad. It was their *reaction* to being out of work.

At the time when Japanese import cars were making a run at Detroit's dominance of the auto industry, layoffs were not uncommon. Many of the unionized autoworkers were reduced to sitting around doing nothing while union leaders tried to work out new contracts with employers. In one community, the owner of a bar, out of sympathy for the autoworkers who had lost their jobs, went out and purchased a used Japanese import. He put it in the back of the bar and charged idled autoworkers five dollars apiece to take out their frustrations on it with a sledgehammer. They pounded that import to a pulp, venting all their pent-up anger at the loss of their jobs. The Japanese automakers were the villains, and the smashing of the car was a symbolic way of sticking it to the bad guys.

But not everybody shared their anger. One newspaper writer, writing a column about the smashing of the auto, admitted his confusion. If these autoworkers were so convinced that Japanese import cars were responsible for decreased sales of American cars, why were they pounding the Japanese car to smithereens? Wouldn't it make sense, instead of *tearing* it apart, to carefully *take* it apart and see what made it so good? If people were buying Japanese cars instead of cars made in America, maybe it was the Americans who had a problem, not the Japanese.

The wake-up call that the American auto industry got from Japan a few years back was typical of how all of us sometimes respond to failure. First, there was an arrogance that said Japanese car sales could never put a dent in Detroit's profits. When the dent kept getting bigger, arrogance became anger as American workers found themselves out of work. Finally, the light came on. Arrogance and anger were replaced by action. Detroit woke up and said, "Maybe we can learn something from the Japanese." Automakers decided that, rather than blaming someone else for falling profits, they would assume responsibility and fix the problem. As a result, the big three American car companies have enjoyed record profits in recent years.

Training, Not Complaining

While it took Detroit a few years to gear up, they finally decided that training was more productive than complaining. So, from the top down, they retrained themselves to make cars more efficiently and more profitably. There is a lesson here for parents. First, we have to understand that "training" is precisely what God has called us to do with our children. Second, we have to agree that, if our children stray off course, we have to retrain them—that is, get them back on course. We can't blame the school, the church, their friends, their environment, or the phase of the moon. In fact, blaming anybody is a waste of time. The real issue is simple: *What do we need to do to help our kids gain the wisdom they need at a given point in life?*

This whole process is what the Bible calls training, discipline, or instruction. Unfortunately, parents often equate discipline with punishment. Granted, corporal discipline, such as spanking, is part of the process of training. But here's the primary difference between training and punishment: Punishment is an end in itself, while training is a means to an end. Punishment exacts payment for a wrong committed, while training has the goal of changing one's character or behavior. Because we know that Christ died as punishment for our sins, we can assume that God does not punish us when we get offtrack. We also know that His goal for us is to be conformed to the image of His Son in our character and behavior (Romans 8:29). Therefore, God relates to us on the basis of training, not punishment. That same task falls to us as parents with our children. In fact, if we do not biblically train and discipline our children, then the training they receive from God as adults will be a total shock to their systems. They'll think God is an ogre if He ever brings the slightest bit of discomfort to their lives. In reality, it would be the parents who were the unloving ones since they failed to train their children in a godlike manner. Parents are the first line of trainers in God's family, and we learn how to train our children from how God trains us.

Hebrews 12:5,6 tells us, "My son, do not regard lightly the discipline of the Lord, nor faint when you are reproved by Him; for those whom the Lord loves He disciplines, and He scourges every son whom He receives." In verse 7, the Word says it is for "discipline" that we endure hardships, and that God deals with us as with sons: "For what son is there whom his father does not discipline?" If the Father disciplines us because He loves us, then we need to discipline our children because we love them. In verse 10 it says,

"For they disciplined us for a short time as seemed best to them, but He disciplines us for our good, that we may share His holiness." Remember that I said training has a goal? God's training of us is that we may share His holiness (be conformed to the image of His Son). Our goal for our children is the same. We want them to learn to live lives that are pleasing to God. Is it fun? Not really, but that's not the point. The point is to achieve the goal. Verse 11 says, "All discipline for the moment seems not to be joyful, but sorrowful; yet to those who have been trained by it, afterwards it yields the peaceful fruit of righteousness."

Hebrews 12:12 continues: "Therefore, strengthen the hands that are weak and the knees that are feeble." This is such a great word picture. Training involves strengthening—taking that which is weak and making it strong. Whether in sports, in the military, or in any endeavor, training involves discipline, exercise, and strengthening. If we do not strengthen ourselves for the spiritual race, we will not succeed, and neither will our children. We're supposed to stand up and be strong under discipline. We are not to consider it lightly, but neither are we to be overwhelmed by it. That is, if we get offtrack in life, we are to be strengthened (disciplined, trained) so that we can get back in the race.

Life in a fallen world is not easy. It's a challenge most of the time. One of the great temptations is for bitterness and resentment to set in. We'll get out our sledgehammers and start pulverizing, verbally or physically, whoever or whatever we think is responsible for our troubles. In reality, it may be that we need some more training. That's why Hebrews 12:15 concludes, "See to it that no one comes short of the grace of God; that no root of bitterness springing up causes trouble, and by it many be defiled."

We need to purpose to train our children not to get bitter when life deals them a hard blow. We as their parents need to bring some pressure to bear on them. We need to show them how to identify the problem, discover the solution, and move on successfully. That's what disciplining our children is all about. To put it simply, we need to give our children the skills to live life fruitfully. The Bible has a single word that sums up what it means to live life skillfully: *wisdom*. The goal in training our children is wisdom, which leads to righteousness.

The Goal of Wisdom
I can't tell you how thoroughly I enjoy our teenage children. There have been times when I've actually lost sleep at night from simply praising the Lord for what I see in their lives. We are reaping the fruit of righteousness that Hebrews 12:11 mentions. Don't misunderstand me—we are not reaping perfection. That's fine, because perfection is not our goal. But we are reaping the peaceful fruit of righteousness as we see our children demonstrate wisdom in critical areas of life. As a result of training in their younger years, they are rapidly moving from being children who have to be trained, to young adults who are manifesting skill in living life from God's perspective.

I know of no more helpful concept to communicate to our children than the goal of attaining biblical wisdom and understanding in their lives. As Proverbs 1:7 says, "Fools despise wisdom and instruction." We do not want our children to become fools, to be persons whose lives evidence a pattern of foolish choices. We don't even want them to make the occasional foolish choice, because in today's world the stakes are so high. A generation ago, a foolish choice might have resulted in being reprimanded for a neighborhood prank. Today, a foolish choice might result in jail time, or pregnancy, or even death. The higher the stakes, the more critical the need for training. Let's face it, in the military, who gets the most training? The pilot of a $100 million aircraft armed with laser-guided weapons, or the driver of the mail truck? Both roles are critical to the success of the mission, but the stakes with the former are higher than with the latter. Therefore, the training is more intense. Our young people today are facing the highest stakes of any generation in history, and we as parents must impart to them the wisdom—and the skills to get wisdom—they need to be successful.

What is wisdom? As I understand the word that is used in the Old Testament, *wisdom* is basically the word for "skill." It was used to describe those who sailed boats and those who crafted the fineries of Israel's tabernacle. Sailors need skills. Craftsmen need skills. When we use the word *wisdom*, we are essentially talking about the "skill of living." Think about the Book of Proverbs: Isn't the father imparting to his son advice about how to *live life skillfully?* Life is like a sailor navigating his boat through dangerous shoals, or a craftsman taking raw materials and constructing a beautiful edifice. Life is filled with dangers and opportunities, and the father in Proverbs is communicating how to watch out for the one and capitalize on the other. The father wants his son to be wise—to live life skillfully.

Let me give you two examples on opposite ends of the training spectrum, but which both illustrate the need for transferring life skills to your child. First, let's suppose your four-year-old son gets a new learning toy for his birthday that requires some explanation. Here's where it starts: "Daddy, how do I do dis?" From the perspective of wisdom, here's what your child is saying: "Dad, I'm at a point in my young life where I'm up against a challenge that is greater than anything up to this point in my first four years. I'm lacking the wisdom to use this toy properly. I really need you to teach me how to do this. Could you help me?" And, of course, you are (presumably) more than willing. Down on the floor you go to get a quick look at the instructions, and in no time you're showing him how it works. "Watch this, pal. See how it works? Watch again. Now you do it. Almost! Try it again. Ohhh, so close! One more time. All right! Way to go!" And he's got it. In a matter of five minutes your child has become wise (skillful) in an area of life. You were able to help him because the skill level required to impart wisdom on this particular topic was not greater than the skill you possess.

Now, fast forward about 15 years. It's the end of your

son's freshman year in college, and he has come to the realization that his ability to manage his finances needs to move to a new level. Sure, he's had a checking account for a couple of years and has managed it (semi-)skillfully. But life is getting more complicated. He's got a job at school, so he's got more discretionary income. He knows he wants to give money to the Lord regularly, but he's not sure how much, and how to keep it from being spent on other things. He wants to start saving for a car. And he's gotten pumped about investing in a mutual fund because of a course he took at college. And he's become the de facto manager of the rent and utility money among the guys with whom he shares an apartment. *And* he needs a credit card because of a financial emergency he had on a trip a few months back. And on and on. So the man-child comes to you and says, "Daddy, how do I do dis?" Or at least that's what you hear. It seems like just yesterday you were giving him wisdom about toys. Now your son is a child no more. He has an adult's questions. Do you have the adult answers? Not only answers about money, but about the myriad of other emotional, spiritual, marital, vocational, and personal issues your children will face.

Have we as parents acquired the skill ourselves in the serious arenas of life so as to pass them on to our children? Do we know how to manage our finances? Are we giving faithfully to the Lord? Are we spending discretionary income in a godly fashion? Do we have the self-control to keep credit cards in check? Are we obeying the proverbial injunctions to lay up in times of harvest enough to get us through the lean years? Explaining how toys work is one thing. Explaining how life works is another. How can we impart wisdom—the skill of living—if we do not possess it ourselves? Parenting, first and foremost, is not about giving our kids wisdom. It is about getting it ourselves. We cannot pass on what we do not possess.

It takes discipline to mature in Christ. It takes discipline to grow up. It takes discipline to say "no" to our own way and "yes" to the Lord. More than anything, it takes discipline to make good decisions. I've seen far too many young people ruining their lives with lousy choices because they never developed discipline. It may be because their parents never developed it. Susy and I decided a long time ago that, if our kids were going to grow up to be contributors to the kingdom of God, to impact our world for Christ, they were going to have to learn discipline and gain wisdom. There is no more pressing motivation for parents to gain wisdom themselves than a desire to see their children gain wisdom.

So let me clarify exactly how parents train their children to be wise. First, when they are young, we define wisdom for them. Second, as they grow, we help them know where to look for wisdom. For instance, when our kids are young, we explain to them that telling the truth is wise, and lying is not. Sharing your toys is wise, being stingy is not. Obeying your parents is wise, disobeying is not. In the concrete world of a child, wisdom is easy. They trust you and believe you as their parents. But then they grow up, and life changes from black and white to multiple shades of gray. We cease telling them what wisdom is, and begin teaching them how to find it on their own. Hopefully, they still tell the truth, share, and obey when those needs arise. But the most important thing that our children ultimately need to learn from us is *how to gain wisdom from their heavenly Father.* If, when they were young, we led them to Him, taught them principles from His Word, and lived as examples of how to discover and manifest wisdom, then we will have done the most critical part of our job as fathers.

When they're small, it's all us and very little them. When they're older, it's very little us and all them. The challenge is to make the transition carefully and effectively as they grow older. Letting go and letting our children discover wisdom on their own can be scary, but it is a parent's responsibility. I would like to talk about passing on wisdom to our children in four critical areas of life: sexuality, choosing a marriage partner, handling money, and choosing a vocation.

The number of adults who are struggling with one or more of these areas is a clear indication that wisdom is not a function of our chronological age. God gives parents the years of their children's adolescence to nail down basic skills in living life—that is, to move confidently into adulthood. If the task isn't accomplished by the time those adolescents leave home, then they enter chronological adulthood as teenagers in terms of their skills. The current state of our culture in the areas of sex, marriage, money, and vocation is a clear indication that we have a lot of teenagers running around disguised as adults. That doesn't bode well for the next generation.

Wisdom in Sexuality

The issue in raising children today is not "whether" they are going to learn about sex but "when" and "from whom." While there are many issues that could fall under the heading of sexuality, our primary concern as parents has been to establish marriage as the backdrop for sexuality. From a biblical perspective, most issues of sexuality either have their immediate application in the marriage relationship or are best illustrated within the context of marriage. For instance, all things regarding sex between a man and a woman have one application: the joyful and fruitful relationship between a husband and a wife. Additionally, even individual issues of sexuality are best illustrated for children by husbands and wives fulfilling their God-given spiritual, emotional, and physical roles in contrast to one another. Susy and I agreed that we would work hard at having a strong and healthy marriage which would provide a secure environment for our children to learn comfortably about sexuality. (Think about that before you read further. No couple sets out to have a bad marriage. Most couples set out to have a good marriage and hope they achieve it. But how many couples have *purposed* to have a good marriage, knowing that if they don't, the chances are excellent that their kids won't either? We purpose and achieve other far-less-important things in life. Why don't we *purpose* to have a permanent, productive marriage?)

Even in writing this, I realize what a narrow view it is in our culture to confine issues of sexuality to marriage

Talking About Purity

+ Exercise modesty in your home.

+ Explain that no part of our body is bad, ugly, or unwanted, but some parts are simply private.

+ Convey modesty by explaining that private body parts are for a future husband or wife, and not for anyone else except a doctor or parent in the appropriate context.

+ Don't treat the inevitable walk-ins while undressed with fear, anger, or shock, but simply say, "Excuse me, I was dressing" or "Excuse me, I didn't know you were dressing," and close the door.

+ Be honest about sex—it is pleasurable, but it is something reserved for marriage.

+ Teach your children about purity and sexual reproductive details long before they experience the temptations of adolescence.

+ Explain to your daughters what men see when women's undergarments are revealed or a woman bends over with a low-cut blouse.

+ Explain the signals that people send when such things happen, and the consequences of attracting someone physically instead of by one's godliness and character.

+ A four-year-old cannot comprehend the importance of all this as much as a 14-year-old, but both children should learn that they don't take off their clothes in front of strangers or let other people touch them in their private areas.

alone. Stop and think of all the ways that sex is expressed in our culture outside of marriage, and you will quickly realize what a daunting task it is to convey wisdom in this area. You are paddling against the cultural current, to be sure. So when our children reached eight or nine years of age, we would begin to explore with them, from the Bible, God's plan for men and women to be joined together as one. We wanted our kids at an early age to understand that marriage and family are the building blocks of the human race. Marriage is God's most sacred earthly institution, to be honored and held in the highest esteem. We went to Genesis to discover that Adam and Eve were joined by God in the Garden of Eden, and that from their union all other marriages draw their design: two coming together as one.

I tell the kids that God wants to use a dad and a mom to create a new person, and I ask them how they think He would do that. As they sit there with a question mark on their faces, I say, "You know, what God would probably want to do is to take a part of both of us, kind of like how you would take a seed and plant it, but He would want it to be done in such a way that it would be very personal." Since my goal is to be the first person from whom they hear about sex, I then show them physically (using any number of excellent illustrated resources which are available) how two people—not just any two people, but a dad and a mom—are joined together. Susy and I together describe the wonderful way by which God provided for husbands and wives to become one physically as an expression of their love for and commitment to each other. When children learn that they are actually the fruit of their parents' sexual union, there is an emotional bonding and security which is incredible. When they understand that sex is the privilege that married couples are able to share together, as well as being the method by which God creates children, it provides a sensible and reasonable explanation for all things sexual.

Obviously, this is not a one-time discussion. But when we as parents initiate the topic, and therefore make it a "safe" area for discussion, it is much easier for children to feel comfortable about bringing up questions later. We open the door of sexuality and keep it open, so that the free flow of communication and understanding is not hindered. As I said, if they don't hear it from us, they're going to hear it somewhere—and most likely incorrectly. This pattern has worked pretty well with our five older children because now we are able to talk openly with them about all kinds of sexual issues. We simply never allowed sex to become a taboo topic. From day one with our children, sex was considered normal, healthy, and easy to define since we have God's perspective on it in Scripture.

In talking to our children about sex, we need to leave the position of a lecturer or instructor and get down on the battlefield with them as another person trying to live a wise and holy life. For instance, when my son Paul was 12, he accompanied me on a ministry trip to California. At the end of the week we went to church with a friend, and on the way home from church, my friend and I were sitting in the front seat discussing some personal matters. I mentioned that I was struggling with my heart's attitude toward a person who had said some hurtful things to me. My friend said that he was wrestling with improper thoughts about some women he had seen at the church.

Turning to Paul in the backseat, I asked him if he had any personal matters that we could pray about together. He said yes, that he was struggling with the same thing my friend had mentioned—temptations in thinking about girls. In our culture, children can start pretty early with struggles in their thought-life. But if a safe and understanding environment has been created, they will also open up and ask for help and prayer in that area. What a joy it was that day for the three of us men to pray for pure thoughts from the Lord and ask Him to help us with temptation and purity! As the Bible promises us, "No temptation has overtaken you but such as is common to man; and God is faithful, who will not allow you to be tempted beyond what you are able, but with the temptation will provide the way of escape also, that you may be able to endure it" (1 Corinthians 10:13). Our frank discussion gave Paul and me the ability to continue that accountability, which we have over the years since.

Our oldest child, Abigail, and I often talk about some of

the challenges both teens and parents are having with respect to purity. I sometimes relay stories, without identifying my friends' names, about some of the challenges adult married couples are having with respect to these issues. I also describe some of the tragic results people are experiencing when they fall into compromising God's principles.

Do these discussions ever get embarrassing? Would it be easier to ignore the subject? Of course, but we do so at our peril. Here's an illustration: We were talking about sexual purity in our family one day when Abigail was about 10, and it was clear my wife and oldest daughter were getting a little squeamish the further I went with my explanations. Never being one to mince words, I persisted. I finally said, "Abigail, I'm still not sure you understand the way in which men are attracted to women. Actually, it's pretty similar to how a male dog is attracted to a female dog." (Since we had three dogs, Abigail perked up. I had found the common ground I needed to get the point across.)

One of our two females dogs had been in heat, and we had had her away from the house for a few days at a kennel to keep Prince, our big male, from bothering her. But after we'd brought the dog home, Prince was still making a nuisance of himself, sniffing and following her around. He knew the party was over, but was looking for any last-minute opportunity. I asked Abigail, "What did Prince do to Sandy after she came home from the kennel?"

"Oh, Dad," she squirmed, "that's disgusting!"

"It certainly is," my wife chimed in. "Let's change the subject."

"I don't want to change the subject," I replied in my most-gentle, Marine-like voice. "We have in-your-face billboards, movies, music, and television commercials about sex. They are not changing the subject, and I want to make sure you know what is going on. These media are carefully orchestrated, and you need to understand how. Now what does Prince do to Sandy?"

"Well," Abigail ventured, "he walks around and sticks his nose in her rear end."

You're right. But a month later, when Lady goes into heat, what does Prince do?"

"Well, he stops following Sandy around, and he follows Lady around, doing the same things to her."

"That's right," I told her. "And you know what motivates the male? God put in *dogs* the attraction of the sense of smell to the female. In *men* he put the attraction of the sense of sight. Everything you have seen Prince do by nature with a female dog is exactly what men do visually. If a husband and wife are in a huge crowd of people, they are both seeing things. The woman is primarily seeing aesthetic things—clothes, decorations, relationships—while the man is seeing sexual things. Men are motivated and attracted by sight, Abigail, the same way Prince is motivated by smell."

My daughter was completely surprised by that. As a female, there was no way in the world she would ever have become aware of that on her own. She needed to be told, and her mother and I were the best people to tell her. Then we discussed the point of application, which is how she needs to be careful about her own standards of dress and physical appearance. All it takes is citing a few examples of modern marketing, and the way sex is used as a visual stimulus when there is a male audience to reach, to convince your kids that commercials and advertisements are accomplishing more than one thing. I want my daughters to understand that if they attract a man just by their physical appearance, he'll last only as long as it takes to find someone more physically attractive. Those examples, coupled with some Scriptures on modesty and true beauty in God's sight (not to mention what it means not to become a stumbling block for young men) were enough to help my daughter gain a whole new understanding of the value of modesty in dress.

The bottom line on teaching about sexuality and raising children is this: There is a direct correlation between the healthy understanding and practice of the parents and the healthy understanding of their children. There are so many parents who still struggle with their own fears, insecurities, and inhibitions regarding sex—even sex in marriage, God's ordained domain. If parents want their children to be wise and biblical in the sexual areas of life, then they are going to have to be that way as well.

Wisdom in Choosing a Life Partner

When it came to establishing standards for our own children in the choosing of a life partner, Susy and I have been greatly impacted by some godly friends, Ted and Gladys Hubbard. Married more than 40 years, the Hubbards have raised four children of their own. Ted has been a pastor, lawyer, and a judge in England, and came to some strong convictions about choosing a life partner through his own study of Scripture as a young man. First, he believed that God meant for one man and one woman to spend a lifetime together. He also was convinced that God was sovereign in His knowledge of all persons, and therefore knew who would make the best wife for him. As a result, Ted decided to ask God to lead him to a wife.

He decided that he would not date, kiss, or sexually touch a woman until he met the woman he believed God was giving him as a wife. As he went through life, this gave him a great protection from temptation. It gave him confidence around women so that he could interact with them comfortably and not feel pressured to become involved in the "dating game." He was saving himself physically, emotionally, and spiritually for the one that God would lead to him. He met Gladys, a Christian woman in one of his classes, when he was about thirty, and he felt sure that this was the one God was leading him to.

After much prayer, Ted began talking to Gladys, who was already convinced that he was going to be her husband. They eventually married and have had a tremendous, fruitful, and godly marriage ever since. The story of their waiting upon the Lord for a marriage partner made a tremendous impact on our children.

The idea of Christian young adults avoiding the dating scene is almost unheard-of in Western cultures like America. Instead, we teach kids how to date according to Christian standards. But people with positive experiences like the Hubbards are beginning to cause the dating scenario to be questioned. Our kids know plenty of young people—Christian as well as non-Christian—who are the walking wounded as a result of failed dating experiences. Think of it. Every dating relationship is going to end in one of two places: marriage or a breakup. We know where the vast majority of them end. If you knew that the vast majority of airplanes crashed before reaching their destination, would you board the next flight? Dating is making less and less sense to a lot of Christian young people and their parents. Susy and I are so thankful that our children are developing strong commitments about avoiding the dating scene and waiting on God to direct their steps to a marriage partner.

It seems to me that dating is more a preparation for divorce than marriage. She explained to her friends how young people begin dating in high school and college, move into an exclusive relationship, begin saying "I love you," getting more and more deeply involved physically, and spending all their free time together—in other words, acting as if they are married. And then they break up. It's just a junior version of marriage and divorce. If the average young person has been through several of these cycles by the time he or she actually marries, is it any wonder that people treat divorce so lightly once they are legally married? Except for the legal part, they've been emotionally, and often physically, married and divorced several times already!

Because of the emotional and spiritual trauma that Abigail has observed in so many broken relationships and marriages, she has decided to simply wait—to hold high the ideal of a pure and protected relationship with her future husband physically, emotionally, and spiritually and to focus on using her single years to serve the Lord undistracted. She is preserving her physical, emotional, and spiritual well-being in order to present herself to her husband one day without spot or blemish.

This point of view has also made a great impact on our 15-year-old son Paul. He has made the same commitment to wait on the Lord for a marriage partner, and is already finding a real freedom that his friends, who are getting involved in the "dating game," are not experiencing.

Wisdom in Finances

What do the experts say is the number-one problem cited by couples who are divorcing? Money! Isn't it amazing? Dirty, green pieces of paper become so important in the lives of couples that they break up over them. But it's not the dollar bills, it's what they represent: independence, control, and possessing things. Is there something unspiritual-sounding about that list? Since when did God encourage us to live independently (as opposed to in dependence upon Him), in control (as opposed to allowing Him to be in control), and in pursuit of things (which are destined to rust and be eaten by moths)? Giving our kids wisdom about money and making sure they know the principles that will lead to future wisdom are absolutely critical to their skill in living.

Susy and I grew up with the miracle of compounding debt as opposed to the miracle of compounding interest. We got married and had two great incomes in one account, but until we got some counsel and practical help from a Christian financial adviser, we were spending more than we were making. After making progress in our own financial stewardship, we began looking for ways to pass on biblical principles about money to our children. Happily, Susy and I have found that our kids are already way ahead of us on the learning curve. For example, when we sold our house on one occasion, we were discussing how much of the proceeds we should use to pay down some debts. Abigail, who was then 13, offered her advice: "Well, just pay off as much debt as you possibly can. That way you won't have to worry about paying it off later." We were quite surprised,

Talking About Money

✦ While going through the drive-through window on a bag-lunch date, ask the attendant how much the starting salary is at the restaurant.

✦ Point out the cost of things you do and purchase.

✦ Let your child handle the budget and finances on a weekend trip or outing.

✦ Tell your kids about a time you failed to carefully manage your finances, and the trouble it caused.

✦ Get one of the many good Christian books on finances written by Ron Blue or Larry Burkett. Discuss one principle at a time from the book with your child. (If your children are strong readers, suggest that they read a portion and comment back to you about it. If they are not very interested in the subject, begin with an interesting fact from the book.)

✦ Discuss tithing and "giving cheerfully."

✦ Contrast investments you've made which will burn up with some eternal investments you have made that will last for eternity.

✦ Share as many ways as you can the principles of sowing and reaping and how God will trust us with a little to see if we are faithful before He trusts us with much.

not realizing that she had developed those kinds of convictions about remaining debt-free.

With personal indebtedness and bankruptcies running at an all-time high in the history of our country, it appears that Christian families are as guilty as any others about ignoring biblical principles of financial stewardship. And this makes it difficult for parents to set high standards for their children. It's difficult to talk what we're not walking. In this area, I speak from experience. But once Susy and I got on the road to financial wisdom, we were able to impart some of the things we were learning to our children. Here are the areas that I believe are most teachable and most achievable with children:

1. *Where does money come from?* My kids know I work hard for my salary. Talk to your children about allowances, working for income around the house, and the importance of doing some chores without pay because it's a family responsibility. 1 Corinthians 29:11, 12

2. *Why do we tithe?* Giving faithfully to the Lord's work is an essential part of every Christian's life, but giving away money doesn't come naturally to most people. We're all selfish sinners saved by grace, and have to learn that God owns everything, and that it our responsibility to give back to Him a portion of what He has so generously given us. 2 Corinthians 9:6, 7

3. *How do we save money?* Open a small bank account for your child and help him or her save money regularly. They'll soon learn the joy of watching their savings grow, and they'll have a skill they can use the rest of their lives. Proverbs 22:7

4. *Who are we called to help?* God doesn't give us money solely for our own selfish pleasure, but so that we can experience the grace of giving. The Bible is clear that those who have been blessed with much are required to give much, so ask your children to help you decide where to give money. Who needs it most? What are the best organizations and causes that need your support? What results from your gift? By becoming involved with some Christian ministries, your child's heart is opened to the needs of a lost world. Proverbs 3:9, 10

5. *Where does the money go?* If you teach your children how to create a budget, comparison buy, and control impulse spending, you'll have given them one of the most important skills in life. You will also help them to keep focused on the Lord, rather than on the latest advertisements, and prepare them to stay away from one of the biggest snares in marriage: fighting over money. Proverbs 21:20

6. *How do I keep records of my finances?* Let your kids see where you spend your money and why, and they'll develop a whole new appreciation for what you go through each month. 1 Corinthians 4:2

By discipling your children in the art of handling their personal finances, you not only give them practical skills, but you also are offered a wonderful opportunity to impress upon them the values of the Lord. God wants us to love others by sharing generously with them, not simply by sending up a prayer and offering a pat on the back. When you care for others practically, you begin to develop a heart for people. One of the most important skills we've offered our children is the skill of understanding that wealth is a tool to be used for God's glory rather than for our own gratification.

Wisdom in Vocation

In bygone days, vocational choices for young people were simpler—not altogether better, but at least simpler. Here was the pattern: Young men learned to do what their fathers did, and young women learned from their mothers to manage a home and care for children. That was the plan, and, I confess, much about it is attractive. Before the days of mass communication, worldwide travel, and courses on every vocational specialty imaginable, vocational choices were easier. Because there were not a lot of vocational options available, the choice of a path to pursue was less complicated.

Marketing experts today tell us that providing consumers with too many options breeds passivity. People are overwhelmed when they walk in the drugstore to get a cold remedy for their child and are presented with 87 different cough-and-cold remedies. They step back and are afraid to choose for fear of not getting the best product for their child. So what do they do? They ask the pharmacist. They put the health of their child into the hands of a total stranger who, because he is wearing a white coat and stands behind a counter, qualifies as an expert. Granted, he probably is more qualified to make a recommendation than the average parent. But facing too many choices leads to passivity, and that makes it easy to turn the important decisions of life over to an expert. Yet that is often exactly how our children "discover" a vocational path.

To put it bluntly, the average middle-class child in America today has an unlimited range of possibilities when it comes to a vocation. This has spawned an entire industry in our public high schools: guidance counselors, whose job it is to help students figure out what to be when they grow up so they can take courses appropriate for that goal. While I am grateful for the help they offer and sympathetic to the need, I can't help but hurt for many young people today who have no clue about what to do with their lives.

What can parents do to be "guidance counselors" for their children? There is one basic answer to that question: *Get to know your kids*. Who could possibly have a better feel for the talents and aspirations of children than their parents? Actually, there is someone: our heavenly Father. Psalm 139 records verse after verse of incredible statements about how well God knows each of us. I especially like verse 16, and have used it as a promise to encourage our children about God's knowledge of their future path in life: "Thine eyes have seen my unformed substance; and in Thy book they were all written, the days that were ordained for me, when as yet there was not one of them." God says He knows the days ordained for us even before those days have come to pass. That is an incredible promise from God to us and to our children.

Before I share a couple of principles that have helped Susy and me develop a sense for our children's possible vocations, let me give you a snapshot of each of our children and what some possibilities are that I have begun to sense from the Lord about their lives.

Abigail loves people, enjoys science, and is very good at counseling and exhorting people. She has become very excited about becoming a Physician's Assistant and following the example of her aunt who is a PA in Illinois. In discussing this area with Abigail, we have presented other options to her in the same vocational field—not to change her mind, but to help her think and establish solid reasons for why she has the preferences she does. For instance, we suggested she also consider becoming a physician. I loved her answer. She responded that she would rather be a Physician's Assistant and avoid the much-lengthier training required to be a physician. Why? Because she is lazy or not willing to pay the price? Not at all. She really believes that ultimately she would like to stay home, be a mom, and raise her kids during their young years. It wouldn't make sense to invest the years of training in becoming a physician only to set it aside in order to be at home for 10 to 15 years raising her children. I was so pleased when Abigail thought through her own long-term priorities and set her sights on being a godly wife and mother. But until God gives her that privilege, she has targeted a very fine vocational area totally suited to her temperament and talents, and in which she will be able to minister to hurting people who are being treated in the medical community.

Paul, on the other hand, has a very mechanical bent. He loves numbers and how things work. He also has a flair for design and building. One of his favorite inventions was a catapult that he built in the backyard which he used to shoot baseballs, rocks, and whatever else he could make fly. He has been very interested in talking with our friends who are in the engineering and architecture professions. He's a project person, and we have encouraged him to take part in projects that would further his experience in the area of designing creative inventions.

Matthew is a people person who loves sports. He has mentioned law and also engineering. He has gained a lot more motivation for his schooling by realizing how much will be required if he does go into one of those areas of endeavor.

Joshua we always kid as being the expert in everything. He is always quick to give an opinion, particularly to correct Dad when he has violated one of the household rules. We are all convinced that Joshua will be in some kind of position where we will all be paying for his advice when he is an adult. We don't know if he will be a financial consultant, theologian, or a lawyer, but we are all convinced that Joshua will be making money with his mouth and mind, whatever his vocation is.

Anna is the only one in the family who has the gift of mercy. She is the one who gives the best hugs when you smash your finger. She has talked about being a nurse. Though she is still young, I already feel that God has gifted her to be in a setting where great compassion and tenderness are needed.

Susanna is just five and although we're not sure what she will be we are sure it will involve people.

What do the above descriptions represent? Nothing more than parents who love their children, try to observe them, gather and hold onto insights about them, and spend time talking with them about their future. They are the things that any parent can do and should do, but that sometimes don't get done until the senior year in high school.

Here are some principles that have served us well as we've tried to impart wisdom to our children about their vocational futures. First, *don't typecast your child with your desires or expectations*. There is danger in announcing, "Johnny is going to take over the family business one day." The Lord may have an entirely different idea than you have. Second, *remember to pray consistently* with your child about his/her future. Your kids need to see that you are lovingly concerned about their future careers, not just your own. Third, *promote the sacredness of all vocations*. God called one tax collector in the New Testament to be a preacher, but He called another one to remain a tax collector. Don't elevate full-time ministry over any other vocation—Zaccheus's vocational choice was dictated by the Lord, and was just as valid as Matthew's. Fourth, *connect your children with other adults* from whom they can learn about a possible vocational interest. Exposure to mature Christians is one of the best ways of broadening your child's horizons.

Fifth, *teach your children to major in their strengths*. I constantly see people talking about improving some weakness in their child, but I think most of us would be better off to simply encourage the child's strengths. If your son is artistically gifted, God designed him that way, so don't force him to give it up in order to develop a career in mathematics! Sixth, *teach your kids to observe the areas in which God gives them successes* or grants them favor as evidence of His leading. The Lord bends each person a bit differently. Encourage your child to discover his or her "bent." Seventh, *prepare them to live in the real world,* not a fantasy world. All vocations require hard work and dedication. The Bible tells us that we all live by the sweat of the brow, so let your kids learn at a young age the importance of hard work.

Eighth, *give your kids the long view.* Good grades in high school mean better choices in college; good grades in college mean scholarships and opportunities for graduate study; et cetera. Life is a series of connections. The stones we lay in grade school are the foundation upon which we'll build much of our lives. Don't take the short view. Set your sights on a goal and seek to achieve it.

Finally, *make sure to share with your children an eternal perspective.* God has a plan for our lives, and for this world, and each of your children is part of His plan. Whatever we do, we should do it all to the glory of God. Our responsibility as fathers is to prepare our kids to be able to hear God's voice and to be willing to follow that voice. This is the essence of discovering wisdom and knowledge, of developing the skill of living in the area of vocations. "The fear of the LORD is the beginning of knowledge," it says in Proverbs 1:7. No young person who is confident in his or her walk with the Lord, and has been raised in an environment of affirmation, discipline, and love, should ever lack for a confident vocational path.

Are your children growing in wisdom in matters of sexuality, choosing a life partner, managing money, and choosing a vocation? Even more important, are you and I? May God grant us wisdom in helping our children to discover the skill of living.

Quotable Quotes

✦ *An Attorney Outlawyered*: Somewhat harried, Susy said she was simply not able to read Susanna a book unless it was very short, to which Susanna replied, while handing her a rather long book, "Mom, could you read this one real fast?"

✦ *Weighty Responsibility*: Mom, the great negotiator, having obtained from each of the children a five-dollar contribution, was off with Joshua to pick out our Christmas tree. Concerned about the size of the tree the salesman was now lashing to the top of her van, Susy asked if it were too heavy to get off the van. Joshua added, "What she really means is, can a 50-year-old man and a 15-year-old kid get the tree off the van?"

✦ *Bumped to the Second String*: Finally succumbing to a deep sense of responsibility and desire to help his wife, Phil caved in and agreed to sand, prepare, and paint their bedroom, if Paul would help him. At that Susy responded, "Oh, no! He's too valuable to use on a paint job. I need him to hang doors!"

✦ *Stool Pigeon*: The usually diligent Paul, forgetting to dust while cleaning the living room, was exposed when Matthew exclaimed to everyone, "Hey, look! I can write my name on the TV!"

✦ *More Humble Pie*: Dad, the seasoned traveler, after several sermonettes on "how to hold onto your gear," was indeed red-faced when informed by his 11-year-old son that he had left his beloved suitcase in the overhead compartment on the plane to Portland—which would have taken it to Brazil, instead of Tokyo, the desired destination.

Study Questions

1. What skills do you wish you had developed as a teen?

2. How did you explain sex to your kids? (Or, if you haven't yet, how do you plan to?)

3. What approach do you plan to take in helping your children find their life partner? Why?

4. How have you mentored your children in the use of finances, whether for good or bad?

5. What two steps could you take to foster your child's vocational development in some way?

II

Home Ministry

J ust as a father has compassion on his children, so the LORD has compassion on those who fear Him (Psalm 103:13).

Families in America are in crisis. From the highest levels of government to the humblest homes in the land, the cry of the American family is heard. The most pitiful cry of all is the cry of children. Hurting, fearful, and lonely children are reaching out to anyone who will embrace them and give them a hope for their future. Over and over we are told by "experts" that the average young person in America has no picture, no mental or emotional image, of what a normal or healthy home is like. As a result of changing expectations, definitions of normalcy are changing as well. "Since kids don't define 'normal' as a traditional two-parent family," the reasoning goes, "why keep trying to preserve it? We'll redefine life's basic structures in order to meet evolving expectations."

Those of us who know why God designed the family, and what He desires to accomplish through it—especially as it relates to raising the next generation—will never settle for such reasoning. Yet there was a time in my life when I was in the process of evolving my own definition of family. Before coming to know Jesus Christ, I was like many in our land: trying and failing to create a home that would accomplish my self-centered goals. Having come to understand God's design and desire for the family, I can now reach out with a measure of compassion and grace to those around me.

In this chapter, I want to relate how God has accomplished two eternally significant works in and through our family. First, He showed me that the most effective way to disciple my own children—to delve into and meet their deepest needs—was to involve them in ministry to others. I was totally unprepared for that reality. In fact, when we began to have children, Susy and I pulled back from ministry in order to devote more time to our own family. That was the wrong strategy. If what Jesus said is true, that it is more blessed to give than to receive, then I needed my thinking corrected. God did indeed graciously correct it.

The second thing God has done, and continues to do, is allow our family to reach out to a number of people in our circle of influence, both children and adults. The crisis of the American family is not "over there" somewhere; it is right in my neighborhood. The crisis is happening next door, down the street, and around the corner. We don't have to go to seminary or become a foreign missionary to get involved at the most intense levels of human need. All we have to do is walk out our front door and be Jesus to our neighbors. This was a profound and life-changing discovery for me. Nothing has had a greater impact on the security and self-confidence of our children than our family uniting together as a team in ministry to others. I want to tell you how that developed, how God gently gave us the confidence necessary to extend His love to those who need it, and how He gave us His love back in return.

Mission and Maintenance

Psychologists tell us that a person's emotional and temperamental outlook on life is pretty well set in the first six years of life. When I look around at our society today, it makes me wonder what happened or didn't happen in the first six years of life of many teens. What were the seeds that were sown in the first 2000 days of their lives? Were they seeds of submission to authority, or seeds of rebellion? Seeds of security, or of insecurity? Seeds of hope, or seeds of desperation? Given the crisis of the American family today, what fruit will be born 15 or 20 years from now by today's preschoolers? Who and what are they becoming? Studies over the years have been remarkably consistent, showing that 85 percent or so of all people who come to Christ do so before their fourteenth birthday. That is why I believe the Christian homes of today are perfectly positioned to bring the gospel to one of the world's most strategic mission fields: children.

But, I confess, I did not always know that. After Susy and I became Christians, as the Lord began to rebuild our marriage and our lives, we began to practice what had been modeled for us: ministry in our home. We ministered in our home for several years before having children, hosting Bible studies and frequently having guests in for meals and social occasions. These were times of great strengthening for us as we grew deeper in our own understanding of the Christian life. In fact, we became so serious about the Christian life that, when we started having children of our own, we stopped using our home to minister to others. With great piousness, I remember thinking, "We don't have time to minister in our home anymore. We need to disciple our own children." We had fallen into a trap that many Christian families encounter when their children are young. Let me explain.

There are some things in life that are products, and some that are by-products. Often, in retrospect, the by-products turn out to be the most important in the long run. For instance, few people who set out to create a famous or historical event ever do. Those who ultimately go down in history do so not because making history was their goal, but because there was something at the moment that needed to be done, and they did it.

The same is true in the spiritual life. Two things that the church is almost obsessed with, "fellowship" and "discipleship," rarely occur when those are the goals. They are most often produced over time as the by-products of another venture. For instance, if you have a service team in your church that meets together two Saturdays per month to keep the church facilities in shape, over time a real oneness—a koinonia or biblical fellowship—begins to develop between the members of the team. But if that same group simply gets together twice a month for the purpose of having "fellowship" (which usually means having doughnuts and coffee), they will gain some calories but probably little else. Fellowship arises out of unity of purpose, out of colaboring together in the gospel.

The same is true for discipleship. Jesus Christ declared that He came into the world to make disciples. He also stated that He came into the world to seek and save the lost (Luke 19:10), to serve and give His life a ransom for many (Mark 10:45), and to destroy the works of the devil (1 John 3:8). But He made disciples in the process by involving other people in a mission, a task, and a purpose which captured their hearts.

When we began to have children, I recognized that we have been given a mission by Jesus Christ. He has commanded us to take the gospel message of salvation into all the world and make disciples so that lost people may come back into a relationship with their Creator through the forgiveness of sin. If I am single, I do that by myself. If I get married, my wife and I do it together. If I have children, then *I get my children involved in the process of reaching out with God's love to those around us.*

I am not for a moment suggesting that I allow my wife or children be neglected for the sake of the gospel. Unfortunately, some in ministry have allowed that to happen. What I am suggesting is following the pattern that Jesus set for His own life and for the lives of His disciples: a balance between *mission* and *maintenance.*

In my mind, life can be divided into two overarching categories. *Mission* is what we see Jesus doing when He was directly involved in healing the sick, casting out demons, teaching the multitudes, confronting the Pharisees, and discipling the 12. But not even Jesus did this 24 hours a day. Scripture records a number of instances when He pulled away from the crowds, often with His disciples, for times of *maintenance*. They needed to rest, regroup, refresh, and refocus in order to remain effective in mission. Churches and families ought to have the same mentality. Life requires both mission and maintenance. Our challenge is to keep them in balance.

My mistake when we began to have children was thinking that my sole mission in life was to pour myself into my children's lives and stop reaching out and ministering to anyone else. I had gotten out of balance between mission and maintenance. I began to realize that we were becoming inwardly focused. Had not the Lord intervened, I would simply have reproduced my error in the lives of my children.

When I said to the Lord, "We don't have time to use our home for ministry," He said back, "No, Phil, you don't have time *not* to minister to people in your home." And then He proceeded to explain what He meant.

Teaching Ministry by Modeling Ministry

A few years after beginning to have children, Susy and I attended a CBMC couples' conference. We came home from the conference feeling convicted that the Lord really wanted us to become more involved in ministry. At that conference, it became obvious to us that, without realizing it, we had become isolated and less effective than we had been in ministry before having children.

As a result of that weekend conference, we began a Bible study in our home for young single adults from our church. This started a process of ministry in our family that I never could have imagined. Trust me when I tell you that I hadn't thought all this out. I had no grand plan. I didn't know that what the Lord was telling us to do had anything to do with discipling our children. Susy and I just felt that we needed to open our home for ministry as we had done earlier in our lives. In fact, I did so even a little hesitatingly, wanting to make sure that our "ministry" didn't encroach upon my "ministry" to my children.

I taught the Bible study on discipleship, and after six months, we had a group of young single adults so excited about sharing their faith that they decided to have an evangelistic outreach for their friends, family members, and coworkers at our home.

When we began making plans for whom to invite to the evangelistic gathering, we started thinking about our neighbors. Our children got involved by walking around the neighborhood with Susy and inviting the parents of their friends. At their age, I didn't sit down and explain maintenance and mission, I just said, "Hey, kids, we're inviting some of the parents of your friends and their families over for dinner to learn about Jesus. Let's go walk around to their houses and deliver the invitations, okay?" Of course, they didn't need to be asked twice. They gladly went—they were going to see their friends!

I began to realize that several things were happening at

Building Vision in Your Kids

✦ "God has something very special He wants you to do."

✦ "What do you suppose God is telling us?"

✦ "My job is to train you to listen to His direction, because you won't believe what He has in store for you to do!"

✦ "I can't wait to see the godly man or woman you will become."

✦ "You are going to have a great impact in this world for Jesus Christ."

✦ "I don't care if you make a big splash, as long as God counts you as one of His faithful ones."

once: We were evangelizing our neighbors, our kids were our warmest links to our adult neighbors, and our kids were involved in the evangelism process. To think I almost missed this by thinking it would have been more spiritual to teach my kids a Bible lesson on evangelism.

The next practical "clinic" that we got involved in was prayer. Now that the invitations had been delivered, we began praying for people to come. Getting the children involved in praying for their unsaved friends and their parents was more "on-the-job training" in our process of disciple-making. The children began to look at their friends, their parents, and their families in a whole new way. No longer were they just people in the neighborhood. Now they were people in the neighborhood who needed to know Jesus. And because our family knew Jesus, we became the spiritual link that could result in a spiritual connection. Our children, with no pressure from us, readily adopted the spiritual burden of praying for their friends' parents to come to the dinner. I was impressed—not with the children's spirituality, but with the process I saw unfolding around me.

When the night of the dinner arrived, everyone was pumped. We had borrowed lots of tables and chairs from the church. Some friends performed bluegrass music and we had piles of barbecue. Susy and I shared our testimonies in a casual and informal way. It was a great evening. Lots of neighbors met folks they hadn't known very well, the young adults in our Bible-study group practiced "friendship evangelism," and our kids got to see the Christian adults reaching out to others in a friendly and effective way. Bluegrass, barbecue, and backyard gospel. To think I had almost forfeited this ministry experience *with* my kids in order to minister *to* my kids.

After the dinner was over and all the guests had gone home, we began to look through the response cards that we had passed out to the guests. We had simply asked them to indicate whether they had placed their faith in Christ when we presented that opportunity after our testimonies. A number of our guests indicated they had prayed to receive Christ! And who do you think was as excited as anyone? Our kids. They had been praying for a couple of weeks for some of those people. But they also experienced the disappointment of some whom they had prayed for but who didn't accept Christ.

Around 11:00 p.m., as Susy was tucking our five-year-old son into bed, she said, "Paul, it's late, and I know you're tired. You don't have to pray tonight." He said, "No, I really want to pray, Mom." And this is what he prayed: "Dear Lord, I just ask that all those people who didn't accept You tonight would get another chance."

Susy told me later she thought to herself, *"Lord, I didn't think I had time to minister in my home because I was discipling my children. But if I really want our children to be sold out for You, I don't have time not to minister to others in my home. What better way for our children to see firsthand the joy and the fruit of giving one's life away to another."*

More Children's Ministry

Soon after the evangelistic dinner, we decided the most effective way of continuing to involve our children in ministry experience would be to involve them with their peer group. Since we had five children within six years of each other, we had a pretty tightly packed peer group of our own.

We had heard about Good News Clubs, which are Child Evangelism Fellowship's weekly Bible classes for children ages 5-12. The clubs are usually held in homes on a weekday afternoon during the school year. We had been exposed to the C.E.F. materials in our children's classes at the CBMC Family Conference we had attended for many years. It seemed like a good place to begin.

As much as Susy wanted our family to lead a club, she was really overwhelmed with her current responsibilities. Our children were ages 7, 5, 3, 1, and 1, we were still hosting the singles' Bible-study group in our home, and were in our second year of homeschooling. Susy was at her practical limit. So she called the local C.E.F. representative and said, "Our family would love to host a Good News Club, but I can't be the leader. If you could provide the teacher, we'll take care of the logistics, refreshments, and getting the kids there." C.E.F. was more than happy to team with Susy and the kids in putting on the club. They sent a wonderful teacher who came faithfully and did a marvelous job at communicating the truth of the gospel.

Just as we learned some valuable lessons through the evangelistic-dinner experience, the Lord was opening my eyes to some additional things about priorities. Remember, I had thought I was being obedient to Him earlier by backing out of ministry in our home. That was actually the problem in a nutshell. I was doing more thinking than I was listening. It was beginning to dawn on me that the largest part of our responsibility as Christians and as parents is to stop long enough to listen to His voice and discern how He is leading.

The Lord has continued to confirm to Susy and me over the years what we were beginning to learn back then. When I believe He is calling me to a ministry or project, but I feel that I'm too busy, then I need to do several things.

First, I need to assume that *whatever He is calling me to do is more important than anything else I am doing*. Sometimes we think God is like we are. For instance, if I need Susy to give me a hand with something, and I call out to her from another part of the house, I usually end up apologizing because I didn't know she had six other things going on at the same time. God is not like that. He knows everything we have going on at every moment, and is calling us in spite of what He knows. Therefore, I assume He is trying to get my attention for an important reason.

Second, I've learned that *I need to look over my schedule and ask the Lord what it is He wants me to change* so that I can obey Him. Maybe a commitment I've made can be changed, or maybe it's time to reevaluate a current priority. It is possible that some of the things I invest time doing in my life can be changed. That is doubly possible if it's something I have grown attached to. God is, after all, in charge. My life is His. If the Master wants me to reorder my life—well, that's what servants do.

Third, I asked the Lord to *show me what I need in order to obey Him*. Do I need new skills? Do I need additional resources? Do I need the abilities of another person who has gifts I don't have? It's a matter of saying, "Okay, Lord. I agree that we're going to do this. But I don't know how. Please give me practical wisdom to accomplish this thing we're going to do." I have never had that prayer go unanswered. God doesn't toy with us. He wouldn't call us to do something for Him without giving us what we need to do it.

Fourth, I've learned that *if I will make that commitment and accept what I feel the Lord is prompting me to do, then He can do miraculous things with my schedule*. I have abused that principle in the past, which is very dangerous to do. But at the same time I have seen that when I do keep my life in balance, He has supernaturally rearranged my schedule. I have seen Him save time for me when I least expected it. Of course, He is the Master of time, so I shouldn't be so surprised.

We had a number of children come to Christ during the two years we had our Good News Club in Atlanta, and not only did we see spiritual things happening with the children who attended, but we found a growing spiritual interest on the part of the children's parents. Some of the same adults who had turned down our invitations to come to church, attend a Bible study, or go to hear a Christian speaker suddenly became more open to spiritual things because their children were involved in the Good News Club. That, of course, gave us an entrance into their lives. It was just one more way the Lord confirmed getting involved with our children in ministry was His plan for us.

Our family, though far from perfect, represented a little patch of light or hope to some others. Warts and all, we were demonstrating to others that it was possible to be married, raise kids, be happy, be spiritual, and be good neighbors and friends—without being totally weird. We experienced the truth that the normal Christian life, at least at the family level, is just "doing the stuff Jesus did" with everybody involved. Be honest, be transparent, be friendly, be generous, be kind, and a hungry-for-hope world will beat a path to your door. That's what happened when we decided to get back in the ministry—kids and all.

Moving On Up

By the time Susy and the kids had finished a couple years of Good News Clubs and we had continued to experience the great fruit of the young single adult Bible study in our home, we were hooked. You couldn't have dragged me with wild horses into the mentality of "cutting back on ministry in order to minister to my children." When we moved from Atlanta to our present home in Chattanooga in 1991, and had to leave behind the Good News Club we had been hosting, we began going through CBMC's life-style evangelistic program called Living Proof. Although the program is actually designed for adults, we felt our children could profit from it. We joined another homeschooled family and went through the 12 sessions together.

The Living Proof materials are especially interesting to older children since each of the sessions includes a 15-minute video. The videos track the experiences of a Christian couple who are making an effort to reach a non-Christian couple that has moved in next door. The videos are exceptionally well-produced, and pull at all the same heartstrings as would the finest television drama. Since today's older children are so used to seeing drama on television, the videos are perfect for the "media generation." You laugh and cry with the characters in the video as they go through the ups and downs of life from both a spiritual and a nonspiritual perspective. By the time our children saw the Living Proof videos, they had come in contact with so many varied evangelistic and family situations that they totally understood the conflicts and resolution presented in the videos. It was a true blessing to see our children watching these training videos so intently, knowing they had personally been involved in similar situations in our outreach efforts as a family.

When we finished the Living Proof series, the children began praying for their friends on their softball and base-ball teams. All it took was for the kids to begin praying for the salvation of their friends for Susy to become interested in starting another Good News Club. This time, Susy decided she was ready to teach it herself. Plus, she felt the children were old enough to begin assuming some respon-sibility for the club and helping in different ways. We agreed this was the next step for our family's ministry together—giving the children an even more active role in reaching their friends for Christ.

Susy enrolled in C.E.F.'s teacher training course on how to evangelize children effectively. She was given creative ideas on making the Good News Club both fun and spiri-tually challenging, as well as clear instructions on how to sensitively lead a child to Christ. Once our Signal Mountain Good News Club was organized, we invited both neigh-borhood children and those who were on our children's softball and baseball teams. Since many of the children invited have mothers who work, the majority ride a bus to school each day—a lengthy, time-consuming process. So Susy organized car pools with other mothers on the after-noon we have Good News Club, which allows her to develop relationships with the mothers.

All the kids who were coming to the club were picked up at school so we could "redeem the time" by getting them to our house as quickly as possible. This car-pool caravan became quite a weekly event for the kids. In fact, on club day, one of the little boys called Susy from the principal's office at school. This eight-year-old was in a panic: "Mrs. Downer, today is Good News Club, and you forgot to call me and tell me who I'm supposed to ride with to Good News Club." He wasn't about to miss club.

Besides our own six, we had approximately 20 children coming to the club. At first, Susy kept them all together in one large meeting, but then experimented with dividing them into an older and a younger group. It worked beautifully, as some of the older children have gotten involved in leadership, helping with younger children, assisting with the Bible lesson and the play times, and serving refreshments. Abigail assumed the role of teaching the Bible verse and missionary story, with the other four children helping Susy with the Bible lesson and lead the songs. It was a wonderful experience for Abigail at such a young age to take on the role of "teacher" for the younger children and it was an incredibly stretching experience for Matt, Anna, and Josh to learn to stand up and teach Bible truths to their peer group. In this setting, Susy and our children have really functioned as a team to lead the club and minister to the kids who attend.

Nuts and Bolts of Success

Of course, having a Good News Club takes time. What worthwhile task in life doesn't? But the results that we have seen in our children's lives have made the time we've invested seem trivial. Here are just some of the things that have impacted our children through our hosting a Good News Club in our home:

1. *They are learning the Word and not just hearing the Word.* They are learning it within a format designed just for children. The stories, illustrations, songs, and teaching aids—everything is geared toward giving a child an understanding of Scripture. When I think how much more effectively they are learning the Word than if I had been their sole teacher, I praise the Lord. I love to teach, but teaching children is the calling and gift of C.E.F. I would be foolish not to take advantage of what they have to offer my kids.

2. *They are learning to communicate the Word.* Whether it is Abigail actually teaching a verse, or the other children helping with the lesson, the children are getting the opportunity for "on-the-job training" in communicating truth.

When Susy started the club each child was quite panicky and "wooden" about presenting just three or four sentences in front of the group. Over the years, as they gained experience and confidence, they have been increasingly able to speak extemporaneously as they travel with me.

3. They are learning to serve. Paul was in charge of a group of boys one club meeting, and one of the kids found a Nerf gun. He began shooting everybody, even during the story time. When my son asked him politely to stop, this kid shot him right in the eye. "How did you feel about that, Paul?" I asked him. "I wanted to strangle him," he told me. "But I knew that if I had done that, or yelled at him, or not forgiven him, then the Lord would not have been able to use that situation in a way that would have been effective for him later. If I were to teach or say something about how God can give us self-control, he wouldn't hear it. He would just remember me yelling at him. So I bit my tongue, and we went on with the lesson."

4. They are learning compassion. One boy, a ten-year-old bruiser, caused trouble at some of the meetings. I remember one day everyone was complaining, "Did you see William do this? Did you see William do that?" One by one our kids said, "Somebody ought to discipline William. If he were my kid, I would spank him. I wonder why his dad isn't teaching him some discipline." Because one of our goals for our children is to see them develop compassion for people, I said, "Look, guys, I wasn't excited about William coming to Good News Club either. But your mom saw a vision to reach a little boy that had needs. What chance does William have if every time he messes up, people turn away from him? God wants us to reach out to William the same way He reaches out to us when we mess up. Maybe our family can be a little bit of the family William doesn't have right now."

5. They are learning that people can change for the better with Christ. Frank was mean, rude, and just no fun to be around when he started coming to club. Then he became a Christ-ian, and you wouldn't believe it was the same kid. Just to see him grow and soften, and to see the Lord make him so much sweeter and gentler has been a blessing to our entire family. At one meeting, when Susy asked the kids if any would like to share their testimony about how they became a Christian, Frank's hand was the first one up.

6. *They are learning that God can change families.* After accepting the Lord, one little boy begged his father to go to church until he finally agreed. His father hadn't been to church in 20 years. Another little boy who was saved in the club is faithfully praying for his father who he says is not a Christian. This little boy is just five years old. Here's what our children are seeing: Kids from hurting homes come to our house and find love and encouragement. Then they start taking their newfound spiritual perspective back to their own homes. We've seen this cycle time and time again.

7. *They are learning about sowing and reaping.* We had a friend call and tell us that on his recent trip to Israel, one of the teenagers in their group had asked to be baptized in the Jordan River. When she gave her testimony, she told every-one that she had been saved when she was eight years old at our Atlanta Good News Club. Her story helped our chil-dren see that spiritual seeds sown in our backyard could lead to a testimony halfway around the world. They are beginning to understand that God is a Tapestry-weaver, knotting and tying threads together on the back side of life to produce a beautiful picture on the front side for eternity!

8. *They are learning that leadership requires sacrifice.* As part of the leadership team for the Good News Club, our children have had to begin preparation early and clean up late, get everything ready and help put it away. They've also discovered (to their chagrin) that they can't ask other children to "behave" and then get involved themselves in

goofing around. But they're also learning that leaders have
to keep growing spiritually. Because they've seen so many
children take spiritual giant steps as a result of coming to
club—learning to offer prayers aloud, memorizing Scripture verses, reading their Bible, inviting other friends to
club—they have had to redouble their own efforts to keep
growing spiritually. There's nothing like a little peer pressure to keep us all accountable and growing.

   9. *They are learning that God will use anybody who's willing.*
We remind our children that God is not using our family
because we are unique or superspiritual. Our kids know all
too well that our family has its share of struggles, and that
their parents are not saints in disguise. Sin is alive and well
in the Downer household. That's the whole point. Because
we do fail at times, we can point the kids to Romans 5:20
and remind them it is always God's grace that allows us to
accomplish anything good for Him. If we sin, we don't wal-
low in it. We confess it, ask forgiveness, purpose not to do
it again, ask for more of God's grace to empower us, and
get moving—"Let's go, club's starting!" We want our children to know God will use—in fact *prefers* to use—weak
vessels like us. He gets all the more glory when He does.

God Still Changes Lives
Think back to your own early years. What captured the
coveted spots in your long-term memory? Something
scary? Something happy? Something sad? Probably some
of all three, and a lot more. One of our most important tasks
as parents is to so involve our kids in life—and I mean real
life, not TV, movies, and video games—that their memory
banks are overflowing with fruitful and positive remem-
brances of what they accomplished as children. Don't
accuse me of being idealistic here. We've got to aim high if
we're going to hit the target at all. Susy and I want our children to look back on their developmental years in our family and be *amazed* at what we did and what they learned. I
don't want them to be like so many young people who,

when asked to describe their childhood, sort of look at you with a blank stare. Honestly, it's as if they can't remember the last ten years! The reality is that perhaps those years weren't very stimulating, weren't very happy, and weren't very, well, memorable.

Perhaps I'm driven by my own memories of childhood. I remember the precise spot on our driveway where I stood as a ten-year-old when I made a decision never to hug my dad again. I also decided I would never cry again. It happened on the day my dad introduced me to the woman who would be my new mother. My real mother had attempted suicide and was in a mental hospital, but she was still my mother, and I didn't want a new one. My memories run generally downhill from there.

There are children being forced to choose between going with their mom or their dad today, every day, in this country. Their hearts and minds are being filled with memories that will haunt them, not help them, for the rest of their lives. And those children will reach adulthood trailing a string of painful memories behind them—memories they will pass on to their own kids one way or the other.

We must first, in our own families, do everything we can to give our children what God wants them to have: hope, love, security, and a family that is making a difference. Then we must teach them to reach out to those who hurt—to provide a shelter from the storms that are raging against the lives of children by the thousands. If we don't, those children will do what I did.

I took the anger and frustration I felt as a child and carried it throughout a tumultuous series of transitions in my life as a young adult. I went off to college and flunked out—the college where my father had been student body president. I went to Vietnam and compounded my rage by seeing many of my friends die before my eyes. I came home and tried to atone for my failures—and my father's—by getting back in school and working hard and marrying Susy. We acted like the perfect married couple. We attended church. I taught Sunday school and served as an elder. But the perfection was short-lived. On the second day of our married life, Susy began considering a divorce. She realized she had married a ticking time bomb, and that she needed to get out before it went off. She stuck it out for five years, but as a woman with a crushed heart.

What was wrong with me? What was I doing to my wife? What was I doing to myself? I had so much turmoil bottled up inside me from my youth that I couldn't contain it. It was seeping out and poisoning my marriage, and would have poisoned my children.

And then God saved me—and my family—from myself. A man invited me to attend a CBMC luncheon where a Christian businessman was speaking, and I caught a glimpse of the peace that I had been seeking for so many years. Several months later I received Christ as my Lord and Savior. Susy couldn't believe the changes she began to see in me, and she received Christ, too. As we began to walk with God, He started putting our lives back together. Actually, He started from scratch, because there was almost nothing left to build upon.

Susy asked God to give her a new love for me, which He did. We learned how to love one another, and discovered how God intended for life and marriage to be. We both were so hungry for real, genuine life—the life that God created us to know—that we soaked up God, His Word, and His love like dry blotters. Since we didn't have children yet, we began to reach out to others, which is the story I told at the beginning of this chapter. Do you understand better now why I was tempted to retreat when Susy and I started having children? I didn't want to get so busy, even with being a Christian, that I would sacrifice my kids the way I felt I had been sacrificed. I wanted to protect them, but in reality I was trying to protect myself.

Gradually, as God began to free me from the prison of my past, I began to look at my own children in a more relaxed fashion. I began to sense that God was going to help our family keep together. Susy and I were learning to live with and love each other. Our first children were doing okay. We were making it. I was learning to trust God. I learned to release my fears and my memories and believe that if we got in step with what He wanted for us, our children would be safe—far safer than with me trying to engineer a protected, pain-free childhood for each of them. I saw that God could heal our family's pain, and in seeing that, I discovered He was giving us enough love to help heal others' pain as well. The more we reached out, the healthier we became. It was as if the medicine we needed came to us in doses tied to giving away our health to others. That's how and why we began to involve our children in ministry.

Teach Your Children Well

I referred earlier in this book to Judges 2:10, which describes an entire generation in Israel that was lost because their parents failed to tell them about God. They didn't know the Lord nor His works. In this country our children are growing up without knowing the Lord or His work around the world. The parents in Israel failed to teach their children to "love the Lord your God with all your heart and with all your soul and with all your might," so the generation was lost, and eventually the nation. No nation is ever more than a generation away from destruction.

Kids today are being parented by their peers. They are lying down with Leno and Letterman, and rising with the radio shock jocks. If there is going to be a spiritual next generation tomorrow, we're going to have to teach them the truth today, then show them how to minister to those who have no one to teach them.

We are witnessing the last vestiges of parents in this country who have faint memories of the Eisenhower era, the idyllic 1950s. Christianity was respected, most families attended church regularly, and the culture at large supported many biblical values. With a modicum of instruction from home and church, the average family could turn their children out into society and stand a decent chance that they would succeed. The last echoes of this sad strategy are too faint to even hear, yet some Christian parents still think this will work. But it will not work. It probably never worked, not even in the fifties. As the Christian theologian and apologist Francis Schaeffer told us in the 1970s, we have entered a post-Christian era in America. Parents who think that society is going to help raise their children are in for a rude awakening.

We must minister diligently to our own children, and get them involved in ministering to others. Susy and I didn't want to rely on our children just catching a vision for ministry from the ministry we as parents were doing. We thought it would be more effective if they would do it themselves—if ministry became an extension of their lives, not just ours. So we have looked for ways to put the children into ministry. I thought I didn't have time for home ministry because I was discipling my children. But if I really want them to catch a vision for giving their lives away to others, I don't have time *not* to open my home for ministry.

When we look over the goals we have for our family—including that the children would learn the Word and be able to communicate it—we have seen over and over how effectively ministry helps us reach those goals. It gives them truth and the confidence to impart it. It gets them actively loving and serving others, and causes them to focus on someone else's needs. Home ministry has made them more aware of the non-Christians around us, and has given them a vision for the lost.

May your home and mine remain a lighthouse of salvation for those in a dark world.

Quotable Quotes

✦ *Your Wife Called:* In the community at the bottom of Signal Mountain, a sign at the bakery said, "Your wife called and said to pick up some bread." Down the street, a second sign in front of the Baskin-Robbins retorted, "Your wife called and said, 'Forget the bread. Bring home ice cream!' "

✦ *Correct, Not Very Polite*: Joshua, attempting to reassure Phil on his fiftieth birthday, offered what he thought was a compliment: "Wow, Dad, you may not look that old, but you are!"

✦ *Legal Action Threatened:* Actual voice-mail message on the CBMC message center for Derrick Merck: "Hi, Mr. Merck, this is Joshua Downer. My basketball got run over. My dad, who you know drives a CBMC leased van, came home and I helped him unload CBMC materials from the CBMC van when my dad was returning from a CBMC trip. My responsibility is to help him unload when he has too much to carry. In doing that, I carried certain CBMC materials as he instructed, which required me to put down my basketball in the driveway in his plain sight before I took the CBMC materials into the house. Sometime later, Abigail, while driving the other van which used to be a CBMC van, drove over my basketball, exploding it. And Mr. Merck, I was just wondering, does CBMC have an insurance policy, and if so, how can I make a claim for my basketball?"

✦ *From Fee to Free:* Not particularly impressed that her two brothers Josh and Matt were declaring themselves aspiring young lawyers, one of their sisters was heard to say, "Well, they might as well get paid for arguing . . . they do it so naturally anyway."

Study Questions

1. How did your life change when you met the Lord?

2. Who discipled you? How did they do it? Who are you discipling?

3. Why do you think ministry involvement fosters spiritual growth?

4. What sort of ministry would you like to do with your family?

5. How would you respond to a man who said, "I don't have time for outside ministry. I'm too busy working on my own family"?

12

Getting Ready to Change the World

*B*ehold, children are a gift of the LORD; the fruit of the womb is a reward. Like arrows in the hand of a warrior, so are the children of one's youth. How blessed is the man whose quiver is full of them; they shall not be ashamed, when they speak with their enemies in the gate (Psalm 127:3-5).

I have always appreciated the metaphors in Scripture having to do with soldiering—not just because I was in the Marines, mind you, but because I see the Christian life as a war. For example, Psalm 127 talks about our children becoming like arrows in the hands of a warrior, and Paul refers to Epaphroditus, Timothy, and Archippus as soldiers for Christ. Why did Scripture's authors choose soldiering as a metaphor for the spiritual life?

Certainly, military metaphors were readily available in the ancient world, especially during Old Testament times. Warfare was a constant part of life for Israel in the early days of her monarchy. By the time of Christ and the apostles, Rome and her soldiers were omnipresent parts of life in the Middle East. But was it just the presence of soldiers and the ready familiarity with military images which made the writers choose these metaphors? Certainly there were other equally familiar occupations, objects, and events to choose from. I think there was something about "soldiering" that went beyond the mere familiarity of the image in the geopolitical environment of the day.

The most amazing insight regarding this in Scripture is Jesus' conversation with a Roman soldier (Matthew 8:5-13). When the soldier's servant was about to die, he asked for Jesus' help. Jesus was about to go to the soldier's house and heal the servant when the soldier intervened: "Lord, I do not deserve to have you come under my roof. But just say the word, and my servant will be healed. For I myself am a man under authority, with soldiers under me. I tell this one, 'Go,' and he goes; and that one, 'Come,' and he comes. I say to my servant, 'Do this,' and he does it" (NIV). The text of Scripture then says that Jesus was astonished at the soldier's words: "I tell you the truth, I have not found anyone in Israel with such great faith."

Jesus and the Roman soldier connected on the level of *soldiering*. I think there was something in the world of a Roman soldier that allowed him to understand perfectly the world of Jesus Christ. It absolutely amazed the Lord. Why? Because here was a Roman soldier who seemed to understand more about the kingdom of God than any of the top people in the nation of Israel, who should have understood the kingdom better than anyone. The Roman soldier had obviously heard that the Jewish rabbi named Jesus had the power to heal people. Otherwise, he wouldn't have come to ask Jesus to heal his servant. We get no indication from the text that he was a religious or spiritually-minded person. But that didn't keep him from having great respect for Jesus' power to heal. Even if he didn't know *how* Jesus healed, the soldier knew *that* Jesus could heal—every time. He knew, for whatever reason, that Jesus Christ had the *authority* to heal people. There are tremendous parallels between soldiering in the Roman army and soldiering in the kingdom of God.

Listen again to the soldier's words to Jesus: "I myself am a man under authority, with soldiers under me. . . ." In other words, he was saying to Jesus, "Look, Jesus, You don't need to trouble Yourself by coming all the way to my house. I understand how authority works, and I know You have authority over disease. In fact, You seem to have the same authority over disease that I have over my soldiers. When I say jump, they ask 'How high?' I speak, they obey. When You speak, diseases obey. I don't know why they do, but I know they do, and that's good enough for me. So save Yourself a trip. Distance doesn't negate Your authority. Your command will be as effective here as it will be at my house."

Now do you understand why Jesus was amazed at this guy's faith? It was on the subject of authority that the two shared an equal understanding. Both the kingdom of Rome and the kingdom of God operated on the basis of authority, and therefore one is a useful metaphor for the other. But that is only one reason why soldiering is a good metaphor for the spiritual life. Think of all the other aspects of becoming and living as a soldier that apply to the spiritual life as well: discipline, training, teamwork, a mission, victories, defeats, suffering, obstacles to the mission, the presence of an enemy, perseverance, weapons, alertness, strategies, chain of command. Do you see the parallels? All of these military terms are referred to in Scripture as having application in our spiritual lives.

We can develop children who are soldiers for the Lord. Our families can make an eternal impact on the world. To do that, we'll need to understand a number of characteristics that make good soldiers—whether in the Marines, the armies of Rome, or the kingdom of God.

Discipline

The number-one characteristic of well-trained soldiers is discipline. The biblical concept of discipline is not punishment or harsh treatment. Rather, discipline is the consistent training, the setting of boundaries and parameters, which leads to success. Discipline is what the Roman soldier knew would cause his soldiers to respond to his commands. Yet discipline is tied to authority, for authority has the right to insist on a response to commands.

As with any raw bunch of recruits which enters the military, our children come into the world needing training. In the Marines, at least, there is an assumption that recruits are a blank slate upon which the concept of soldiering is going to be written. You might be a good person or a bad person when you enter the Marines—it really doesn't matter. All that matters is that you're not a Marine. It is assumed that you know nothing and need to be taught everything. Then training begins.

I grew up with the concept of the greenhouse approach to child-rearing. I assumed that you had these little plants that grew up from seeds and you provided them with a nice environment, watered them twice a day, and they would grow into fine adult children. Of course, that would require stopping plagues, spraying for insects, and pulling away weeds; but basically, once started, the growth process would go in the proper direction. The Marines don't assume that, and neither does Scripture. In fact, Scripture assumes that when children are born they are headed totally in the wrong direction. "Foolishness is bound up in the heart of a child," Proverbs says (22:15). So with our children, there is a definite need for instilling discipline which leads to training.

Susy and I started instilling discipline in our children very early. I've always felt sorry for the oldest kids in any family, because they are like the lead goose in a V-formation. They're having to cut through the wind first in order to make it easier for the ones following. But training the first kids well does make it easier on the younger children who come along. If the older ones have been disciplined (trained), then the younger ones pick up the good behavior patterns. But the young ones still test the system. The challenge for parents, after years of disciplining the earliest children, is not to give up. I have seen in many families a tendency to start off with the first child or two with strong convictions about discipline, only to have the convictions get watered down with each successive child.

However, one of the most *ineffective* things to do is to discipline without a relationship. If you discipline without a relationship of love, you often get resentment and anger. It's like the child is saying, "Wait a minute. Who are you? You haven't earned the right to discipline me!" They would have the same response if a total stranger walked into the house and tried to discipline them. I am not saying that, from an authority point of view, parents have to earn the right to discipline. But from a family's point of view, the relationship is the key to the receiving and applying of the discipline. (Of course, this analogy between soldiering and the family eventually breaks down. In the military, the drill instructor doesn't care if you think you're loved when he yells at you. And I wouldn't recommend saying back, "Who are you to yell at me?" However, there is a commitment, a closeness, and a trust that develops among soldiers who serve together.)

I have a friend who destroyed his relationship with his kids. He had let too many things, over a period of time, come between them. Their relationship was shot. So to fix the situation, he literally spent one whole year "on the carpet" with his kids, wrestling, playing, reading, talking— just rebuilding his relationships. He did minimal amounts of disciplining that year, but it seemed the more time he spent with the kids the less they needed discipline. It worked. He won his kids back. After "earning" the right to exercise authority over them by consistently demonstrating love over a long period of time, he was able to impact their lives and discipline them.

Remember: The ultimate goal of discipline is not the elimination of bad behavior; it is the incorporation of godly behavior. So if the children's speech became hurtful toward one another, or biting or sarcastic, we would ask them to memorize a Scripture verse on wise speech and kind words. Or if they were being an irritation to one another, rather than a blessing to one another, we would have them learn a verse on being a positive blessing in each other's lives. Once they had memorized the verse, it gave us a reference point when future infractions occurred: "Did your speech just edify and build up your sister? What should you have said instead of the words you used? Since God has called us to be a blessing to one another, tell me what sort of blessing you are being to your brother right now. And what could you do to be a blessing to him?" We also used the technique of asking the offender to serve the person they offended for the next hour, to clean up a room or do a chore for him or her. Obviously, different children will respond more positively to one type of discipline than to another, and it is up to us as parents to find the key to each child's behavioral heart.

Two principles are essential in this area. First, Hebrews 12:3 says, "For consider Him who has endured such hostility by sinners against Himself, so that you may not grow weary and lose heart." When we lose heart or grow weary of being righteous, we have to consider that Christ died for us on the cross. We have a saying around our house. We say, "What do we deserve? We deserve the cross." All of us, including my precious children, deserve the cross. It was our sins that put Christ there. Sometimes my kids will say, "I don't deserve this. That's not fair." I will say, "Wait, wait! What do we deserve?" They will say, "Well, we deserve the cross." It takes our focus off "fair" and puts it on what Christ did for us.

The other principle is found in 1 Peter 3:17. It says, "For it is better, if God should will it so, that you suffer for doing what is right rather than for doing what is wrong." Therefore, if we do wrong and suffer for it and take it patiently, of what credit is it? But if we do right and suffer for it and take it patiently, then we have God's approval. Those two Scripture verses undercut the "it's not fair" routine because what's "fair" is for all of us to be dragged out and hung on a telephone pole right now—kids included, once they reach the age of accountability.

If you get stuck in the "it's not fair" cycle, just stop, devalue the currency down to zero, and start over. Discipline those who need it when they need it, with as much justice as you can. Since "fairness" is not a kingdom value, you are not obligated to spend a lot of time seeking it.

One final word on discipline: I want to so live my life before my children that they cannot use my behavior as an excuse for their own. Granted, we as parents are not perfect, and we are not to suggest to our children that we are the standard they should look at. Christ is their only standard. But if I am correcting them for unkind words or a bad attitude or a slovenly spirit, I do not want them to say, "But, Dad, I've heard you use that word before." This is simply being consistent. If I am not going to obey the speed limit, then I won't carry a whole lot of moral weight with my children when I correct their lead-footed ways. It simply does not work in raising children to have a walk that is different from our talk. That's a well-worn message, but because it is biblical (James 2:14-17), it is worth repeating.

Esprit de Corps

Perhaps no branch of the military service is better known for esprit de corps than the Marines. I confess it is a powerful tool for motivating a group to accomplish a goal. Though we wouldn't necessarily use that term with our children, we should teach them about the equivalent in the family: *attitude*. Griping, complaining, lack of repentance, whining, fussing—all these normal expressions are symptomatic of a common childhood disease called "bad attitude" (of course, it's known to afflict adults as well).

How do you deal with a child who does not have a repentant attitude? Since a good attitude is the goal, how do you help the child change his attitude? On one occasion, Josh and Matt had some words with each other over an issue. After hearing both sides of the story, Susy told Josh she thought he was wrong and needed to apologize to his brother. He really didn't think he was wrong, but he said he was sorry anyway, with an "I'm-sitting-down-on-the-outside-but-standing-up-on-the-inside" kind of attitude. Susy said, "Sorry, Josh. I can tell you're not convinced in your heart that you were wrong. Your apology wasn't sincere. I want you to go to your room and pray and think about this, and ask the Lord to give you the right attitude toward Matt in your heart. Then come back and let's talk." So he did that and he came out in about five minutes. He sort of harumphed and said, "I'm sorry." My wife told him, "Well, that was a little bit better, but that still didn't do it, Joshua." He then said something disrespectful and had to be punished. Hours later, he admitted he was genuinely sorry.

There's a lot of gray area here in methodology, but not in the ultimate goal. The biblical principle about sins of the heart is found in Hebrews 12:15: "See . . . that . . . no root of bitterness springing up causes trouble, and by it many be defiled." However you work with your children to get their attitudes corrected, don't fail to do so. If you give them an hour to cool down in their room, don't get busy and forget to go back. Attitudes go sour sometimes, and they need to

---

Soldiers for Christ

✦ 1 Corinthians 9:7: "Who at any time serves as a *soldier* at his own expense? Who plants a vineyard, and does not eat the fruit of it? Or who tends a flock and does not use the milk of the flock?"

✦ Philippians 2:25: "But I thought it necessary to send to you Epaphroditus, my brother and fellow worker and *fellow soldier*, who is also your messenger and minister to my need."

✦ Philemon 1:2: "To Apphia our sister, and to Archippus our *fellow soldier*, and to the church in your house."

✦ 2 Timothy 2:3-4: "Suffer hardship with me, as *a good soldier of Christ Jesus*. No soldier in active service entangles himself in the affairs of everyday life, so that he may please the one who enlisted him as a soldier."

be corrected. That way reconciliation can take place, sin can be laid aside, and life can go on. But attitudes that are allowed to fester will normally spread more poison later. Children should not be allowed to live in the "no-man's-land" between a good attitude and a bad attitude. They need to know the beautiful fruit of the Holy Spirit will be manifest in our lives if we are filled with the Holy Spirit. If love, joy, peace, patience, and the rest of the fruit is missing, we need to discover why. "I'm having a bad day" should not be the reason!

Susy's been good about helping the kids with their attitudes. I look more at behavior, but she really watches out for wrong attitudes. Because we homeschool our kids, we are with them quite a bit. Susy in particular gets to spend much time with the children. When she's with them all day and gives them instructions and chores to do, how can she keep from using a bad tone of voice and having a quarrelsome attitude herself? We have tried to make this a priority of prayer. I ask the Lord to keep me from using a negative tone of voice, and Susy and I pray for each other that we will not do this. Get the children involved in the process. Ask them what they need to work on, and then hold each other accountable throughout the day. Invite your kids to respectfully remind you when your voice or attitude begins to get toward the edge of acceptability. When children see that their parents are willing to admit areas of weakness and to discuss them freely, it will help them open up about their own needs.

Sarcasm is humor at someone else's expense. When Susy and I got married, we were very sarcastic back and forth to each other. Sarcasm sows a seed we don't want in our kids or in our marriage. If you are a married couple and you cut each other verbally back and forth, your kids will do the same thing to their siblings—and to you. If you come home and dig at your wife and make sarcastic comments, you are communicating to your sons that you don't respect their mother and they don't have to respect her either. They begin to think it is okay to laugh at Mom. Sarcasm breeds disrespect. A godly man once told me to get the sarcasm out of my marriage. I did, no questions asked. Sometimes I will start getting sarcastic again, and then one of our boys will say something sarcastic. Right away I realize they are just modeling my behavior. If I straighten up, so will they.

Promotions

When you advance from rank to rank in the military, there is a tremendous sense of pride and accomplishment, especially if you advance ahead of the normal schedule. But promotions have to be earned.

Now I'm not suggesting that families assign ranks to their children ("Private Billy, take care of the dishes after supper." "Yes, sir!"). That's not how a family works. But here is a very helpful way to promote your children from one level of responsibility and maturity to another. Susy and I have found this to be one of the most positive things we've done, especially when some rewards are attached to the promotions, which I'll describe later. Having "handles" to put on our children's phases of life is helpful. We never use these "labels" in any sense except the most informal, and we almost always try to use them as verbs, not as nouns, so that they are descriptive of behavior and responsibility, not a category. Let me summarize the five levels of promotion that we use before describing them in more detail.

The first step in developing a mature soldier for Christ is developing a *worker*. We have found between the ages of six and eight that helping the children become good workers is an achievable goal for them. From eight to ten years of age, we have tried to help our kids become *managers*— not only to do a job, but to motivate others to work alongside and learn to manage the assets and people available to accomplish the task. The next stage, from 10 to 12, is to become a *leader*. Here we're talking about actually guiding, leading, and directing what work will be done and offering a vision for getting the task completed. The fourth step, from 12 to 14, is to become a *discipler*. That goes beyond just leading workers, into actually being part of God's plan to develop other people into workers for Christ. That could mean to disciple someone or mentor someone in secular endeavors. Once they have become disciplers, the next step would be to see our children become *soldiers*, willing to lay down their rights, their fleshly desires, and their very lives for the call of Christ.

1. Learning to work. When I joined the Marines, I realized my mother had taken care of me most of my life. I could not even sew on a button. It was a rude awakening on the first Sunday when we did not get to watch football all day. We were given a scrub brush and a bucket and sent to the water stalls to hand-scrub our own clothes, which we dried by the sun and wore the next day. I will never forget thinking that I did not need to thoroughly rinse my clothes and finding out the next day that my crotch was on fire from the soap rash I had developed from not rinsing my trousers well enough. I found sewing on buttons to be an incredibly difficult task, especially when you put the button in the wrong place. The whole shirt is crooked as a result. I grew up knowing how to water-ski, play some sports, and date girls. But I didn't know anything about how to be a worker. The Marines had to teach me that before I was qualified to do anything, especially get into battle.

I am committed to teaching our kids to work, and have found from six to eight to be the ideal age. At that point they are able to understand simple instructions and accomplish a task. So we set out to teach our kids how to work, and guess what happened. We found that our kids did not naturally want to work (surprise!), and that they needed to be shown *how* to work (surprise again!).

For instance, I had been working with Paul on learning how to do the dishes. The first thing I found out was that verbal instructions are not very effective in teaching kids how to work. Just to tell Paul to clean up his room was really meaningless. I had to get down on my hands and knees and show him how to do it. Showing him how to clean the bathroom floor was more effective than telling him to "clean this place up." Also, in doing the dishes, I needed to show him exactly how to apply the soap, scrub each dish, and put the food down the disposal. Once we got the mechanics down, however, I was still faced with the problem that Paul didn't like to work. Right after dinner, about the time the dishes were to be washed, Paul began to say he needed to go to the bathroom. After several weeks of this consistent routine, I realized he was using the bathroom as an excuse to get out of working. So we were out doing dishes one night and Paul said, "Dad, I need to go to the bathroom."

"No, Paul, you can't go to the bathroom until you finish the dishes."

"Dad, I have to go to the bathroom."

"No, you are going to have to do the dishes first."

"Well, I am just going to go to the bathroom right here."

"Fine. If you go right here we will clean that up after we do the dishes, but you will complete the job of cleaning the dishes."

I simply had to draw a line and let him know that avoiding work was unacceptable. If he wanted to go to the bathroom, he could go before dinner or after the dishes were done. Several years later when we went back to that house, I heard him point out the small bathroom to one of his friends: "That's where I used to hide out to avoid doing the dishes."

Another lesson I learned was not to expect what I didn't inspect. Often I would go back after I thought Paul had finished a job, only to discover that it hadn't been done. But then there was the day when he was about eight years old that we were moving from one house to another. I gave Paul very precise instructions to clean the basement, which was a dirt-floor room. My instructions were to move a certain number of items to different places and then to rake and sweep the floor. I will never forget when I went to check on his progress. He met me at the door, dirty from head to foot, and beamed, "Dad, look at that. Isn't it beautiful?" We surveyed the basement together, and indeed it was beautifully done. When I saw the twinkle of satisfaction in his eye, I realized that was the day Paul became a worker.

Because we are created in God's image, each one of us has an inner desire for excellence and order—even our young children. One of the greatest things we can do as parents is help our children experience the satisfaction of "a job well done."

2. *Learning to manage.* Abigail, as the first child, seemed to be a natural worker. We never had to remind her to begin or complete her tasks. Because she liked to do things herself, our challenge with Abigail was helping her become a manager. As the first child, she worked hard to gain our approval, so her desire was not to share the job and therefore share the credit, which is necessary to be a good manager. So we had to work hard to explain to her that, since she had become such a good worker, we really needed her to help her younger brothers and sisters learn what she had mastered. She could not be a good manager if she did all the work herself, but only if she got others to help along the way and they became diligent in their own right.

As Abigail developed as a manager, and Paul developed as a worker, Susy and I realized we now had two excellent resources on our side in accomplishing the myriad tasks that it takes to run a busy home. Often parents who never teach their kids to work are continually involved in taking care of the children without much reciprocity on their part.

After Abigail developed as a manager, we then began to encourage Matthew as a worker. In that process, Matthew and Paul learned something about managing. Because Matthew is our people person, and Paul is very task-oriented (on the tasks he likes), they would hit rough water whenever they tried to work on a task together. When the two of them were working on a fort in the backyard, just prior to some guests arriving at our home for the evening, Matthew would continually lay down his tools and run into the house to see if our guests and their kids had arrived. He was far more interested in meeting and greeting than he was in sweating on the fort with Paul. This, of course, was a great irritation to Paul, who ultimately lost his temper and lashed out at Matthew. Paul didn't care much about the arrival of the guests, and certainly didn't want Matthew bringing them to see the fort for fear they would mess up what he had worked so hard on. In reflecting on this incident later, we were able to help both boys see that everyone has different strengths and abilities. Paul builds things, Matthew builds relationships, and both are important.

So Paul and Matthew, working together and learning from one another, have each learned not only to be task-oriented, but also people-oriented. Had we left them alone and allowed them to grow independently, Paul would have become a more task-focused person and Matthew a more people-focused person. By having us show them that they needed to work together to manage one another and to be part of a team, they learned the other's strengths and dealt with their own weaknesses. Now as we look at the two of them, Matthew has become an excellent worker and has always been good with people. Paul, an excellent worker, has now become very good with people.

3. *Learning to lead.* From 10 to 12, we worked on developing Paul as a leader. We moved all three boys into the same room to teach them how to serve one another and become workers, managers, and leaders. We continually impressed upon Paul that some of the greatest work he will do in his life will be to help lead his younger brothers into wisdom and maturity. If he is faithful in that, then he will enjoy part of the Lord's commendation and reward for the fruitfulness of his brothers' lives.

As a leader, Paul has needed a lot of coaching from us to develop decision-making processes and learn how to lead with love and encouragement rather than force. But he is on his way to becoming a skilled leader as a result of the simple interactions within our small family unit. We have found the family is a great personnel management workshop, teaching each of us how to motivate, discipline, build and train teams, devise strategies, and evaluate results.

The positive steps we were taking to build soldiers for the Lord in our family began to impact Susy and me in working with other adults. At one point the finances in our ministry were way below what they needed to be. Though as a team, all of our staff were to share in the responsibility of building our donor base, I was trying to carry the burden myself (I was acting as a worker, not as a manager or leader). The temptation for a person with a worker temperament is to try to accomplish things himself, then get angry with others when he can't. I could sense that was the direction I was headed in.

In a particular staff meeting where we were talking about the finances, the pressure finally got to me and I just broke into tears. I shared with them my fears about the finances, and my failure to have pulled us together as a team to address the problems. I heard myself explaining the same principles of teamwork and management that we've taught the children. As a result of my finally being willing to bring the staff in as participants in the need, they willingly became participants in the solution. Hopefully, I'll make that move more quickly next time.

4. Learning to disciple. From 12 to 14, we encouraged Abigail, Paul, and Matt to develop as disciplers. At various times all three have worked with friends in a discipleship program called Operation Timothy. Abigail has also had mentoring relationships with other younger kids through the Good News Club. Now that Paul and Abigail are into their late teens, we are finding that they are even impacting adults as budding young soldiers for Christ.

One particular example is a woman Abigail talked to at one of our children's ball games. The woman asked Abigail about homeschooling, and Abigail described some of the challenges and pressures she had seen Susy go through. She also described the positive benefit of watching Susy wrestle with the challenges of homeschooling. Abigail also outlined some of the tremendous benefits of being able to train our children at home and not be bound by the schedules and curriculum constraints of a school system. There were many other things Abigail discussed, but primarily she demonstrated that homeschooling is an excellent option for training children. The woman who had asked the question had decided that morning to stop homeschooling, but was so encouraged after talking with Abigail that she decided to continue. I was extremely gratified that Abigail had the confidence and poise to humbly share some encouraging words with a woman more than twice her age—and see the woman take her words to heart.

I continue to be amazed at the number of hurting people who are desperately looking for a word of encouragement or a hopeful answer to their situation. While we don't encourage our children to go around giving advice to adults, the times this has happened have made me all the more grateful that we have helped our children understand there are answers to life problems, and they can lead others to those answers. I am especially humbled when I remember how few answers to life I had when I was my children's ages.

On one of our weekly dates, Abigail, then 13, took Anna, 7, along with us because I had missed my date with Anna due to being out of town. As we sat eating lunch and going through our Bible-study materials, I asked Abigail who discipled her. She said, "Well, you and Mom discipled me." I asked Anna who had discipled her and she said, "You and Mom discipled me, along with Abigail." I said, "That's right, Anna. Now, who is going to disciple Susanna?" (Susanna was then one year old.) Anna quickly said, "Oh, Abigail, you, and Mom . . ." She paused for a minute, and it was as if a light bulb went on in her head. Her eyes got big and round, and her whole face lighted up, and she said, "Oh, I will!" I just cheered because Anna had gotten the picture of the discipleship process.

Discipling and mentoring in a family can take place in all areas of family life. For example, the boys help each other develop sports skills. They spend many afternoons pitching and catching with one another to help develop their abilities. Some of the kids work with each other on the piano. Joshua excels at baseball and helps Anna in that area, while Anna helped Joshua when they were learning to read. Also, our older kids have helped our younger kids work on their reading and mathematics skills.

Another advantage of teaching our kids to disciple others is that they are much less likely to follow the poor leadership of their peers. When they see so clearly demonstrated that they can impact what people do for right or for wrong by their words and actions, it gives them a clear picture of how they need to be careful whom they are following. During devotions I have given them many examples of how I followed the wrong people into bad activities and, in fact, was a leader of other innocent people into bad activities.

This has helped the kids stand up to temptation. One time when Matthew was returning home from the batting cages with his baseball team at the age of 11, they stopped at a very large cave on the side of a mountain. All the kids piled out of the car with two coaches and one of the wives and went running into the cave, having fun, yelling, and then throwing rocks at the pond that was in the cave. Matthew's coach was surprised when Matthew remained at the entrance of the cave, refusing to go in. The coach asked him why he would not go in. Matthew said, "Well, I just can't go home and tell my father that I went into a cave without asking his permission."

One very important aspect of the process of growing into "soldierhood" for our kids has been rewards. The cave incident with Matthew won him a gold medal. We had seen the motivational value of awards during the children's involvement in sports, so Susy and I went to a trophy shop and bought medals that we would present to them. For what purpose? For exceptional displays of character in their lives. We hold a family award ceremony and praise whoever is getting the award. These ceremonies make the recipient feel special, and go a long way in teaching that righteousness is rewarded.

5. *Learning to be a soldier.* There is an ultimate goal in learning to work, to manage, to lead, and to disciple. The goal is to become a committed member of the Lord's army, ready to give your all for His glory, whatever the cost. It is still too early at this point in our children's lives to draw final conclusions about their commitment to this level of their spiritual life. But I am confident that each of them will ultimately grow into the place of being an active and sold-out member of the Lord's army. But even in their youth, we've seen signs of the children being willing to risk their reputation—and whatever else might be required—by standing up for Christ and His kingdom.

It is difficult to teach sacrificial commitment to Christ because it is something that eludes even adults as we go about our daily lives. But there is a lot of teaching in Scripture about those who took a stand without fear of the consequences. We have told our children the stories of Esther, Daniel, Joseph, Paul, and other greats of Scripture so as to paint pictures for them of what sacrifice looks like. Introducing them to heroes of the modern missions era, informing them of the unbelievable persecution many Christians are suffering, and taking them to see and hear national Christian leaders and speakers from other countries, gives them a steady stream of input regarding the prices many in our day are paying to follow Christ.

We have a practice of praying for our kids very specifically before every sporting event that they compete in that they would do the following four things: One, that they would do their best. Two, that they would be good sports. Three, that they would honor the Lord with their thoughts, words, and deeds. And four, that they would have fun doing it. Paul decided one year to write those four principles on each of the four fingers of his baseball glove. He knew his teammates would eventually see it, ask him what it meant, and possibly ridicule him for it. His other team members immediately saw his glove, and Paul was able to explain his motivations and goals in playing sports and how we pray together for his success in the four areas.

At a summer camp, Abigail met a young lady deeply involved with a boyfriend. Both the boy and the girl wanted to be in full-time music ministry, but they were both only 17 years of age. The girl expressed some concern that the relationship was moving her away from the Lord. Abigail discussed with her some concerns about dating, then suggested she and her boyfriend put off dating for a number of years until they believed they were old enough to be married. The girl seemed relieved at that suggestion, realizing they could see each other as friends in large groups but protect their hearts and their purity until they were old enough to consider marriage. At that point, Abigail was moving from leadership through discipleship into the commitment of a soldier—willing to take an unconventional and unpopular stand on an emotionally charged issue for most teens.

Being a soldier means we are willing to suffer for the cause of Christ if need be. Our children are going to grow up in a time where they are probably going to have persecution unlike any American generation has known. If they are peer-dependent, weak-kneed, and shallow in faith, they are simply not going to be able to stand against the temptations of the world or the wiles of the enemy. It is soldiers we are after, but it takes a lifetime to build men and women whose faith will stand against great opposition.

I make no apologies: *I want to change the world.* To do so will mean shaping my children into soldiers for the cause of Christ, so that the vision God has planted in my life will continue to grow through my kids. I'm not completely responsible for how they turn out because they each have free will, but I want them to grow up to make an eternal impact, so I have decided to intentionally disciple my children into maturity in Jesus Christ.

Of course, the jury is still out on my family. None of my kids are fully grown yet, none have moved into careers or had children of their own, so I write these words with some fear and trepidation, knowing the possibility exists I'll have been judged a failure as a father. But with God's grace, I'm doing the best I can to shape the next generation of Christian leaders. My father's reward will be to know that I did all I could to see my children walking in obedience to the Lord. I may not change the world, but what a blessing to know I've passed on to my kids the only means of doing so: living in the power of God. May you join me in the celebration.

Quotable Quotes

✦ *Massive Cleanup—Runaway Mother At The Store:* While proceeding in her perennial packing of too many projects into too short a period of time, Susy was darting down the grocery aisles, basketing the essentials for the next day's feedings. Turning down aisle two for the final item of hamburger buns, which were stacked on a folding table on the right, Susy quickly turned her basket back to the left toward the checkout, forgetting that she had just passed through a narrow passage between the buns and a three tiered display of approximately 150 bottles of Worcestershire sauce that he grocer obviously wished to move rapidly. Careening into the inappropriately placed display, Susy virtually exploded close to, if not all the 150 bottles of Worcestershire sauce! As she looked at the white tile floor, now cascading with a wake of brown aromatic sauce, her lawyer's mind quickly reviewed the elements of the defense known as "negligent placement" of a display. Her thoughts were interrupted by a grocery worker, obviously sent from Heaven, who quickly admitted that

Quotable Quotes (continued)

the display was poorly placed and too highly stacked for the heavy grocery cart traffic, and told her not to worry about the cost of the breakage. Breathing a sigh of relief, but still feeling the shock of the explosion, Susy continued toward the checkout counter trying to be inconspicuous, which was foiled by the supermarket speaker blasting, "Massive cleanup on aisle two! Massive cleanup, aisle two!"

✦ *Best Illustration of the Economic System of Supply and Demand:* Dad selling a "very special" two dollar bill to Matthew for ten dollars.

✦ *Reproducing One Capitalist at a Time:* Remembering well his loss earlier when he paid $10 to Dad for a $2 bill, Matthew made 1996 his year-of-business as demonstrated by Anna's excitement that Matt was teaching her how to throw a football for 25 cents for every 10 minute lesson.

✦ *Let Your "Yes" Be Yes and Your "No" Be No:* After Dad's great pronouncement that Matt and his cousin, Tim, would pick their respective touch football teams, he began to divvy up the players by size, weight and experience to which Matt replied, "Hey, Dad, I thought you were going to let us pick the teams!"

✦ *Calling a Combat Unit Under Attack:* Sometimes my morning calls home are received at a time of great stress wrought upon members of our home school by one or more of the recipients of my flawed male genes. I barely said hello when Susy voiced her distress the "Joshua's and Matthew's incessant whistling is just driving us all crazy, but how can you fuss at children who are whistling the Hallelujah Chorus?"!

Study Questions

1. Where is your discipline strong? Where is it weak?

2. How do you foster *esprit de corps* in your family?

3. What sort of "promotions" do you offer your children?

4. What has been the most helpful thing you've learned from this book?

5. After having read this, what three things can you commit to change in your life?

CBMC of USA

The Christian Business Men's Committee of USA (CBMC) is an interdenominational, evangelical and discipleship ministry comprised of more than 50,000 people involved in 1000 committees and ministry teams nationwide.

Ministry Opportunities in CBMC

Citywide committee teams: More than 500 teams of men meet weekly across the United States for prayer, Bible study, outreach, and discipleship.

Ministry teams, Bible studies, and home groups: Additionally, over 500 teams of men and couples meet in homes and other settings for evangelistic Bible studies, outreach dinner parties, and discipleship groups.

Living Proof teams: These are groups of men and couples who meet to focus on the biblical processes of life-style evangelism and discipleship.

Small groups: Hundreds of CBMC-sponsored couples' groups meet weekly to discuss topics ranging from principles of financial stewardship to building godly marriages.

Outreach: CBMC sponsors more than 2000 outreach meetings each year, presenting the truths of Jesus Christ to more than 200,000 uncommitted and unchurched people.

Discipleship: Annually, more than 25,000 discipling teams are formed using *Operation Timothy*.

***Eternal Impact* groups**: Around the country, groups of men and couples are reading and studying the book *Eternal Impact: Investing in the Lives of Men*, building into their lives a greater recognition for and practice of the biblical process of making spiritual reproducers.

Conferences/retreats: CBMC sponsors more than 30 family, men's, and couples' conferences and retreats, including a national men's conference.

Leadership prayer breakfasts: CBMC participates in over 25 community prayer breakfasts to acknowledge God's role in civic affairs and to present the gospel of Jesus Christ to civic leaders.

Forums: Business owners and top executives meet monthly in small accountability groups for problem-solving and support.

Resources

Living Proof 1. Evangelism As a Lifestyle
This 12-session video training series dramatically portrays the challenges and joys of building friendships with non-Christians, allowing them to observe your life and begin to understand what it means to be a follower of Jesus. Especially effective for use in small groups.

Living Proof 2: Lifestyle Discipleship
This sequel to *Living Proof 1* offers another 12 video sessions and takes the material a step further, showing the opportunity and difficulties new believers encounter in their desire to become faithful, consistent, and growing followers of Jesus Christ.

Eternal Impact: Investing in the Lives of Men
A profound book by Phil Downer with Chip MacGregor that details how to make a positive impact on the world in a way that will endure for countless generations. Teaching the principles of "life-on-life" discipleship the way Christ practiced it, this book has helped many develop a greater recognition of ministry opportunities, and helped them put into practice the biblical process of making spiritual reproducers. A group or individual study guide is included.

Operation Timothy
This printed series, four booklets and a leader's guide, has been used to nurture and equip thousands of new believers. Now available in a revised and updated edition, it starts with the basics of the Christian faith and proceeds to address the important issues of personal discipleship.

If you would like to order any of these resources, or to find out more about *CBMC* and the conferences and retreats in your area, call 1-800-566-CBMC (1-800-566-2262), FAX (423) 629-4434, E-mail: info@cmbc.com, or contact their web page at www.cbmc.com.

Biography

Phil Downer is the president of Christian Business Men's Committee of USA (CBMC). Prior to that he served as a senior partner in a large law firm with offices in four states. In 1967-1968, he served as a machine gunner in Vietnam with the Marine Corps. Phil received his Bachelor of Business Administration from Southern Methodist University, and his Juris Doctor from Emory University School of Law. He is an author of four previous books, including *Eternal Impact: Investing in the Lives of Men.* Phil and his wife, Susy, have six children and live in Chattanooga, Tennessee.

Chip MacGregor is senior editor at Harvest House Publishers in Eugene, Oregon. A former pastor and seminary professor, this is Chip's third book with Phil Downer.